I0465411

Urban Art:
Creating the Urban with Art

**Proceedings of the International Conference
at Humboldt-Universität zu Berlin
15-16 July, 2016**

Urbancreativity.org

Title:
Urban Art: Creating the Urban with Art
Proceedings of the International Conference
at Humboldt-Universität zu Berlin
15-16 July, 2016

Editors:
Ulrich Blanché
Ilaria Hoppe

Graphic Design:
Pedro Soares Neves

Proofreading:
Maximilian Lehner
Paul Hockenos

©Authors and Editors
Lisbon 2018
ISBN: 978-989-97712-8-4

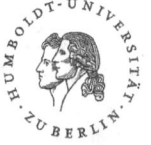

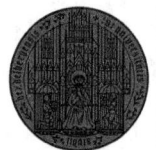

**UNIVERSITÄT
HEIDELBERG**
ZUKUNFT
SEIT 1386

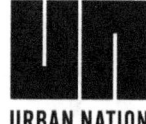

URBAN NATION

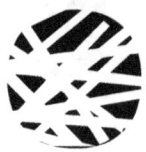

Street Art & Urban Creativity
International Research Topic

Funded by the Günter Rombold Privatstiftung

Table of contents

Acknowledgments

As organizers of the conference Urban Art. Creating the Urban with Art at the Humboldt-Universität zu Berlin in 2016 and editors of this publication, we would like to express our gratitude not only to our partners, but also to the many helping hands on both sites of production. We would like to thank our academic institutions: the University of Heidelberg and the conference host, the Institute of Art and Visual History at the Humboldt-Universität zu Berlin. The former institute director Prof. Dr. Kai Kappel made the opening remarks at the conference and supported us in many ways. Furthermore, we would like to acknowledge the committed and professional work of our chairs during the conference: Thierry Maeder (Geneva), Peter Bengtsen (Lund), Heike Derwanz (Oldenburg), Jacob Kimvall (Stockholm), and Caroline Loeb (Michigan). Finally, our gratitude goes to Lichtenberg Open ART in Berlin (LOA) for their contribution in funding the conference.

For the publication of the conference papers, we would like to thank our partners the Urban Creativity Network Lisbon, Urban Nation Berlin - The Museum for Urban Contemporary Art (Stiftung Berliner Leben), Lichtenberg Open ART in Berlin (LOA), the Humboldt-Universität zu Berlin and finally the Günter Rombold Privatstiftung at the Catholic Private University (KU) Linz.

Ilaria Hoppe & Ulrich Blanché

Introduction

Ulrich Blanché

1) Urban Art, Graffiti, Street Art, and Public Art

In April 2016, Ilaria Hoppe and I received 73 international proposals from our call for papers: from researchers from 27 countries and diverse academic backgrounds. Our subject matter in this book, as does the conference, makes use of four main terms: urban art, street art, public art, and graffiti. Graffiti was not our main focus but many of the authors in this volume deal with street art and graffiti. Urban art has become an art-market term, as Johannes Stahl states in the first essay of this volume. But, as Ilaria Hoppe will expand on in the second part of our introduction, urban art as a term can exceed self-authorized, often indoor street art and graffiti.

It seems that each author has a different understanding of street art, graffiti, urban art, and public art. There are tendencies, however, to differentiate between the terms. Street art is often more picture-based and tries to reach a general audience. Like graffiti, it is usually illegal or self-authorized. Graffiti could range from historical graffiti (in Pompeii, latrinalia, scratchings in medieval churches, etc.) to contemporary graffiti (style writing) or just about any illegal activity in urban public space involving first and foremost the writing of words or letters. Urban Art is the legal and/or indoor variant of street art and graffiti. Urban art and street art are also related to performance activities and urban development, graffiti is not. Public art usually comes into being with public money, community involvement, and it is usually sanctioned.

Still most researchers understand street art and graffiti, but also urban art, as outdoor art practices (former) street artists or graffiti writers do. Street art, graffiti and urban art, however, can also be terms outlining a certain visual style (like Baroque can be a style) and are understood more and more this way. Practitioners who never worked illegally or self-authorized on the streets might create urban art, namely art "in the style of" and media known from graffiti and street art: without location, without illegality, but for instance with stencils, with spray cans, on urban furniture, car wrecks, pieces of walls, removed doors, trash cans, etc.

Furthermore, urban art, graffiti, and street art can be a period (like Baroque can be a period) that might be over, or not, as various researchers pointed out in 2016, for instance Alison Young at the Street Art & Philosophy conference in New York, Christian Omodeo at the Urban Creativity conference in Lisbon and Raphael Schacter on hyperallergic.com.

In terms of artists, style, and period, street art or style-writing graffiti does not differ from other art terms, such as Baroque or impressionism. Public art or graffiti (and to a certain extent also street art) could be "timeless" as well, an alternative art history as these phenomena existed in variations in all times and places.

2) Street art researchers and their background

Most researchers who applied for our urban art conference had a background in art history, art and design or/and were artists/curators or specialized, for instance, in street photography or performance studies. The second biggest group came from architecture and design, urban planning, metropolitan studies or (urban) geography. Sociologists or social anthropologists formed the third group; some had studied art and cultural sciences, cultural studies or cultural anthropology. Other researchers had a background in media studies, psychology, philosophy, political sciences or Asian studies.

The reason why so many art historians (17) applied might be that we, as art historians ourselves, organized this conference in an art historical context. I suppose other academic urban art/street art conferences might attract more sociologists or anthropologists or more philosophers, such as the Street Art and Philosophy conference in New York in 2015. Other street art researchers (not in our sample) have academic backgrounds for instance in criminology, law or in modern languages.

3) Tendencies in our Urban Art Proposals

It was interesting to read through the different understandings of these four key terms, urban art, street art, public art, and graffiti. Quite a few researchers use these terms (or some of them) interchangeably as if they had the exact same meaning. Many researchers commonly use "graffiti and street art" as a pair, but seem to know acknowledge differences, similarities and intersections (personal, stylistic, historical, and intentional). Most understandings have in common that all these practices happened outdoors or are inspired by outdoor practices.

Quite a few, including the author of these lines, differentiate between legal and illegal activities (or as I call it: self-authorized). As concepts of style, all of these terms could be used in a legal and institutional context as well. Each could be an umbrella term or a synonym for at least two others. Often graffiti is assumed to be non-legal and public art legal. City planning, (non-)institutional actions, performance art in public spaces and ephemeral urban interventions are often considered to be urban art as well, no matter if illegal/self-authorized or institutional. Some researchers consider carnivals, museum-scapes, art biennales or other art events in the city, psychogeography and urban walking, protest camps or urban archaeology forms of urban art.

The name of Über-street-artist Banksy appeared in more than 10 percent of all submissions, Shepard Fairey in 4 percent. More than 10 percent of all proposals were monographic. Artists, wanted to talk about their own work. Nearly 10 percent were interested in speaking about street art in their home country or city.

4) The papers in the conference sections

In the 16 papers and two introductions in this volume, there are nearly as many understandings of urban art, street art, public art or graffiti, although not everyone defined what they meant by these terms. However, from the context their understanding of these terms is often obvious.

a) Section 1: Public or Urban Art? On Terminology

In our CFP, the topics Urban or Public Art? About Urban Art Research (Terminology, history of the core concepts) attracted the second greatest number of all applicants. It formed the basis of our first conference section Public or Urban art? On Terminology.

Johannes Stahl is the first art historian who wrote academic books on graffiti and street art in Germany, in the 1980s. In his essay, Stahl describes the historical development from graffiti to street art to urban art and points to the inconsistencies in the usage and motivations to use these different terms since the 19th century. Pedro Soares Neves from Lisbon, a graffiti pioneer in Portugal -- spark plug of the Urban Creativity network - who turned to research and publishing about street art and urban creativity, discussed the differences between urban and public art. Finnish street art researcher and street art in "Asia" expert, Minna Valjakka, opted to use the term "urban creativity" and the value of non-art instead of discussing street art, urban art, and public art in an art context.

b) Section 2: Digital Media & the Urban (Art)

The largest number of proposals dealt with New Media (Internet and social media in the production and reception of urbanity). It formed the basis for our second section entitled Digital Media & the Urban (Art).

Landscape architect and urban designer Meltem Sentürk Asildeveci pursued how specific identities of meeting places are changing in accordance with social media impact (especially Twitter) and how mobile communication is redefining urban design theories. Katja Glaser shared one chapter of her German Ph.D. thesis "Street Art & Neue Medien" (2017) in which she investigated the mutual interactions of street art and new media technologies. In her paper, Glaser discussed QR codes and digital archiving practices in street art.

Italian street art researcher Marco Mondino1 described street art as an interdisciplinary object, a language of urban visual culture that is important to study through an integration of theories and tools about media studies and a semiotics perspective. Art historian Annette Urban analyzed some examples of (institutional) media art from the 1990s and from today. She concluded that similar issues occurred regardless of recent digital mobile media and that the dialectics of de- and reterritorialization are a valuable analytical tool for urban media art in general.

c) Section 3: Affect & Performance

The topics Performativity (Action and reception by moving in the urban space) and Emotions and the City formed our third section Affect & Performance. In Agnieszka Gralińska-Toborek's "Art of Serenity. Aesthetic Function of Humor in Street Art," the author states that even very activist street art usually uses laughter as a weapon. With the help of humor, things we are afraid to see in the public realm are uncovered. Susan Hanson's essay "Street Art as Process and Performance: The Subversive 'Streetness' of Video-Documentation" differs from the original paper she gave with Danny Flynn at the conference "The Active Role of the Viewer in Urban Art: From Reception to Material Engagement." Hanson's chapter emphasizes the role of street artists' videos as performance and as a more authentic way to transfer the street into an indoor art space. Elisabeth Friedman and Alia Rayyan gave a paper on "Re/Viewing Jerusalem: Political Art Interventions in Occupied East Jerusalem." The authors discuss the political potential of participatory urban art interventions in the contemporary context of occupied East Jerusalem.

d) Section 4: Territories

Peter Bengtsen visually and contextually analyzed some site-specific street artworks by Spanish artist Isaac Cordal that address how humans relate to nature in an urban environment and how site-specific street art might have an impact on our perception of nature. Jovanka Popova discusses participation in democratic regimes and where art practices in urban public space can exceed traditional, institutional boundaries.

Although we did not mention graffiti in the CFP, a few proposals dealt exclusively with graffiti. In these proposals, graffiti meant ego-style writing graffiti in the US-American style since Philadelphia and New York in the late 1960s. Our applicants were not referring to historical graffiti in Pompeii, not bathroom graffiti (latrinalia), or graffiti as more or less spontaneous often political messages on the street, which are a part of street art and graffiti research, too. Henrik Widmark's contribution about graffiti by football supporters in our conference (volume) can be seen in this context. These supporters do not have to have a style-writing background. They usually do not have to have an art background either; they are more than spontaneous messages, often quite organized and interested in spreading their message widely. Like street artists, they speak to a general public or like graffiti writers to a certain peer group: other supporters.

e) Section 5: Urban Imaginary & The City

Architecture and City Planning (Medialization of architecture and alternative forms of urban design/city planning) is the last section Urban Imaginary & The City. Johanna Elizabeth Sluiter opened this panel with her paper "'The Man In The Street' Shadrach Woods & the Practice of Everyday Architecture and Urbanism." Postwar urban planner Woods used urban structures like stems, webs and bazaars in his texts and his architecture and was geared to care more about pedestrians and streets, less about cars and roads. Pamela C. Scorzin's chapter "Urban Art as a Laboratory - New Approaches to Architecture and City Planning" deals with new approaches by the urban art collective Office for Subversive Architecture (osa). Renée Tribble's essay "From Urban Interventions to Urban Practice? An Alternative Way of Neighbourhood Development" discusses urban interventions as new form of urban development, reflected in the recent win of the Turner Price in 2015 by radical young architects group Assemble.

f) Section 6: Networking Panel

An international conference is also a great opportunity to meet researchers and practioniers from different street art, graffiti or urban art backgrounds. From Here to Fame Publishing from Berlin continuously stage, curate and collaborate with international Urban Art and Hip Hop projects around the world since 2008. Their founders Akim Walta and Don Karl spoke about their work. Street Art & Urban Creativity is a network of international street art and graffiti researchers founded in Lisbon in 2014. Members Ilaria Hoppe and Ulrich Blanché gave a short introduction about the network, its aims and possibilities.

In her essay Yasha Young, director and curator of Urban Nation, informs about the development and the goals of the forthcoming Urban Nation Museum for Urban Contemporary Art in Berlin. Jens Besser, a Dresden based (urban) artist and curator introduced his work and also contributed a short essay about the idea of a travelling Urban Art Library to document the development of contemporary muralism.

5) PS: About our cover photo

On February 14, 2009 I took a photo of one of the so-called "human beans" by British street artist Dave the Chimp (*1973) in Berlin. This ongoing series of stick figures with an orange bean-shaped body was started at the latest in 2008. When I saw the motif I liked the contrast of the characteristic human-bean-orange with the bluish green wall. Obviously, a house owner had sloppily painted over the upper part of the bean. It was impossible to say what the original bean had done. Then someone added astonished, slightly angry eyes to the bean where once its face was.

When Ilaria Hoppe and I were looking for a key visual to use on our poster for the urban art conference in Berlin in 2016 I remembered the photo. It was site-specific and showed a dialogue, multiple authors on the street, over time, as well as street art's ephemerality.

When I gave our flyer with the motif to urban art curator and former graffiti writer Stefan Winterle, who had worked with Dave the Chip before, he said he was quite sure Dave the Chimp added the eyes himself. In 2017, we contacted Dave the Chimp per mail and he kindly gave us permission to use the motif for the book. I asked him if he had added the eyes as Stefan Winterle said. Dave's response: "The bean wasn't painted over. I painted it to look like it had been painted over!" So it was an illusionistic dialog referring to the many dialogues that happen on the street all the time.

Urban Art:
Creating the Urban With Art

Ilaria Hoppe

Institute of Contemporary Arts and Media,
Catholic Private University Linz
i.hoppe@ku-linz.at

1) Urban art as an umbrella term

The aim of the conference and this publication is to discuss "urban art" in its broadest sense: as an umbrella term that encompasses a great variety of creative expressions in the urban environment on a global scale. I am aware of the use of the term urban art for products of the art market that are related to graffiti writing and street art. I do not disagree, but would like to propose a much broader field of denotations. Firstly because this term was used by artists and activists themselves at the beginning of the great renaissance of street art around the millennium. In Julia Reinecke's first academic monograph on street art, submitted as a master thesis at Humboldt University in Berlin, we find the following quotation from stencil artist Logan Hicks: "(…) Urban art best describes the movement. The art that signifies this movement is influenced, and primarily lives within the city environment. (…) The people, the mediums, surfaces and showcases that exist within this movement are all born from the city streets" (Reineke, 2007; Blanché, 2010). Onema points in the same direction: "It sums up what we're doing: creating art in/for/inspired by the urban environment that we live in. It is simple and easily understandable to those who don't do art, while still maintaining the idea of creativity and intelligence, not just 'vandalism'" (Reineke, 2007; Blanché, 2010). Curator Adrian Nabi also coined an encompassing term for the Backjumps exhibitions in Berlin after 2003 by naming the phenomenon at large as urban communication and aesthetics (Nabi 2003).

The broad implications of the term "urban art" allow summarizing very different outcomes, styles, media, and techniques ranging from illegal graffiti writing to performative, participatory and architectonical interventions (Hildebrandt, 2012), from adbusting to legal murals and so forth. We do not need to be imprecise by describing the single form of urban creativity, but neither do we have to restrict them by definitions. To adhere to terms, as graffiti writing and street art is on the one hand useful to stress their critical potential, on the other hand it can be excluding, if the artistic or just creative expression does not fit in their characterization. If we use the term urban art in its broadest sense as a model for analysis, then it is also possible to overcome polarities that were already described and criticized by several authors, that is to say, the oppositions between art and vandalism, art and non-art, high and low art or art and advertisement and so forth. The objective here is, of course, not to overlook these discussions, but to acknowledge them as part of the phenomenon itself. The aim is to deal with every creative expression that appears on our large urban screen. Also, for this reason the interdisciplinary approach is so important as it offers a multi-perspective of urban practices, produced by many and often anonymous authors using a great variety of media.

The multitude of expressions poses a great challenge for scientific research, especially for art history, which still privileges monographic approaches and has difficulties to recognize, e.g. street art as a genuine form of art. Even though academia as well as the established art world have claimed to overcome the categories of high and low long ago, both are still working with hierarchies. Here methods of visual culture studies or the German Bildwissenschaft come into play by allowing us to analyze non-artistic forms of creativity or just signs in the urban fabric, moreover the reception of urban art through photographic and film documentation. These images find their ways mostly into the internet and in photo books, and in return shape the urban imaginary. The idea is not to elevate forms of urban art artificially, but to consider the phenomenon at large and see it as a contemporary epistemic model for a way of processing knowledge via images in a dynamic way. The challenge here is to think about a form that includes many forms, a multitude of perspectives, which are constantly networking visually and virtually.

2) Creating the urban

Furthermore, the term urban art opens the field toward the discourse on the contemporary city that has precisely changed in the period of the street art boom since the 1990s. Actually, the static notion of the (post)modern city was given up for a much more flexible conception of the contemporary urban, understood as a process, which is constantly changing, ephemeral, mobile, entertaining, virtual/digital and also chaotic and difficult to control (Bourdin, Eckardt, Wood, 2014). These characteristics meet perfectly the criteria of urban creativity as the contributions of this publication demonstrate. Street art, in particular, has shown to be not only constantly changing, ephemeral, mobile and entertaining, but also developed at the same time and together with the web 2.0, and is therefore also virtual. It represents and produces the contemporary urban multidimensional space. This process is of course not linear, but implies oppositions and contradictions, such as gentrification. Street art is very often accused (or praised) as a motor of urban renewal because it attracts people to live in such an environment, which in turn allures to real estate developers. However, after the process of gentrification is completed, especially graffiti writing and street art disappear from the respective area, a process that has happened in Berlin. The intensive investment is accompanied by control of property that leads to the again more static notion of the city. Processes like this show how conflicts within the contemporary city very much depend on the urban imaginary: Who has the power to decide about the overall image? Who is permitted to develop the ideas about communal living (Bourdin, Eckardt, Wood, 2014)?

From this follows that the urban is also political in different ways: it has begun to assume the meaning of the public sphere (Öffentlichkeit). Recently, it wasn't just in European cities that opinion polls during election campaigns named a so-called "urban electorate," which cannot be defined so clearly. After the controversial media law in Poland was enacted early in 2016[1], the Polish foreign minister Witold Waszczykowski stated in an interview that the law would cure Poland of different kinds of diseases, such as the new mix of cultures and races, a world of cyclists and vegetarians, who want to use only renewable energy and fight against any form of religion.[2] In this neoconservative position, which we encounter these days not only in Poland, we see a reflection of this urban public that apparently is hard to define. Of course, I think that this kind of urban public is the prime audience of urban art, maybe even the agents of it. They and their urban culture constitute forms of a global development that challenge many people and lead them toward neo-conservative parties or even further.

Finally, the discourse on the urban has replaced the one on the city itself and has its own semantic history. Until the end of the 20th century "urban" had a positive connotation: It was idealized as the Mediterranean city with the central piazza in the tradition of the Greek agora, representing the ideal of historic democracy. Strangely enough,

---

1 - It puts the national broadcast companies directly under the influence of the government that claimed his right to appoint the directors directly. For more information see: http://www.humanrightseurope.org/2016/01/poland-jagland-raises-media-law-human-rights-concerns-with-president-duda/ (24.07.2017).

2 - For the original text see http://www.bild.de/bildlive/2016/14-polen-minister-44000764.bild.html (24.07.2017).

this concept was only realized in shopping malls and artificially built districts like Potsdamer Platz in Berlin. These models are not urban in themselves; they artificially just represent urbanity. Participation here is clearly limited to consumerism and controlled labor. These concepts were criticized by contemporary urban theory that stresses more the conflicting aspects of urbanity. From this perspective, the urban is not conceived as a concise space, but more as an open process negotiating claims on urban territories and the struggle on the symbolic significance of its places. However, it is at this point that we see again the potential of urban art as a creative tool to influence and shape the symbolic meaning of urban space itself, and in doing so reclaiming that very space. Its inclusive characteristics often tackle static notions of city planning and oppose policies of governance, as was also the case in Birgit Mersmann's talk about Korean practices (Mersmann, 2018). The analysis of urban art is therefore a valuable tool to make such processes visible. The contributions to this volume show an understanding of the contemporary urban that takes into consideration the inconstancy of the public sphere (Helbrecht/Dirksmeier, 2013) and the possibilities of its shaping.

References

Blanché, U., 2010. Something to s(p)ray: Der Street Artivist Banksy. Eine kunstwissenschaftliche Untersuchung, Tectum, Marburg.

Bourdin, A., Eckardt, F., Wood, A., 2014. Die ortlose Stadt. Über die Virtualisierung des Urbanen, transcript, Bielefeld.

Helbrecht, I., Dirksmeier, P., 2013. Stadt und Performanz, in: Mieg, H. A., Heyl, C. (Eds.), Stadt. Ein interdisziplinäres Handbuch, Metzler, Stuttgart and Weimar, 283-298.

Hildebrandt, P. M., 2012. Urbane Kunst, in: Eckardt, F. (Ed.), Handbuch Stadtsoziologie, Springer, Wiesbaden, 721-744.

Mersmann, B., 2018. Lacing Places: Situationist Practices and Socio-Political Strategies in Korean Urban Art Project, in: Dornhof, S., Hopfener, B., Lutz, B., Buurman, N. (Eds.), 2017. Situating Global Art. Topologies – Temporalities – Trajectories, transcript, Bielefeld, 27-44 (in course of publication).

Nabi, A., et.al. 2003. Backjumps – The Live Issue, catalogue, Vice Versa, Berlin.

Reinecke, J., 2007. Street-Art. Eine Subkultur zwischen Kunst und Kommerz, transcript, Bielefeld.

The Virtual City:
From augmented urbanism to urban hacking

Frank Eckardt

Bauhaus-University Weimar, Germany

Belvederer Allee 4

99421 Weimar

Frank.Eckardt@uni-weimar.de

Abstract

In recent debates, the question on how new information and technologies influence urban life has been reformulated to include aspects of a more profound change. This has to do with the technical ability to lay information on spaces, which remains visible to others. In this way, places can be identified with mobile phones and also allow the user to share information on this place with others. In this "augmented city," communication among users can create new geographies. In this article, the author underscores the impact of the ICT (information and communication technologies such as smart phones, tablets, Augmented Reality technologies, social networks) innovations in urban life. In a second step, the concept of augmented urbanism will be understood as part of a more profound societal change in which the diversity of urban life styles is at stake. As for urban hacking, the options for norm-changing strategies are taken into account. It is argued, it needs to be framed as being linked to the spheres of art, sport and urban planning; urban hacking must be regarded a potential vehicle of local adaptation to global codes.

Keywords: virtual urbanism, urban hacking, augmented city, urban theory, urban sociology

1. Introduction

The permanent innovations of ICT since the 1990s have raised questions about the impact on "space" in the widest sense, but also with regard to very particular questions of urban life. In the most profound reconsiderations, space appears to be shrinking and compressed by the diminishing of distances. The appearance of economic, social and cultural phenomena as being "just-in-time" and transmission of "real time" have questioned the basic order of time-space-connections where the gap between two moments in time have been produced, signified and controlled the experience of distances and by doing so, enabling space as a chronical idea. With the emergence of ubiquitous communication, the perception of space has overcome the dual before-and-after order; ICT enable us to be present at the same time in different qualities but simultaneously.

Many considerations about the implications of this new space-time order have taken into account that profound changes in perspective on cities might need to be assumed (Boudin, Eckardt, Wood, 2014). In particular, the so-called "end of geography" has either led to overoptimistic claims of a decentering world where connectivity has become the main concern or produced dark fantasies about chaotic and ungovernable spaces. In the discourse on the effects of globalization on cities, the general assumption has been that cities were not dissolved as important living spaces for most people and that the spread of ICT does not solve the problems of hierarchies, and social and political inequalities - neither in states nor within cities

Another perspective concerns the micro level of cities: the personal interaction in shared spaces. One critique is that the meaning of public space has become challenged as people are more concerned with the communication that is displayed on their electronic device rather than with the persons physically around them. Underlying the assumption that "in former times" people interacted with their bystanders randomly, this rather nostalgic view misses the innovative spatial production that is undertaken by ICT users in public spaces today. In the modern city, communication enables meeting by travelling from one point in space to another; this function of communication has been added up by "staying tuned." Research shows that communication does indeed enable meetings with absent persons. Mobility is increasing because of better and faster communication options.

Nevertheless, the logic of ICT-based urbanism has changed with regard to its spatial frame. The most striking difference between a permanent online communication and its space to the former modern urban life might be seen in its need for constant production of visuality. This has to do with the distracting effect of ICT that require a large amount of concentration, even if this is rather diffuse. The psychological focusing on two permanent layers of presence creates a different regime of looks (cp. Graham, Zook and Bolton, 2013). For the cities, shaping and designing space in its built environment has so far had a function for interactive communication on the basis of direct sensing. Still, large parts of the urban environment function according the rule of direct-stimulus interpretation. Basic urban semiotics like traffic lights, shopping logos, official indications like school banners or police station signs, territorial claims like borders and gates were not abolished and still learned by urban dwellers in early childhood as an important symbolic order. What is common to all of these semiotic settings is that they are part of an introvert map that is created step by step in the run of the primary socialization of the individual and based on personal communication with (parental) authorities. Becoming a stranger meant that one has not undergone this process of personalized and space bound socialization in a particular place. This implies meant that the learning of the semiotic layer needs to be repeated. The modernization of life had, however, followed the same principles, so that traffic lights and house gates can look different but they can be understood in its functionality regardless the cultural context. The content side of this observation of a strange symbolic order was not touched by this estrangement and can be reconstructed by careful looks and in a directly sensed manner.

With the spread of ICT communication in the public realm, the meaning of public space has become a different, which not only dissolves the idea of space as distance but also of presence. While progressive architects have regarded public space in its functionality as meeting places and fostered their quality to comfort people to stay, the meaning of "being present" in a holistic way has become doubled or irritated by the presence of a "virtual other." Still, it is hard to find the right terminology, which is not normative, and using metaphors that might be misleading for this transformed experience of virtualized public space. Like Kitchen and Dogde (2011) speak about the "digital shadow" that is left behind with our traces of ICT communication, the analysis mostly starts from the point of view of the ICT user. Few critics have so far reflected on the fact that the perception and experience of the shadow was predicted and foreseen by the public or private providers of spatial arrangements.

The main aspect of the ICT-related analysis is the personalization of individual perspectives. As we know from the classic essays by Walter Benjamin on the Parisian flâneur, the walk through the city is highly motivated by desire and emotional needs of the individual trying to find his personal place in mass society. In this regard, contemporary personalization of the use of communication and public space is only in the line of this process of individualization. In this, it can be regarded rather as a kind of radicalization of modern urban behavior than as a profoundly different way of interacting in the city. This means, that while the physical gaps no longer are as important as they have been, the longing of city dwellers to "embark" mentally on different levels is the essence of urban dynamics. In Benjamin's time, the dissociation from the present surrounding came as a shock and brought in memory of the past. Today, it appeared that the complexity of sensing and feelings in the city are parallelized and embedded into commodity spheres. The commodification of these feelings is realized by the production of security and safety. The major tools to achieve this stabilized emotional urbanity are the creating of shared codes, which are recognizable in the virtual and the built environment. Instead of the shock of difference and the unsolved problems of the past, this process of virtualization of urban aims at using symbols and aesthetic concepts which are enabling flows between both worlds without any kind of irritation.

2. Augmented urbanism

The basic principle of urban development can be described as a highly controlled and themed construction of symbolic landscapes in the city where ICT firstly has been made present to become a widely accepted tool for communication. This is in particular true for the first generation of ICT-related urban projects, such as the theming of cities according to particular narratives. Already in the early 1990s, this principle has been realized by paradigmatic concepts like Disneyland and Times Square. The dissemination of internet cafés followed up and made ICT-related communication popular and trendy. In this phase of urban development, the spread of electronic billboards and screens was paradigmatic. It symbolized a semantic hegemony of the idea of a superior form of communication and in this way broke the ground for the preference of norms that superpose existing perceptional freedom. In other words, the permanent change of uses of the public space that required a certain flexibility of norms—on what is allowed to be seen and done— subtly gave way to an understanding that being in touch with global communication lines and their codes of viewing are most important. Setting up screens became a kind of power demonstration that devalued other forms of non-virtual communication. Consequently, many cities adopted the idea that a city needs to have one identity and a pictorial appearance that can be branded globally by the code of ICT. While in the beginning, cities have been augmented to foster and enable virtual communication, from a certain point onwards, the cause-and-effect relation turned around: virtualized interaction affected urban life and augmented the urban reality in a variety of ways.

Augmented urbanism therefore implies not so much that cities offer spaces to link up to virtual communication like looking at screens, rather it means that virtual communication flows into the very logic of urban life. In this regard, the "normal" use of mobile phones and permanent online presence is a technical and social basis for the augmented urbanism. To understand this impact, the city needs to be seen as being both planned and lived by with its daily routines. Apparently, the routines of many citizens have been changed by the personalization of information that they receive, translate into their own spatial behavior, and thereby reinforce. Daily routines have become more effective and therefore have changed the rhythms of a city. Moreover, they shape new urban geographies by following individualized tracks of mobility. The major driving force for the creation of new mobility structures, however, comes from the activity of other users where the individual reacts and so forth. The main aspects of urban life are no longer related to the information given by its providers, such as shops, restaurants, hotels, traffic facilities, schools and others, but they are part of a larger act of communication where the interpretation (with "likes" in its simplest way) are crucial. For urban planning is the choice of residence is essential. Neighborhood descriptions and their visual appearance have become mostly a question of virtualized information.

The character of this augmented urbanism cannot be seen without its technical basis. While these ICT-related communication forms offer more options for choosing places to work, live, recreate and more, the generation of this information follows two main principles. Firstly, it searches for solutions that enable immediate decision. In this way, from "first appearance" the emotional interpretation of "like" or "not-like" appears to be unquestionable. Led by the imperative of decision-making, the recommendations are either ranked or simple "yes" or "no" qualifications. In this regard, ambivalence of information and the need for own research are discredited. This principle of avoiding misunderstanding and thereby neglecting ambiguity leads to the second function of augmented urbanism, which is social sameness. The algorithmic logic of search machines and others seeks recommendations in the light of the individual user profile. By doing so, the search for affinitive other users leads to a filter bubble with the underlying unspoken philosophy that it is always the best to live with people or to go to place where you meet "your kind". In its urban consequence, the shaping and building of people of the same taste – be it traditional, be it liberal-open minded – leads to the rise of gentrified areas and gated neighborhoods where otherness is structurally or by exhibiting your way of life excluded. At least for the European cities, the loss of a certain degree of social and cultural mix is at stake.

3. Urban hacking

Cities have reacted in many ways on the "lived by" augmented urbanism. Globally, the social segregation of cities has increased with a nowadays self-understood principle put into practice that living in your own community is recognized as being "the best way to do". The appreciation of cultural and social difference has been reduced to highly controlled and rather timely arranged coulisses and events. The emergence of the festival and event city falls into this category. While thus urban life has become something of a Potemkin-style cosmopolis, urban planning in its core function, such as realizing public projects, has been confronted with the request for more public participation via ICT. This is even more true for the "digital divide:" this new form of participation does not challenge the basic principle of radicalized individual urbanism. Nevertheless, there is hope for an "augmented deliberation" (Gordon and Manosevitch, 2011). Its main emphasis lies in the potential of ICT to increase discussion about the best solution for planning problems. The ability to include other ways to reach other non-verbal sense helps to improve the creativity, flexibility and the inventiveness of the planning process and altogether they reinforce the norm of necessary conversation. Role play and gaming can even show ways how to manage conflicts of interest, which are often significant in planning processes. Outside the established spaces of planning, the use of ICTs can be indeed also seen as a kind of deliberative or anarchistic practice that does not accept the streamlining of spaces in the light of virtual sameness creation. While it is allowed to shape a layer of information and imagination on the information displayed on a mobile screen with look on a particular place – like getting the recommendations of other users when zooming in on a spatial address - disrupting and irritating informational practices are developing at the same time. As an attempt to classify these activities, the term "urban hacking" has found some acceptance in the academic world. It is introduced to describe activities that are counteracting pre-given codes on the meaning of space or spatial arrangements. In this way, they are invading the internet like hackers and use them for their own purposes by imposing a different code. This kind of urban behavior can be traced back to the 1970s with its culture war: hip-hop music, skateboarding, break dance, graffiti. The cultural logics of advanced capitalism have incorporated these activities into its repertoire of reproducible routines. Despite their successful integration in commodification, potentials of resistance have risen again with the "cultural jamming strategies in the risky spaces of modernity" (Friesinger, Grenzfurthner, Ballhausen, 2010). In their jamming, urban hackers do not necessarily follow any kind of political idea or are aware of their code switching and irritating conduct. Rather, out of a very self-understood feeling for autonomous moving, the new forms of public behavior in cities criticize mass production, cultural homogeneity and social conformism in an implicit way. There is also, however, a politicized part in the urban hacking phenomena if bicycling actions like Critical Mass are considered where many participants are posting political statements against the mainstream preference for car use. Clearly, politically motivated are also activists who strategically target certain companies with "adbusting" where they are laying critical information on the augmented urban spaces, for example pointing out environmental concerns about the companies. So far, the different examples mentioned in the discourse on urban hacking have a more profound and often a less visible communality. This is, in short, the re-interpretation of the norms of homogenous interpretation of a space by both action and representing this in the information layers of the augmented spaces. There is, of course, a massive attempt of companies and public authorities to limit and to even criminalize these activities. One can, however, also find supportive spheres that protect urban hackers. Firstly, the aestheticization of cities allows hacking in the realm of art. This is also a two-fold relationship. As the history of graffiti shows, its disruptive character and freedom has also been tamed and civilized for exploitation by the art industries. Secondly, urban hacking profits from a return of the body and of movements where individual sport has become widely accepted as being normal in the city. To be seen as doing "sport" creates the need for distinguishing one selves from those who do only boring jogging – leave alone Nordic walking – by exhibiting more risky behavior. Thirdly, it is the field of urban planning itself, which paradoxically seeks for unconventional behavior to brand the city as being unique. Guerilla gardening, squatting, temporary use of vacant buildings and all kind of "urban pioneering" are creating a desired atmosphere of creativity and attractiveness. Pictures of these augmented spaces are worldwide creating urban brands that cannot be invented top-down and which are necessary to let the city appear as attractive for visitors, investors and especially the young and highly qualified workforce.

4. Conclusions

In sport, art, architecture, and urban planning exists an ambivalent attitude toward urban hackers who are aware that they are image-shaping actors. Their activities are inspired by mostly uncommon forms of interaction with public spaces, which they know from the virtual world. It is not only the information on how to adbust or to youtube skating on a bench. Urban hacking is an activity that re-adopts spaces that have been mono-normed by global codes of life-style recognition. The augmentation of urban spaces is an expression of power shifts where local needs have been subdued to the imperatives of globally recognizable forms of aesthetics. While ICT can be regarded as helping to establish the better promotion of arguments for the sake of a more participatory planning, the hacking of spaces is an expression of a non-verbal interaction with the already established norms of homogenous spheres. As a simple technique, urban hacking could also be instrumentalized for the sake of place branding and marketing. It can make places attractive as being alternative or "different," which in turn can be exploited for urban branding.

References

Boudin, A., Eckardt, F, Wood, A., 2014. Die ortlose Stadt. Die Virtualisierung des Urbanen, Bielefeld, transcript.

Friesinger, G., Grenzfurther, J., Ballhausen, T., 2011. Urban Hacking – Cultural jamming strategies in the risky spaces of modernity, Bielefeld, transcript.

Gordon, E., Manosevitch, E., 2011. Augmented deliberation: Merging physical and virtual interaction to engage communities in urban planning, New media & society 13/1, 75-95.

Graham, S., M. Zook, M, Boulton, A, 2013. Augmented reality in urban places: contested content and the duplicity of code, Transactions of the institute of British Geographers 38/3, 464-479.

Kitchen, R. and M. Dogde, 2011. Code/Space: Software and Everyday Life, Cambridge, MIT Press.

On Terminology

Some Defining Aspects in Graffiti, Street Art and Urban Art

Johannes Stahl

Abstract

Graffiti has developed in an interesting way: from a craft technique in the Renaissance to a defining difference made in the 19th century between official and unofficial inscriptions. Even then, graffiti was depicted as an art of rebellion. In counter perspective to this tradition of being just politically rebellious, New York writers instead had difficulty defining their practice between art, vandalism and rebellion.

Street art is a speaking term: Defining a phenomenon by its place is just one element of this definition. The connotations of the word "street" and the physical street as a visual subject as well as a site for art should be looked at as defining factors, too. How does street art refer to the fact that street perspective or mobility produces a way for people to look at things? What similarities exist if objects and their reception are compared to advertising or so-called "percentage art"? And where and under which conditions is street art free or applied art?

Urban art opens another defining possibility. Here aspects of urbanism can enable a closer look into these phenomena, but also how factors of urbanity have changed during the last decades.

Keywords: Graffiti, street art, urban art, definitions

I think that many of the terms in use and their definitions mainly follow approaches that are not accorded to art history terminology and which are typical in their time. It is sometimes amusing to consider the claims that definitions make. Typically, in a more business-related approach, a gallery assistant in Munich explained to the author that urban art is the superior term for all forms of art in public, including street art, of which graffiti is part.

Some shortcut definitions try to put it in historical sequence: graffiti later became street art and even later urban art. The graffiti writer Mare 139 wrote in 2007, referring to the 1980s in New York: "What we call street art today is nothing else than what writers made in those times." (Mare 139, 2007: 110) The question rises if this can be regarded as a normal historical development or more like a marketing-minded relaunch of a product, which – from time to time – has not only lost a bit of its attractiveness but was taken out of the game because terms like urban art matched better with business activities.

1. Graffiti

In 1970, a dictionary entry stated: "Rarely used in the 19th century, when it was first used outside the Italian language, the term 'graffiti,' which seemed to be in use for all kinds of scratching, inscriptions, carvings and scribblings on whatsoever surface, takes a new meaning: for the archaeologists and paleontologists, it becomes a general term serving to distinguish popular inscriptions from official inscriptions in antique monuments (…). Today, it is common sense to call graffiti all unofficial drawings and inscriptions to be found on surfaces, architectural ones and others, in which the primary function differs from those [surfaces, J.S.], which are normally in use for drawing and writing." (Curry et al. 1970: 850).

It is remarkable that the authors use the singular *graffito* and mention French users of *graffite*, plural graffiti.

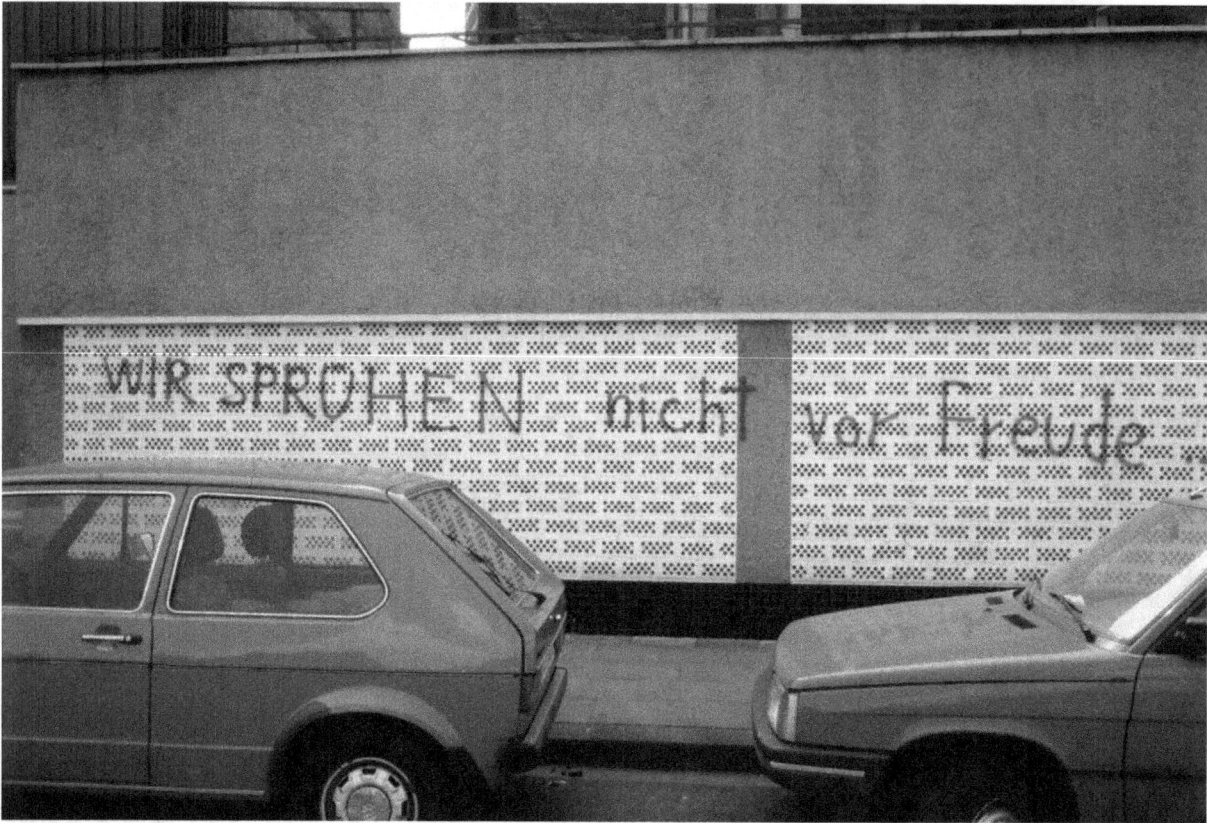

Fig. 1 - "Wir sprühen nicht vor Freude ...," (we don't spray out of fun) Köln, Magnusstraße, photo taken August 1983].

The date when they published this definition is close to Theodore Roszak's (1969) exposition of ideas about counter culture. However, the focus on the unofficial element in graffiti had older roots. In his comments on Pompeian excavations and his discovery of graffiti in the mid-nineteenth century, Raffaele Garrucci (1872-81) introduced and used the term graffite for every unauthorized attribution to public walls, widening the formerly technical differentiation between *sgraffiare* (scratching) and *pentimenti* for legal and thus social aspects.

But referring to graffiti as art is another question than to ask for technical, legal or fashion definitions.

One might ask: How do scratching and related techniques refer to art? Can art be counter culture? At least, scratching made a difference in German legislation discussed in the mid-eighties. It mattered whether you just altered the surface or "harm the substance." Nowadays, the definition of the "substance" is very large. The alteration of this notion has enforced stricter laws. An addition in the 1979 judgment against Harald Naegeli put a related perspective into words (cited by Thoss, 1983: 215-225).

"Harald Naegeli has, over years and with incomparable hardness, consequence and ruthlessness, managed to make the residents of Zürich insecure and to unsettle their faith in the invulnerability of property based on our legal order."

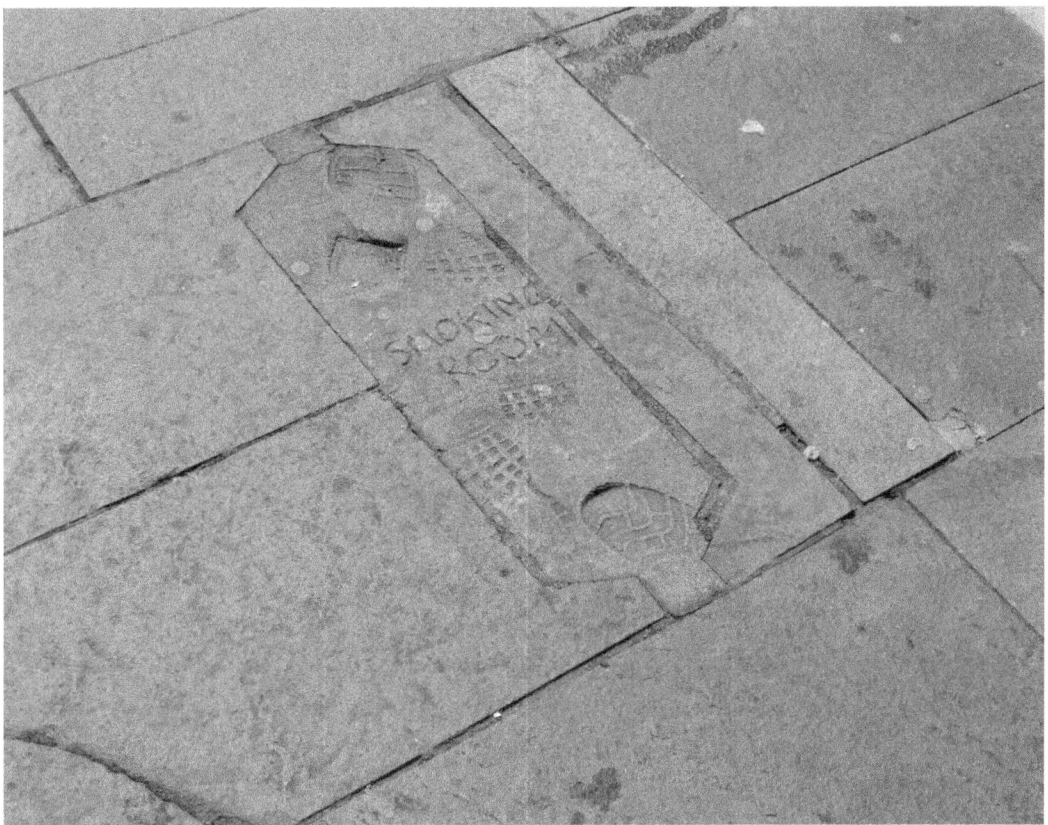

Fig. 2 - Footprint and ghost writing in Edinburgh, photo taken 2012].

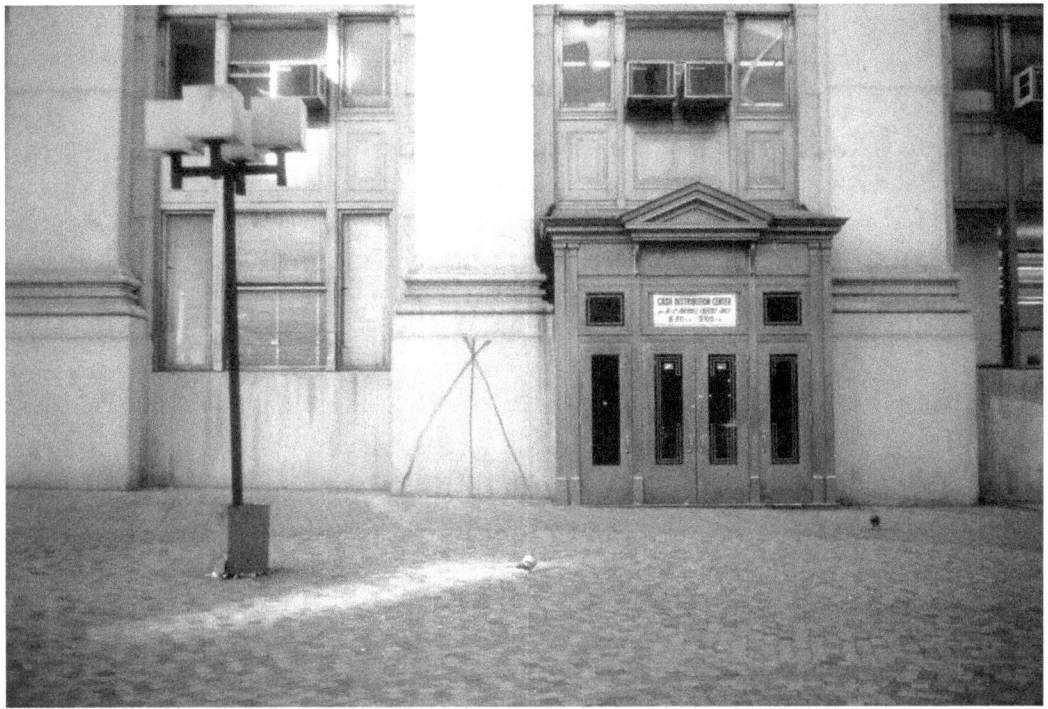

Fig. 3 - Red Indian tent in New York's financial district, photo taken October 1986].

Besides these questions, graffiti has been a hip term. As an example, George Lucas' highly successful film *American Graffiti* (1973) used it, but in no way referred to the cultural impact the first gallery show writers of the *United Graffiti Artists* had in 1973.

As late as 1986, a bookshop catalog, which was structured according to art eras, was entitled *Graffiti*, as the most current art movement (Delivery catalog, 1986). It might be asked if mentioning a word in a context like this is a sign of something that has already ended. However, compared to the everlasting public phenomenon, graffiti never has been just an art era. This is one of the main differences with wordings deriving from the art scene.[1]

It is worth considering how and why its forms have spread worldwide, how the promotional process took place. Nevertheless, the question remains: how much of it was a youthful art movement, how much of it a media phenomenon and how much a class-related item?

Looking at the wording of "subway art" and "spraycan art," the definition is obvious, but a show by Sidney Janis Gallery in 1983 modified it to "post Graffiti Artists" (Janis 1983). Can a growing segregation be felt here? For art marketing, it is definitively better to leave the illegality behind and maintain the wildness.

The gallerist was very disappointed with his "wild" guests:

> "These boys are not very reliable. (...) You're doing business with people who are merely irresponsible. There are few who are very sincere about it, but there are others. For example, when I took them to Madrid we made a big exhibition, maybe 75 paintings, they gave me two big galleries and (...) they got into trouble on the social side. Between their paintings, they were bad boys and I had a lot of trouble with them. So it was a chance for a reliable gallery like ours to really sponsor that kind of art because the whole thing might develop into something or the whole thing might collapse..." (Stahl 1990: 138).

Gallerist Tony Shafrazi has had similar questions. While acclaiming graffiti artists like Futura 2000 as "heirs to the continuing tradition of rebellion, play and adventure which is art" in 1982 (Shafrazi 1983), he was more reluctant to deal the case in 1986:

> "It is interesting as a young phenomenon, but unless they learn about the rest of the culture (...), you can't go very far with that because it's totally naive, uneducated and gradually very limited. Up onto a certain amount of time it has a certain interest of dynamic energy because it comes from the street, is very raw, very rebellious and that's all it is. But after the first year, the second year, the third year you expect some correlations with given things of the world" (Stahl 1990: 144).

In a letter to the author, artist Phase II made his controversial point of view clear: his aim was full acceptance, at least as a remarkable cultural impact, if not as art:

> "Words like graffito and graffiti only minimalize, direct and control an art of tremendous magnitude, endless direction and unpredictable aspects. (...) Titles have admittedly been used to satisfy an unreceptive >public< unprepared to deal with the beauty of this art and its existence" (Phase 1989).

---

1 - Similar question is asked by Raphael Schacter, (with the doubtful attempt to replace the term with "intermural art"):
   http://hyperallergic.com/310616/street-art-is-a-period-period-or-the-emergence-of-intermural-art/. Thanks for the hint, Ulrich Blanché!

2. Street Art

It is worth giving a second look to a central essay in the growth of an esthetic view of graffiti. In 1933, Hungarian-French photographer and essayist Brassaï wrote his famous *Du mur des cavernes au mur d'usine*, an essay accompanied by photos that he had taken of graffiti in Paris. He wrote: "The art of the streets with bad reputation becomes a valuable criterion. Its law is formal, turning over all the canons which have been established with big efforts by the aesthetic theories" (Brassai 1933).

It is remarkable that the term "street art" is almost in use here, decades before Robert Sommer published *Street Art* (Sommer 1975). Used even earlier (Schmidt-Brümmer 1974), this term meant wall paintings. The objects shown there were mainly commissioned or tolerated murals trying to express dreams for and by ethnic minorities. It seems the term has undergone a basic change since then.

In order to get closer to defining sources, some questions might be helpful. If the street is regarded as a functional space, how does street art deal with this functional aspect? First, I think street art should have to do with streets: as form, site, functional space and cultural phenomenon.

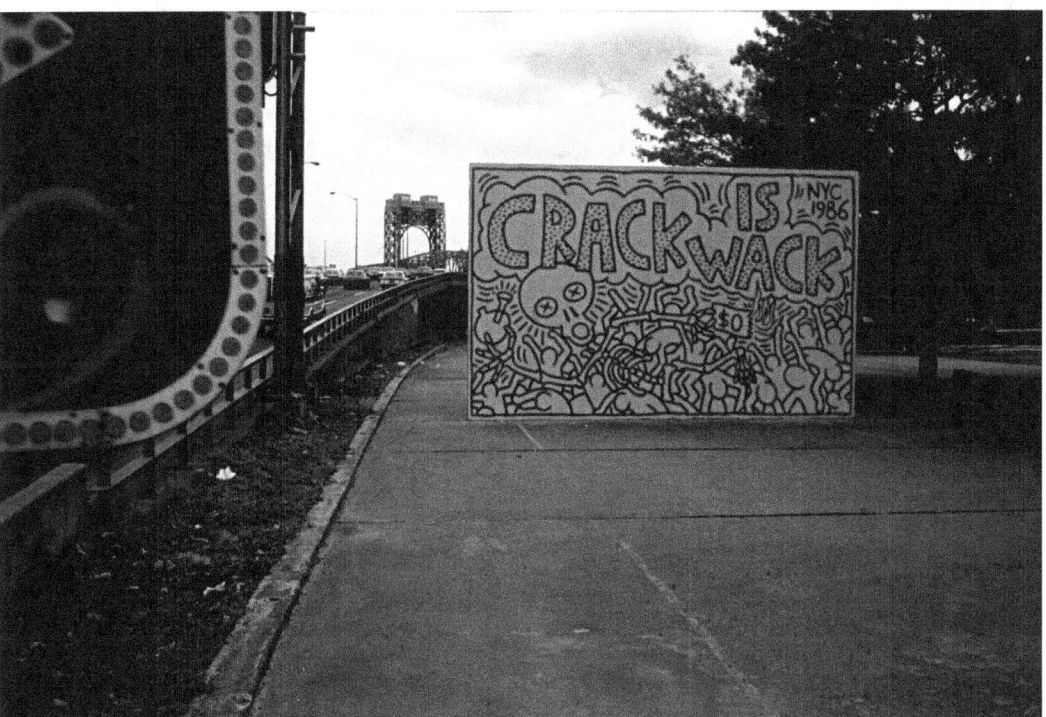

Fig. 4 - Keith Haring, Crack is wack (II), commissioned version of the mural, NYC, FDR Drive, photo taken in October 1986.

If street is regarded as a site, being site-specific can be basic for street art. Remember, the discussion about so-called drop-sculptures, which might have been placed anywhere.

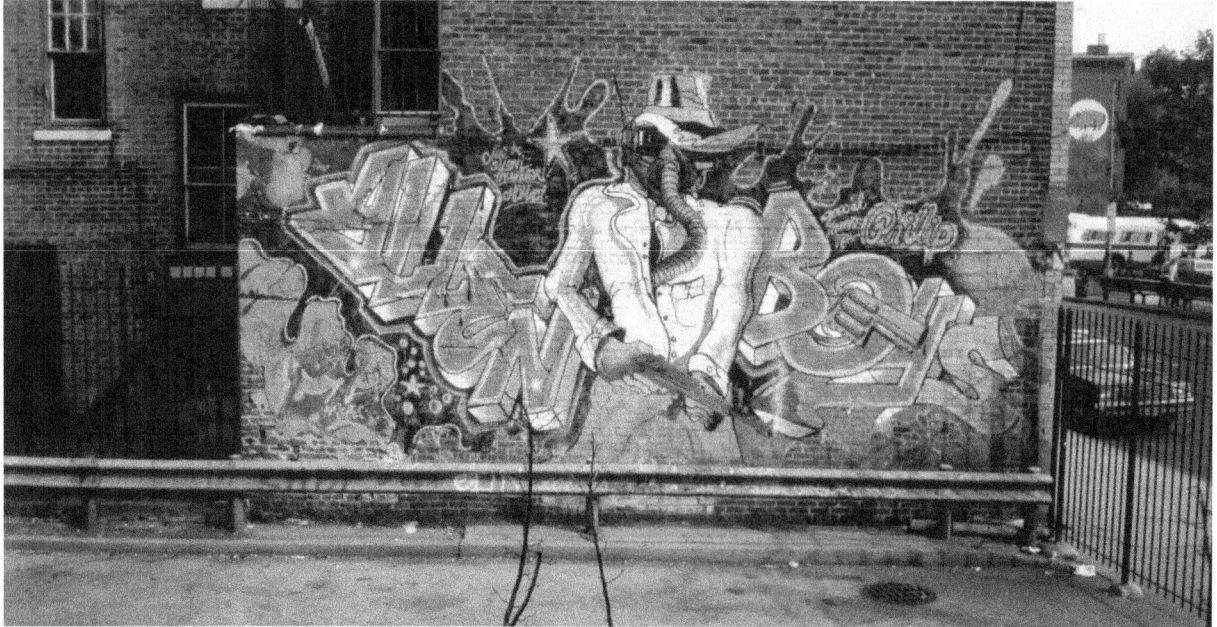

Fig. 5 - Lee Quinones: Allan Boys, NYC, Allen St, photo taken October 1986.

If people regard the street as an image, street art should refer to this role as part of the scenery - or at least as action space.

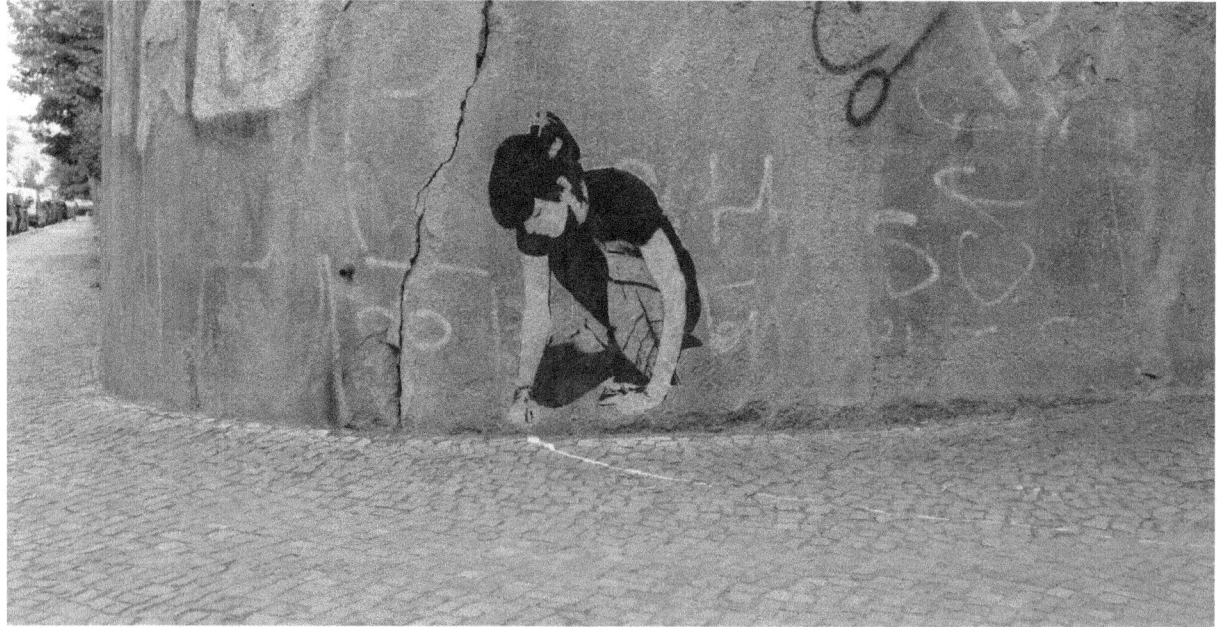

Fig. 6 - Using Street as canvas; Halle, Rathenauplatz, photo taken 2008.

If street is considered as a meaningful creation, this raises questions about the meaning of public art.

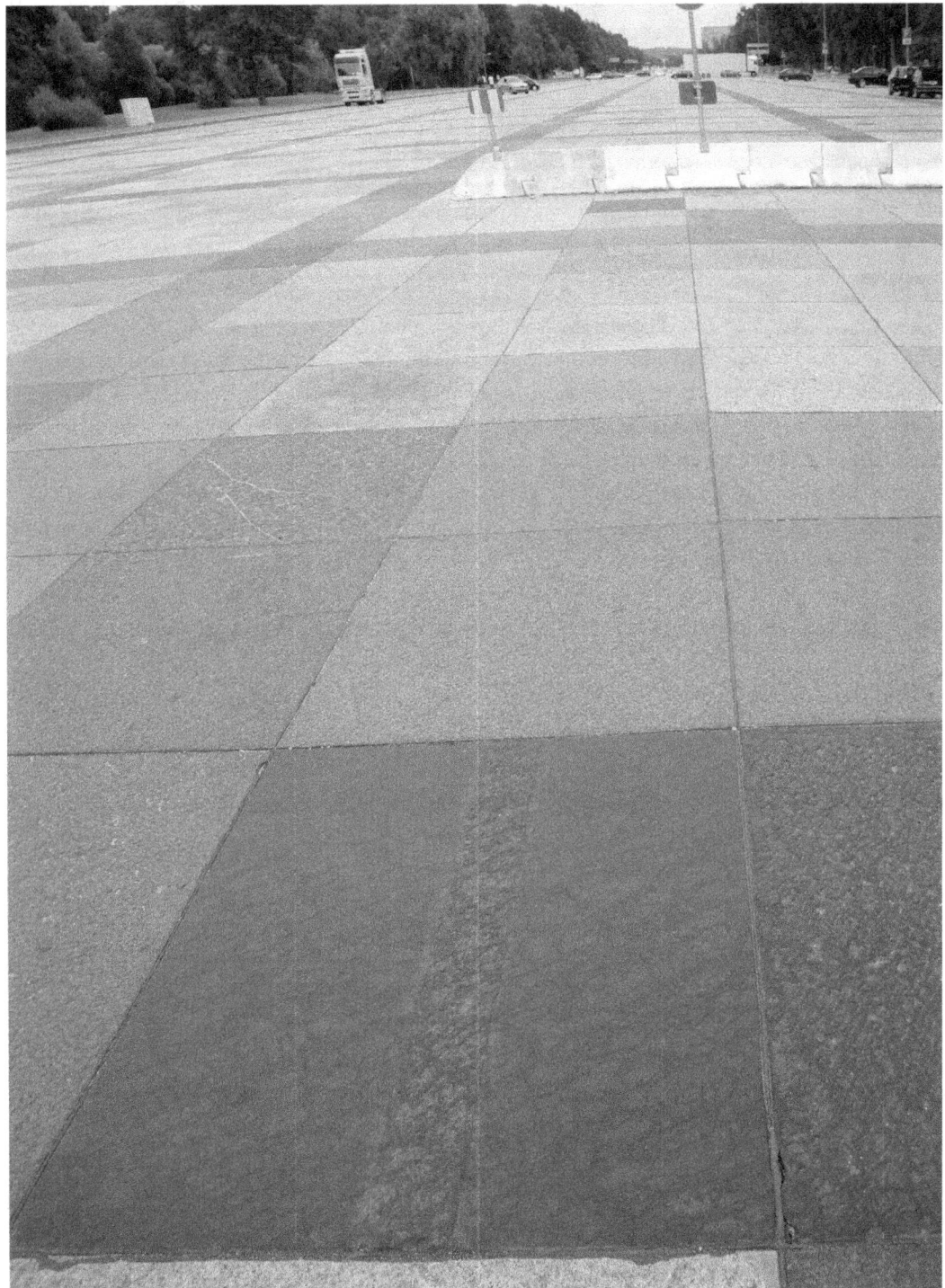

Fig. 7 - Karl Prantl, intervention at "Große Straße", Nuremberg.

The *Große Straße*" in Nuremberg was designed to be a solemn background for the marches of the National Socialist movement in Germany during the 1930s. Austrian sculptor Karl Prantl intervened in 1991, following a conception made by Israel artist Dani Karavan for a sort of aesthetic conversion of this Nazi ambient. If it follows these suggestions for definitions, street art can be an ambitious undertaking.

3. Urban Art

As for street art, here is an attempt to find some basic aspects of the term "urban art." If for urbanity, form, function, design and meaning of public space, and its forms matter, it has to be asked: How does urban art handle this?

Urban forms have long been in focus; urban surroundings determine human lives in so many ways. How streets, places, architecture, and habits form a sense of urbanity is the object of many considerations and even teaching narratives. Does urban art take these formal components serious? Are they possibly defining components?

Many urban forms – whether planned or just developed by human behavior – are the result of common sense. Jean Baudrillard interpreted graffiti as a "revolution of signs," because they disturbed the consensus of society, both by not respecting property and by refusing to give clear signs or topics of a public discussion. However, I doubt whether graffiti writers or other urban artists wanted to leave all common conventions in a sort of an "uproar of signs" (Baudrillard 1975) or if they just wanted to "watch the name pass by" (Mailor/Kurlansky/Naar 1973) and be part of the economics of attention using their own codes. In any case, they succeeded in many ways: They generated media hype and were acclaimed by the contemporary art scene as well as having commercial success. Seen from this point of view, the narrative of style wars appears also to be a mode of social consensus. The media hype about their pieces took them in anyway, be it by the success in an acclaiming art scene or on a commercial level. Seen from this point of view, the narrative of style wars reveals a new layer of the conflicts about consensus.

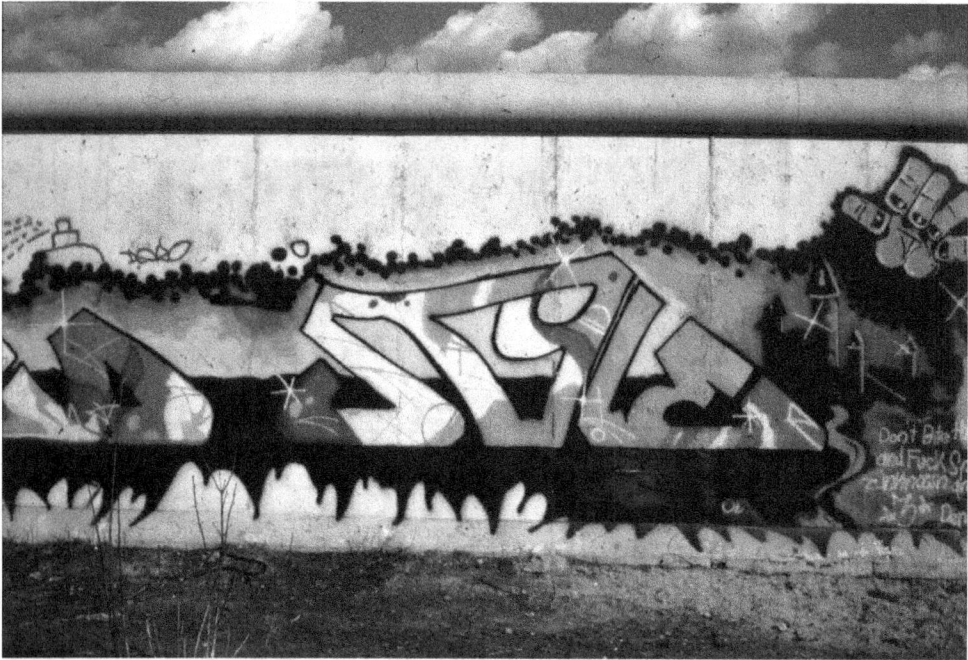

Fig. 8 - Style, Berlin Wall, photo taken October 1986.

If urban space is a construct formulating a public design: How does urban art interfere with this dimension? A similar question might be posed when it comes to spots where the architectural design of a town like Hannover has suffered from too car-friendly policies after World War II that overemphasized the street in the urban fabric.

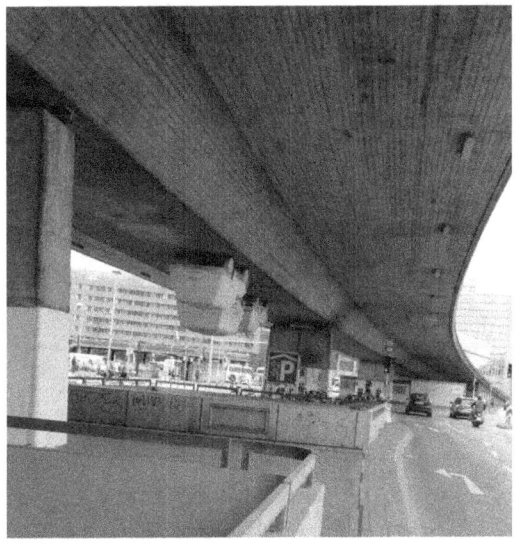

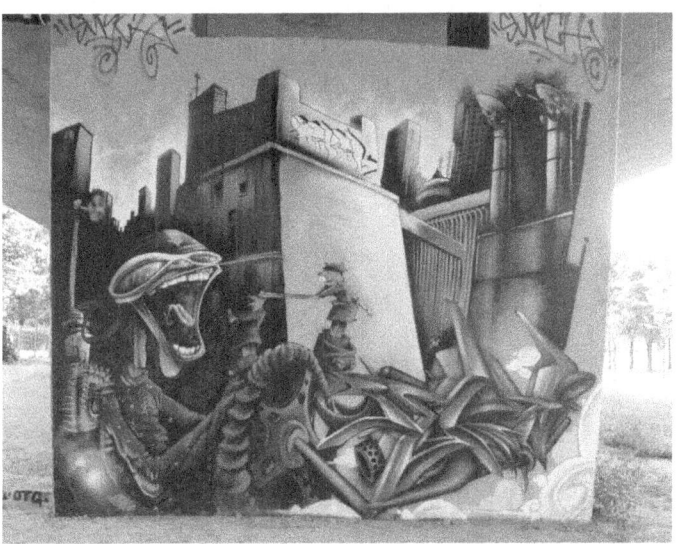

Fig. 9 - Andreas von Weizsäcker: hang over; 1991. mixed media, concrete, Hannover, Raschplatzhochstraße.

Fig. 10 - Inner city interaction, mural in Brussels-Anderlecht, photo taken March 2008.

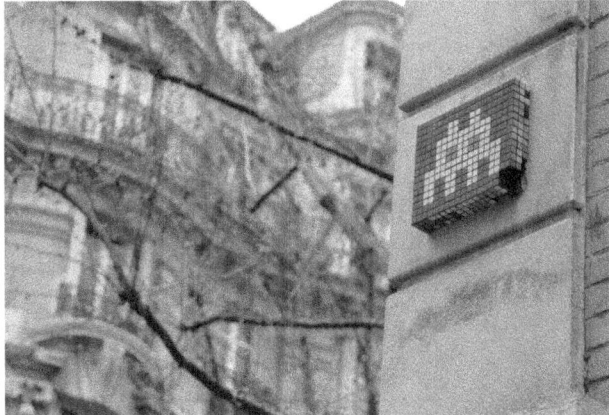

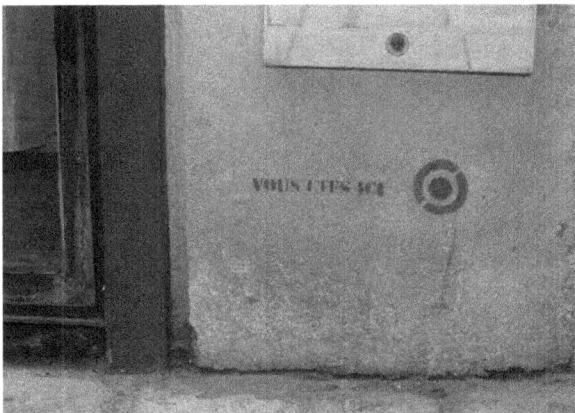

Fig. 11 - Space Invader, Paris, photo taken March 2008.

Fig. 12 - "You are here," position in town, Paris, photo taken March 2008.

Can images of rats fixed to the walls by artists as different as Judy Rupp, Blek le rat or Banksy really interact with the city? Or are they just isolated images with their own narrative disclosed from architecture and citybuilding?

The mosaics from Space Invader, for example, rework the imagery from the 1970s video game; insofar as their iconography originates from outside of the urban narrative, transposing it to the contemporary city. Placed at spots where usually road signs are posted, the mosaics disturb orientation and modify the urban space.

Seht Sigellaub's famous art definition "art is to change what you expect from it," might constitute definition-criterion for all of these phenomena, whatever you call them. And it might depend on your own position, whether you feel this change or not.

References

Baudrillard, J., 1978: Kool Killer oder die Revolution der Zeichen, Merve, Berlin. First in: Interferences, 3 (autumn), Paris, 1975.

Brassaï, 1933. Graffiti parisiens, Minotaure 3-4.

Curry, G.D., Decker, S.H., McLean, W.P., 1970: „Graffiti". In: Encyclopaedia Universalis. Paris 1968; Bd.7, 1970, 850. URL: http://www.universalis.fr/encyclopedie/graffiti, 2017-02-17

Delivery catalog of Buchhandlung König, Köln, 1986.

Garrucci, R., 1872-81: Storia dell'arte cristiana nei primi otto secoli della chiesa, six volumes, Prato.

Janis, S., 1983: Post-Graffiti Artists, catalog New York (Sidney Janis Gallery.)

Mailor, N. / Kurlansky, M. /Naar, J., 1973: The Faith of Graffiti. New York.

Mare 139, 2007: So weit zurück. In: Mai, M., Wiczak, T. (Ed.), 2007: Das Gedächtnis der Stadt schreiben, Dokument, Arsta.

Phase II, 1989: handwritten letter to the author.

Post-Graffiti Artists, catalog New York (Sidney Janis Gallery) 1983.

Roszak, T., 1969: The Making of a Counter Culture: Reflections on the Technocratic Society and Its Youthful Opposition, Garden City (NY).

Schmidt-Brümmer, H., 1974. Street Art, Köln.

Shafrazi, T., 1984. Catalog „Champions," New York 1983, introduction, cited following: Arte di frontiera. Catalog (Galleria communale di Bologna), Bologna.

Sommer, R., 1975: Street Art, New York.

Stahl, J., 1990. Graffiti zwischen Alltag und Ästhetik. Zu Problemen der Wandzeichnung, scaneg, München.
Thoss, P., 1983: Muß der Sprayer von Zürich ausgeliefert werden? In: Schweizerische Zeitschrift für Strafrecht 1983, 215-225. Cited in: Frankfurter Rundschau 281, 1983-12-03, 14-15.

Urban or Public Art?

Pedro Soares Neves
FBAUL/ CIEBA, PhD Scholarship: HERITAS/PD-FCT/BI/2015
sevenpedro@gmail.com

Abstract

The inconclusive discourses around urban art, public art, and urban art have generated an array of terminological designations. In this paper, I analyze the impacts of the terminology's rapidly changing usage in Lisbon between 2008 and 2014. In the Lisbon World Expo '98, open-air sculptures and art installations were labeled under the heading of "urban art program" (arte urbana). This illustrates a growing use of a designation that identified something new and distinct from traditional fine arts, nearer to the concept of public art (Lamas, 2000: 152).

A decade later, in 2008, the Lisbon city council commissioned a series of group paintings in outdoor panels developed with the purpose of graffiti management. The expression "urban art" (arte urbana) was used again, but this time with a totally different meaning, namely "[…] to confirm graffiti and street art as recognizable and recognized expressions of urban art as an artistic subculture globally present in world metropolises" (Carvalho and Câmara, 2014). This paper traces the development and use of this terminology in Lisbon.

Keywords: Urban Art, public art, urban design, street art, graffiti, Lisbon

1 - Public Art

1.1 - The origins of the term public art

In the UK, Morris and Ruskin understood "public art" as a reaction to the industrial revolution in the second half of 19th century, situating it as a natural development of the arts and crafts movement but with ornamental and socially engaged characteristics. It was disseminated through Belgium and Germany by Henry van de Velde (Abreu, 2015; 14 – 27).

The artist Eugène Broerman (1861–1932) coined the term "public art," describing it for the first time in an article entitled "L'Art Régénérateur". In 1893, he spoke of "L'œuvre de l'art appliqué à la rue et aux objets d'utilité publique": "The work of art applied to the street and to objects of public utility" may be what today corresponds to good quality urban environments for public use (Cheron, 2011; 701).

This movement culminated in the organization of international conferences (with wide city council attendance) and generated the foundation of "Institut International d'Art Public," which published twelve volumes of the periodical "L'Art Public" from 1907 to 1912. However, the parallel emergence of the first modern art movements in the early 20th century (i.e., Fauvism, Cubism, Expressionism, and Futurism) conflicted with the conservative aesthetic that was associated with this initial public art movement. This confrontation with the progressive aesthetics of early modernity was fatal, as the public was not interested in the conservative aesthetic adopted by L'Art Public.

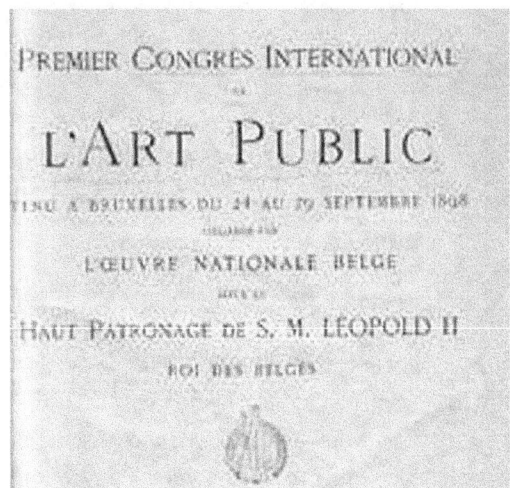

Fig. 1 - Catalogue of the first International Congress of Public Art 1898, Brussels.

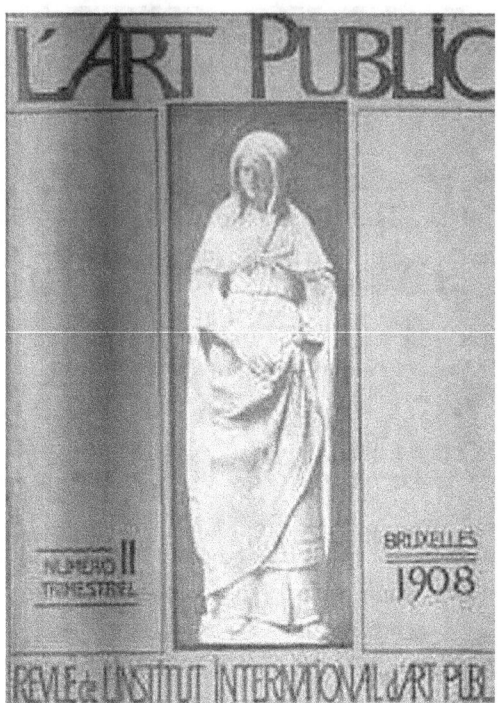

Fig. 2 - L'Art Public, n. II, 1908, Brussels.

1.2 – North American use of the term Public Art

During the same period in the USA, the term Public Art had a different meaning. The City Beautiful Movement, a reform philosophy of North American architecture and urban planning that thrived during the 1890s and 1900s, presented some initial resonance with the European use of the term public art, with its focus on monuments and neoclassical revival. However, the Anglo-Saxon literature supports the view that public art (as we understand it today) originated in the New Deal program called Art-in-Architecture (A-i-A), a structure for funding public art that is still in use today (a percentage of the new building costs goes to art programs.)

According to Knight (2008), public art radically changed during the 1970s following the civil rights movement and its claims on the public space, the alliance between urban regeneration programs and artistic interventions in the late 1960s, and the revision of the notion of sculpture. In this context, public art acquired a status that went beyond mere decoration and the visualization of official national histories in public space as in Europe in the 19th century. It therefore gained autonomy as a form of site construction and intervention in the realm of public interests.

In addition, environmental public art is considered as a means to raise ecological awareness through a green urban design process. And in this context, it is relevant to mention the trial around Richard Serra's *Tilted Arc*,[1] which shows the essential role played by site-specificity in public art – as an element often intrinsic to the art work itself, which sets the parameters for the use of the space it defines.

---

1 - Michalos, Christina. "Murdering Art: Destruction of Art Works and Artists' Moral Rights" in *The Trials of Art*, edited by Daniel McClean, 173-193. London: Ridinghouse, 2007.

1.3 - Is Mural painting also Public Art?

There is a long history of mural painting, from Egypt, Christianity, and the Middle Ages through the Renaissance. However, with the purpose of superficial characterization, we begin our survey of muralism in the early 20th century. Speaking with reference to mural painting at the Bauhaus, Oskar Schlemmer wrote in his diary:

"Mural painting, rightly praised as a genre that is capable of accomplishing an emphatic relationship to space and architecture, in contrast to the autonomous character of easel-painting and the associated danger of l'art pour l'art, must find an appropriate site and solution here at the Bauhaus." (Schlemmer, 1922 cit. in Harrison e Wood, 2003:307).

The political Mexican murals by Diego Rivera or David Alfaro Siqueiros contained clear and direct critics to advertising (Harrison & Wood, 2003: p. 429-431). It was argued that, "the creators of beauty must use their efforts to produce ideological works of art for the people (...)" (*ibidem*: 406-407). Also, the Italian fascists, for instance Mario Sironi (1885-1961) in his manifesto "Mural Painting Manifesto" 1933, praised mural painting as a strategy for ideology dissemination (*ibidem*: 424-426).

In fact, scale and visibility in relation to costs generate outdoor large-scale mural painting as a very effective option for communication and reaching large audiences. The surface support of the creation, the "skin" of the city, the limit between private and public, is common to both muralism and graffiti or street art, but in mural painting there often exists consent for the production of the work, a limit crossed by ephemeral, spontaneous non-commissioned Graffiti and Street art.

A clear distinction between muralism and public art is much harder to make. Muralism is a self-contained genre, which has its own specificities. The question is how many of these characteristics are contained within the public art concept. For instance, some key reference artists, such as Mexican muralists, produced work within the New Deal program A-i-A that constituted one of the main streams of public art expression.

1.4 - The Public Art Problematic

There are a number of competing place and production-oriented definitions of public art. For instance, Hayden (1995, 68) describes public art as, "artwork that depends on its context; it is an amalgamation of events – the physical appearance of a site, its history, the socio-economic dimensions of the community, and the artist's intervention."

Antoni Remesar (2000) provides an even more encompassing definition of public art that accords it an elevated status as a 'generator of meaningful places':

when I speak of public art I use the concept in a very general way, I understand it like a group of "artefacts" of dominant aesthetic characteristics that furnishes the public space. (...) This perspective over the concept allows the conception of public art as a generator of meaningful places "co-production" agent, and not just an "artistic" manifestation placed in public space. As a producer of sense of place and through the capacity to generate meaning and "identity", public art would be one of the key elements to put in practice the social processes of appropriation of space. Therefore, when I speak of public art, I refer myself to things like public space design, landscaping, sculpture, performances, etc. (...) and in conclusion (...) this art is possible when the regeneration program principles are based in the values of sustainability and in social cohesion, put in practice in their real dimension and not just like propaganda arguments, like usual (...)."

Contemporary definitions of public art are limited in that they often do not agree on what the expression means in practice. In turn, this lack of consensus has generated many discussions of the term's usage, which influenced the emergence of other terms that try to escape what some regarded as the problematic flexibility and over-inclusiveness of the term 'public art.'

2 - Origins and usages of the concept of Urban Art

Several aspects influence the diffuse meaning of the term Urban art. For example, one of the aspects is the language in which the reference to the term is made. In this French language article, the expression Urban art is used to identify certain aspects of Alberti's treaty - *De Re Aedificatoria*:

"[...] The constitutive function of this aesthetic requirement was formulated very early by one of the greatest theorists in the history of town planning (or more precisely urban art), the humanist Leon Battista Alberti (1404-1472) who set forth the principle in his De re aedificatoria, published in 1483[...]."[2]

The expression "Urban art" also arises in reference to the work of pre-culturalists like John Ruskin or William Morris or cultural urbanists like Camillo Sitte and Ebenezer Howard (Choay, 2003). As Alberti, these authors identify the "Urban art" concept as Urbanism, or even building, underlining the aesthetic component. The transition from image-based plans to urban planning changed the original meaning and purpose of the term, processes that for instance in Portugal happened since 1954 (Lobo, 1995).

2.1 - 1998 Lisbon EXPO'98 Urban Art concept

In the Lisbon World EXPO' 98, the open-air sculpture and art installations were labeled as an "Urban art program" (Arte Urbana) by its commissaries António Mega Ferreira and António Manuel Pinto. With the participation of national (Portuguese) and international artists, the Lisbon World EXPO' 98 contained approximately 50 pieces, the majority of which were three-dimensional works, but which also contained two-dimensional works such as pavements, murals and tiles, in an open area of 330 acres. The Lisbon World EXPO' 98 offered space and resources for innovative urban experiences created from the desire to realize new philosophies for the occupation of space.

EXPO' 98 was developed as part of a new form of understanding urban space, that created a new urban landscape in the texture of a very old city. In the words of António Mega Ferreira, this Urban art program represents the sum of the parts that had been profiled as indispensable elements for the construction of the landscape, not as decorative figuration, but as a common point for a dialogue about a strategy of deconstruction and re-construction of the urban space that culminates in the EXPO' 98 area, but that inevitably was expanded to the complete intervention area. Because of that, it is not considered a program where the interventions encountered the reason for existing in a specific sectorial strategy dedicated to the visual arts, but in the concrete placement and discourse that should embody the EXPO' 98 area.

In the catalogue, Pinto and Ferreira (1998) identified 24 artists and works. Each piece is part of a greater self, that is present in the whole area, for eyes, hands, body, and intelligence sensitivity. In a discourse characterized by time,

2 - Original quote in French: "(...)La fonction constitutive de cette exigence esthétique fut très tôt formulée par l'un des plus grands théoriciens de l'histoire de l'urbanisme (ou plus exactement de l'art urbain), l'humaniste Leon Battista Alberti (1404-1472), qui en énonça le principe dans son De re aedificatoria, publié en 1483 (...)". *L'urbanisme - De l'art urbain à l'urbanisme* in LA VEDAN, Pierre (1975). *Histoire de l'urbanisme à Paris.* Paris: Hachette

Mega Ferreira writes that the works will not make sense if left to the criminal hand of time or neglect – and indeed, 17 years later, the city council is proceeding with restoration and conservation. Ferreira continues with the argument that there will be a time where the simple removal of one of these works will shock by the amputation of part of the group. And when they are missed, in the noise that these pieces make, they will fully live in the place and memory of what they were, and how they served to say all that the EXPO'98 space wanted to say.

António Manuel Pinto (1998) shares different perspectives on the topic of Urban art as it relates to EXPO '98. He specifically emphasizes his concerns about life in urban public space, and how the urban art program could be a great opportunity for the realization of new experiences, bearing in mind the EXPO '98 conditions of funding resources and space. Pinto also identifies the problem of the ecological validity of many contemporary art projects (called at this point: Urban art) introduced in public space.

The commissaries hoped that the introduction of artistic projects would have an influence on the usage of the territory that was being created, trying through them to overcome general preconceptions that prevail in the understanding of a public art project. Clearly, Urban art as expression is here used to detach any resonance in the mind of some architects and artists that public art consists in a static statuary element in the middle of the square - a paradigm of older definitions of the term. They hoped that this new urban space would accordingly be perceived as more dynamic.

The project aimed to relaunch the image of public space, with an open, shared and positive image. In this way nine of the central (Intervention Zone of the EXPO'98) pieces aimed to overcome the state of anonymity that the public space suffers from, by generating places for permanence, and humanizing the profile of the urban landscape of the new city. Artists and other agents were charged with the task of overcoming the monolithic character of the city, generating new reference places for citizens, building reactions against indifference and apathy, and generating paradoxical objects and discontinuities within the urban grid.

The commissaries aimed to escape the historical restrictions of the role of the public art object in urban landscapes. They sought instead to generate art places. The commissaries understood that the intervention of the artist in public space should result in a transgressive element, not pacified within the city structure. This pushed the works beyond mere aesthetic value or artistic gesture – forcing the artists to question the social value of their work and the place that it occupies within urban spatial logic.

2.2 - Urban Art, Graffiti and Street Art
The records tell us that Urban art was associated with Graffiti and Street art for the first time in the exhibition Spank the Monkey of 2006, in Gateshead, UK (Bengtsen, 2014, 67). The term emerges from the set of problems that appeared as a product of the distance between Graffiti and Street art and the established art world. It was born from the need to solve the issue of addressing and representing Graffiti and Street art in the context of indoor, institutional and/or commercial cultural agents.

Since 2008, the auction house Bonhams promoted periodic auctions specializing in Urban art. In 2009, the discussion forum Banksy.info changed its name into the Urban Art Association. Nevertheless, in both circumstances, there were no definitions or clarifications made regarding the meaning of the term's usage in its essence and in relation to Graffiti and Street art. Divergent reactions occurred in both the Street art world and in the established art world because of this lack of definition (Mathew, 2008).

The occasional use of Urban art as a synonym for Street art frustrates some in the world of Street art. The connotation and commercial viability of the expression Urban art meant that the placement of works in the street and sometimes just the reference to the street became vehicles for a commercial career. In this situation the relation to those who spontaneously produce Street art has become unclear, as it quickly can turn into Urban art marketing that potentially it will later be sold.

In the Portuguese context the expression Urban art is also put in relation with graffiti as "actions that are made in the environment of the cities by graffiti writers (...) potentiated by museological programs or of the big entertainment multinational enterprises like 'Cow parades'" (Andrade, Marques, Barros, 2010).

2.3 - 2008 Lisbon - Urban Art Gallery (Galeria de Arte Urbana, GAU)

In October 2008, the program "Urban Art Gallery" was launched in Lisbon. Physically it was an open-air structure, composed of painted JCDecaux advertising panels, but conceptually it was a city wide program of actions organized by the city council, advised by some authors and agents (in which the author of this text, Vhils, Ram, Mar, among others were involved). For this purpose, a small brochure[3] was published containing a proposal for the usage of the term "Urban art", where a line is drawn to the work of the already mentioned pre-urbanists such as Morris and Ruskin (Choay, 2003). Some years later, the city council responsible for structures in Calçada da Glória, near Bairro Alto released a statement that served to "confirm the graffiti and street art as recognizable and recognized expressions of urban art, as an artistic subculture that is present in the world metropolis" (Carvalho, Câmara, 2014).

By designating "graffiti and street as (...) expressions of urban art", in the context of the urban rehabilitation of the Bairro Alto area, the council clearly do not intend to relate their work directly to the Urban art, Graffiti and Street art. At the same time, this statement represents an attempt to connect to these uncommissioned forms by recognizing their global existence. This is assumed in the context of their parallel connection to the expression "Urban art" as a form of urbanism, or drawing the city, practiced by cultural urbanists within the arts and crafts movement.

Of course, all of these developments were informed by the Graffiti and Street art relevant to Lisbon's historical developments, which are necessarily connected to global dynamics. At this point, it is also relevant to have in mind the proposed three typologies that describe Urban art in Lisbon (Neves, 2015 p. 121 – 134). These are the typology of formation, which includes the cultural urbanists' application of the term urban art as a form of drawing the city, and which also encompasses material signs of use of and in urban territories; the pre-formal typology, which incorporates subcultural graffiti and street art in its non-commissioned aspects; and the formal typology, which includes institutionalised forms of urban art such as muralism, contemporary art, and public art.

3 - Conclusions

In modernity, the term public art emerged without the earlier utopian ideal of the socially engaged characteristics of arts and crafts. Postmodern public art recaptures these socially engaged dimensions but is still located within the realm of the "art world". Thus, perhaps at this level public art is more limited as a concept than it was at the end of the 19th century.

---

3 - This brochure was disseminated with a box containing post cards of the initial paintings in the "Galeria de Arte Urbana", promoted by the Lisbon city council with the support of the Friday's project in October of 2008.

Urban Art was initially related to Arts and Crafts from a planning perspective, and (again) to the utopian ideal of the socially engaged characteristics of arts and crafts. Urban art as a term that now encompasses Graffiti and Street art also incorporates the histories of the usage of these other terms. This phenomenon has emerged in our postmodern context, but (again) is still located within the realm of the "Street Art world". Thus, today in this sense, urban Art is arguably more limited as a concept than it was at the end of the 19th century.

Commissioned murals are a form of (low cost) public Art, now adapted to digital dissemination on social media. The number of mural festivals, internationally, is rapidly expanding, with the ethos of, "give them a wall and a cherry picker". This development is supported by a rapidly growing urban art market and commercial ecosystem (ex:tours).

Given a critical awareness of the particularities of Graffiti and Street Art, and visual signs in general (street usage), perhaps both public and urban Art together may in future generate a critical mass for the expansion of the boundaries of the (Street) Art world(s) and came closer to the socially engaged utopian ideals of the end of the 19th century.

3.1 - Comparison of the **relations between Urban Art concepts in Expo'98 and 2008 (GAU)**

3.1.1 - Similarities in the approach:
- Both have concerns addressing the problematic of public space usage;
- Both introduce influences (or are signs of influence) in the usage practices of the territory;
- Both are distant from the past/old static concept of statuary as the expression of art in the city, this way both search to generate (and or are the result) of dynamism;
- Both have concerns about the role of a piece within the spatial logic of the territory;
- Both work to overcome the monolithic vision of the city;
- Both make considerations and selections about the places of implementation;
- Both search for a reaction to the generalized indifference, suggesting paradoxical and discontinuous elements within the urban tissue;
- Both (try to) escape the mere logic of objects in the landscape;
- Both go beyond the aesthetic value and artistic gesture;
- Both are not decorative figuration (although the 2008 tend partially to configure figurative);
- Both provide a common point for a dialogue about a strategy of deconstruction and re-construction of urban space (although in 2008, this tends partially not to be connected to the urban space construction, mainly if interpreted as murals);
- Not exclusively integrated into a specific sectorial strategy dedicated to the visual arts (although the 2008 have this predominance);
- Shared notion of group of pieces (both 1998 and 2008), collective body;
- Shared accomplishment of desire of new philosophy for space occupation;
- Both operate at the level of the image of the public space, aiming positive (although in the case of 2008 some are just critic, or encryption), shared and open territory (in 2008 by the practice);
- Both consider relevant the transgression and the non-pacified character of the works, although graffiti and street art transgress the limits of the law, working with the public private dialectics, 2 dimensions, the message and the transgression itself, 1998 urban art have the transgression only in the message.

3.1.2 - Differences on the approach:

- The 1998 urban art "works will not make sense if left to the criminal hand of time or men neglect", the 2008 urban art is undefined in time duration or (in the majority of the cases) clearly ephemeral, it will (only) make sense to be called graffiti or street art if works are left to "criminal hand of time or men neglect";
- in 1998 the removal of one piece will damage the collective body, in 2008 the removal of one piece is part of the process;
- in 1998 there were worries about the introduction of contemporary art in the public space, Graffiti and Street Art do not have the (contemporary art) status;
- break the anonymity of the public spaces, generating places for permanence (2008 generically do not have this concerns);
- 1998 has the purpose of humanizing the urban landscape, 2008 does not have this purpose, the humanization of the landscape exists but as a consequence;
- distinct audience purposes, 1998 searches for generating reference places and points for citizens, 2008 generates reference points for (sub) cultural groups, only latter mass culture absorbed;
- 1998 intends above all to generate a place of art, 2008 connection with art is not direct (or inexistent);
- 1998 has concerns about the social values of the works, in 2008 this consideration is not direct, although many works, authors and agents have this concern;

References

Abreu, J. G., 2015. As Origens Históricas da Arte Pública, Convocarte, N.º 1 "Arte Pública", FBAUL/CIEBA, Lisbon.

Andrade, P., Marques, C., Barros, J., 2010. Arte Pública e cidadania, novas leituras da cidade criativa, Caleidoscópio, Lisbon.

Carvalho, J., R., Câmara, S., 2014. Lisboa, Capital da Arte Urbana, revista On the W@terfront, nº30, Barcelona.

Cheron, C.,2011. L'Œuvre de l'art appliqué à la rue et aux objets d'utilité publique (1894-c.1905): étude d'une société bruxelloise d'art décoratif, in: Actes du LVe Congrès de la Fédération des Cercles d'Archéologie et d'Histoire de Belgique, Ao.t. Namur, Presses universitaires de Namur, Namur, pp. 28-31.

Choay, F., 2003. O Urbanismo: Utopia e realidades de uma antologia, Editora Perspectiva, São Paulo.

Hayden, D., 1997. The Power of Place, MIT Press, Cambridge.

Harrison; C. & Wood, P. (eds.), 2003. Art in Theory 1900-2000, Blackwell Publishing, Oxford.

Knight, C. K., 2008. Public Art: theory, practice and populism, Blackwell Publishing, Oxford.

Lamas, J. M. R. G., 2000. Morfologia Urbana e desenho da cidade. 2ª ed. Fundação Calouste Gulbenkian, Lisbon.

Lobo, M. S., 1995. Planos de Urbanização. A Época de Duarte Pacheco,DGOTDU/FAUP, Porto.

Collings, M., 2008. Banksy's ideas have the values of a joke. NY: The Times, January 28.

Neves, P. S., 2015. Significado de Arte Urbana, Lisboa 2008-2014, Convocarte, N.º 1 «Arte Pública», FBAUL/CIEBA, Lisbon.

Pinto, A. M., Ferreira, A. M. 1998. Arte urbana: urban art, Lisboa Expo'98, Parque Expo 98, Lisbon.

Remesar, A., 2000. Waterfront, Arte pública e cidadania, in: Brandão, P., Remesar, A. Espaço público e a interdisciplinariedade, CPD, Lisbon.

Beyond Artification: De/reconstructing conceptual frameworks and hierarchies of artistic and creative practices in urban public space

Minna Valjakka

PhD, Research Fellow, Asia Research Institute,
National University of Singapore

Abstract

The aim of this paper is to provoke more in-depth discussions on the dynamics and power structures underlying the conceptual frameworks of artistic and creative practices among practitioners, researchers, institutions, city officials, and urban planners in the face of growing city branding, social activism, privatization of public space, and a neoliberal art scene. It is based on ethnographic research undertaken since 2012 during extensive fieldwork, mainly in Hong Kong, Tokyo, and Seoul, and has benefitted from comparative perspectives across the regions.

I wish to shift emphasis from providing competing definitions to the more essential questions of what we gain – or loose – by the "artification" (Naukkarinen and Saito, 2012) of artistic and creative practices in urban public space. What kind of institutional and conceptual hierarchies do we de/reconstruct with our choices of definitions? Especially the official aestheticization of public space has often transformed previously subversive forms into tools of regeneration and gentrification. In addition, the common understanding of urban art as a commercial form of street art has become prominent in Euro-American discourse and city branding while artists and, for instance, public art are ever more involved in what Sharon Zukin (1995: 23) defined as the "aesthetic mode of producing space." I posit that more nuanced research on the contingencies and impediments resulting from the growing pressures to conceptualize anything as "art" by the various stakeholders involved in artistic and creative practices is needed for better understanding current societal and cultural changes in cities, the arts, and creativity.

Keywords:

artification, de/reconstruction of conceptual frameworks, hierarchies, urban art, artistic and creative practices

1. Introduction

Cities are filled with artistic and creative practices that de/reconstruct urban public space through varied strategies of, among others, guerrilla gardening, flash mobs, urban furniture, street art, contemporary graffiti[1], urban knitting, and creative activism. Although aesthetic concerns are essential for the majority of these practices, for many the primary aim is to enhance civic participation, sharing, and belonging. The organically emerging manifestations around the globe have gained academic attention as new forms of do-it-yourself urbanism (Iveson, 2013; Talen, 2015), guerrilla urbanism (Hou, 2010), everyday urbanism (Chase et al., 1999), urban interventions (Pinder, 2008) along with more artistically inclined interpretations as art activism (see e.g. Felshin, 1995; Thompson, 2015). Despite the differences in

---

1 - As I have clarified elsewhere (Valjakka, 2015a: Valjakka 2015b), the concepts used in Anglo-American research are not fully applicable to artistic and creative practices in Asia because of the local perceptions and adaptations. In order to make a differentiation from the indigenous forms of writing in urban public space, with "contemporary graffiti," I denote the transcultural forms inspired by American and European graffiti that started to emerge in East Asia mainly in the 1990s.

the conceptual framework employed, what the previous studies (in)consciously share is the emphasis on more socially just future and liveable urban fabric resonating with Henri Lefebvre's (1996: 147-159) often reiterated "right to the city," even though the question of what kinds of right are at stake is not thoroughly addressed (Attoh, 2011). The questions of *who* can interact with the urban public space and *how* are especially relevant amid of privatisation of public space and gentrification.

Many of the artistic and creative practices in urban public space resonate with David Harvey's (2012: 115-154) call for "reclaiming the city for anti-capitalist struggle." Because of geopolitical circumstances, growing social inequity, and intricate interrelations between the local and global art scene, the issues addressed by these practices are not, however, limited to anti-capitalism today. In the shadow of the ever growing instrumentalization of arts and culture for city branding, privatization of public space, and intricate power structures in neoliberal art market, the dynamics and power relations underlying the conceptual frameworks employed are far more complex than previously acknowledged. Furthermore, as Alana Jelinek (2013: 4-5) suggests, most of contemporary practices, including street art and graffiti, have become clichés of resistance that actually maintain rather than challenge neoliberal structures. Hence, I posit that the intricate questions of artistic, aesthetic, cultural, commercial, and social values involved in creation, participation, and evaluation of practices and, more importantly, reflected in the academic discourses are essential for in-depth analysis despite the fact that their continually changing qualities seem to escape permanent definitions.

More research is needed for analyzing the factors that are transforming perceptions and, furthermore, the kind of contingencies and impediments that result from growing pressures to conceptualize anything and everything as "art" by the various stakeholders involved in artistic and creative practices in urban public space. Through nuanced transdisciplinary studies, and better understanding of current societal and cultural changes in the cities, a more critical analysis of the value and power structures reshaping the role of arts and creativity can be gained. One possible way to approach these issues is through the conceptual lens of artification that "refers to situations and processes in which something that is not regarded as art in the traditional sense of the word is changed into something art-like or into something that takes influences from artistic ways of thinking and practicing" (Naukkarinen and Saito, 2012). Although not directly addressed using this specific concept, artification of graffiti and/or street art is one of the core processes underlying the current debates both in academic and public discourses. This is indicated by a more commonly accepted concept of urban art in the Euro-American context. Since the varied manifestations of artistic and creative practices emerged in urban public spaces both in European and North American cities in the 1960s, the mediation processes between urban public space and the "white cubes" of the art world has launched heated discussion on the role, status, evaluation, and definitions of the practices. As Roberta Shapiro and Nathalie Heinich (2012) maintain, the understanding of this dynamic process of social change requires the close examination of symbolic, material and contextual levels simultaneously. To reveal the dynamics of the artification process itself, Shapiro and Heinich suggest "ten constituent processes: displacement, renaming, recategorization, institutional and organizational change, patronage, legal consolidation, redefinition of time, individualization of labor, dissemination, and intellectualization."

What then constitutes the artification of artistic and creative practices in urban public space today and renders them as urban art? What kind of strategies, power struggles and dynamics are in play both on the public level and behind the scenes? More importantly, what can be gained – or lost – by the artification of artistic and creative practices in urban public space? What kind of institutional and conceptual hierarchies do we de/reconstruct with our choices of conceptual and theoretical frameworks; and what kind of values are implied through the chosen definitions and identities? It is beyond the scope of this paper to provide a detailed (art) historical analysis of the transformations or a holistic overview of artification processes across borders. Rather, my aim is to elucidate the major internationally shared trends and the most visible symbolic, material, and contextual features of artification in urban public space. The framework is based on an extensive ethnographic research since 2012 in various cities in East Asia, and on a comparative perspective built through and in dialogue with scenes in Europe, Canada, the U.S., and South Africa. Hence, my wish is to bring forward the importance of comparative and transdisciplinary analyses of artification processes around the globe and how they impact to our academic research.

2. Multiple perceptions, intentions, and use of "urban art"

The understanding of the *varied* prevailing perceptions of urban art – as well as its forms of agencies and intentions – provide a beneficial starting point for the deeper analysis of the dynamics between different disciplines, value structures, and contextual artification in both public and academic discourse. The main tendencies can be categorized in five broad rubrics which are not exclusive but often overlapping: 1) the mediation and re-imagination of a city and/or urban; 2) (un)authorized interventions and/or art in urban public space; 3) promotion of art forms deriving from the practices of street art and graffiti; 4) bridging the dichotomy between street art and graffiti; 5) employing art for branding and social well-being.

The first trend is evident among scholars from varied disciplines who examine how the city or the urban is mediated and reimagined in different forms of arts including literature, film, contemporary art, and photography. Edward Soja (2000) interprets the Neolithic wall painting from Çatalhöyük, the world's first known artistically rendered image of a cityscape dating back to roughly 6150 BC as urban art. For Soja, this mural depicting an erupting volcano and around eighty household compounds is an artistic breakthrough of imaging the city. As the "original example of a distinctively and self-consciously panoramic *urban* art form" he maintains, it "expresses a popular awareness of the spatial specificity of urbanism" (Soja 2000: 40). The definition of this settlement as a city or a proto-city is still debated among scholars, but Soja regards such reservations as a primary example of Eurocentric perceptions. He recognizes the importance of the erupting volcano and the possibility of the meaning of the image lying more in the relationship of the volcano and the city, than on the depiction of the city itself. What he fails to take into account, however, are the contested interpretations of the mural as the oldest known map, a representation of a settlement, which has recently been proved (Schmitt et al., 2014; Clarke, 2013). In addition, it is made on three interior (not exterior) walls of a house. The question remains whether we could consider this as the first example of urban art when it is a realistic representation of the settlement placed inside a building rather than on shared outer space?

Insignificance of physical site to the definition of urban art is especially visible in cultural studies, where research on urban imaginations and representations is well established and the use of urban art simulates the use of urban literature, meaning that the focus is on the depictions of the city, its people, and narratives. In her recent study, Robin Visser (2010) examines the post-socialist aesthetic circumstances in Chinese cities through urban literature and urban art. Unfortunately, she does not provide a definition for urban art but employs it for contemporary art works that examine the varied issues of urbanization in China, both the city as the subject and the subject in the city. While some of the art works are interventions in urban public space, some are oil paintings, installations or sculptures about the new subjectivities in the cities aimed to be displayed in art institutions. In these discourses on (re)imagining the urban, the defining criterion for urban art clearly relates more closely to the *content* of the art work and its recognition as an art form, but is not limited to the city itself or restricted to emerge as interventions in public space.

The second tendency is most represented by scholars from art studies and urban studies with the focus on the interfaces of urban public space and artistic and creative practices. For them the ontological classification based on the position of the art work in urban public space versus private interior space is far more common than the content criteria. The emphasis on (un)authorized interventions and/or art in urban public space versus works displayed inside art institutions is indeed one of the dividing questions in the understanding of urban art today. However, the growing demand of *art* in urban public space along with the privatization of public space are reshaping the urban fabric and art scene not only in cities in East Asia but across borders, bringing challenges to this approach. While museums, galleries, and other art institutions are exclusive to some extent, the majority of them aim to enhance their accessibility and publicness with growing emphasis on art projects reaching out from their material premises to urban public space in forms of events, performances and murals. In addition, urban art and street art museums add their own characteristics to the equation enhancing the presence of art in urban space. The most often voiced question is: Is it urban art regardless of whether it is commissioned or not?

This perception closely intertwines but also questions the third tendency, namely the use of urban art for emphasizing the artistic value and status of various practices based on or borrowing from graffiti and street art by art institutions that wish to legitimize exhibiting and presenting the art forms in question on their premises. Similar to galleries and museums, some established auction houses, like Bonhams since 2008[2], promote urban art as a groundbreaking art movement. In these cases, the key denominator is the emphasis on aesthetic and material resemblance with the artistic forms emerging in urban public space, although the forms are restricted to those easily sold for private or semi-public spaces.

The fourth rubric is visible among the creators themselves who aim to overcome the dichotomy between graffiti and street art. At the same time, they both challenge and gain the acceptance of a larger audience. For instance, the Seoul Urban Art Project in 2012-2013, was a contemporary art collective that included both local and transnational artists working under the "open gallery" concept to provide alternative sites and ways of interaction in the city. According to Junkhouse, the paragon of the project, the main goal was to show "real art on real street" instead of "public art that fits the taste of the masses." The attention was given "to diversity and a daring experimental spirit."[3] Despite the inspiring rendering and inventive experiments in abandoned buildings, the aims of the project did not fully succeed because of restrictions by city officials for safety reasons (e.g. lack of audience access to see the art works in person). In the end, the project needed to rely partially on representations through video and photographs displayed in other sites, such as alternative art spaces, resulting in unplanned artification itself.

Finally, as Sharon Zukin (1995: 23) has elaborated, although artists have become more aware and active of their role as artists and participants in political activism, they are also often collaborating with urban redevelopments as "beneficiaries, both developers of an aesthetic mode of producing space (in public art, for example) and investors in a symbolic economy." The same applies not only to artists but also practitioners from varied backgrounds in East Asia today. Coevolving tendencies bring forward unseen contingencies: while the art markets are promoting the commercial value of urban art, and various private, commercial, and non-governmental stakeholders are reaching

2 - For more information, see Bonhams's website, http://www.bonhams.com/departments/PIC-URB/#/ag1=past&MR1_main_index_key=sale&m1=1, accessed 15 January 2017.

3 - Junkhouse, a local painter and street artist, interview with the author, 7 June 2015, Seoul.

out to public space through art, city officials and urban planners across the world use the instrumental value of any kind of art for tourism and city branding. The growing official interest provides fertile ground for urban art festivals and projects to bloom across national borders with mixed agencies and aims.

In parallel and with official initiatives, also artists and residents can launch large-scale regeneration projects in order to preserve and brand their neighborhoods. One of the recent key examples from East Asia is the Gamcheon cultural village in Busan, South Korea, which has become a highly popular touristic site because of its artistically rendered public spaces. In 2009, the residents participated in the Village Art Project Competition, sponsored by the Korea Ministry of Culture, Sports and Tourism, and received 100 million Korean wons (about US$ 95,000) for the project (Hong and Lee, 2015). Regardless of how these kinds of projects label themselves — whether they are organically initiated or government-led projects and what concept they use — they are often more focused on the aestheticization of the space and artification of all sorts of practices, including but not limited to everyday practices such as cooking together or pot planting outside of one's house. Hence, they more likely add to the cultural, symbolic and/or commercial capital of the neighborhood or city in question.

3. Prevailing hierarchies and their interrelation to power structures

Besides the varied use of the concept urban art in different disciplines and practices, the growing need to promote artistic and creative practices in urban public space by various stakeholders for regeneration, branding, cultural capital, and social well-being brings challenges and contingencies to practitioners, artists and scholars alike. While harnessing art and creativity for various purposes enhances the processes of artification, it inevitably also blurs the line between support and exploitation. Organically or privately initiated projects, such as an annual street art festival in Hong Kong organized by HK Walls, a non-profit arts organization[4], can get the attention of the local tourist board, which then advertises the event in order to create a more alluring city image for younger generations of tourists in Asia. Publicity can bring new audiences to the event but also cause misunderstandings and unjustified accusations of the commercial intentions of the organizers. Indeed, occasionally, city officials, private entrepreneurs and developers employ artistic and creative practices as they see fit to their own agendas, regardless of the creators' own wishes. Art has the ability to catch public attention in today's image dominated world and, consequently, to enhance the notion of a vitality of a place or a neighborhood. Because of the commonly perceived positive impact of art to community, it more easily wins support from different stakeholders. The artification processes of renaming, institutional and organizational transformations, and growing patronage of artistic and creative practices in urban public space in East Asia are both the result and cause of social and cultural reconstruction of the urban fabric today.

Concurrently, this official and government-led artification of artistic and creative practices in urban public space creates pressure for other stakeholders, such as practitioners, artists, NGOs, NPOs, and art institutions to come up with socially engaged art projects to be funded by the local governments, transnational corporations and/or other legitimate institutions. On the one hand, aesthetics and arts may risk to be reduced into a mere instrumental role resulting into what Raminder Kaur and Parul Dave-Mukherji (2015: 15) regard as NGO-ization of art practice. On the other hand, growing support for art projects engaging with communities and social groups provide new opportunities for financial support: conceptual framing of, for instance, a social neighborhood experiment as art in a funding application improves the possibilities of acceptance and is a valid choice for aiming to maintain the practice in question. Artification of artistic and creative practices in urban public space is, indeed, a double-edged sword.

---

4 - For more information on HK Walls, see its website, http://hkwalls.org/about/, accessed 8 June 2017.

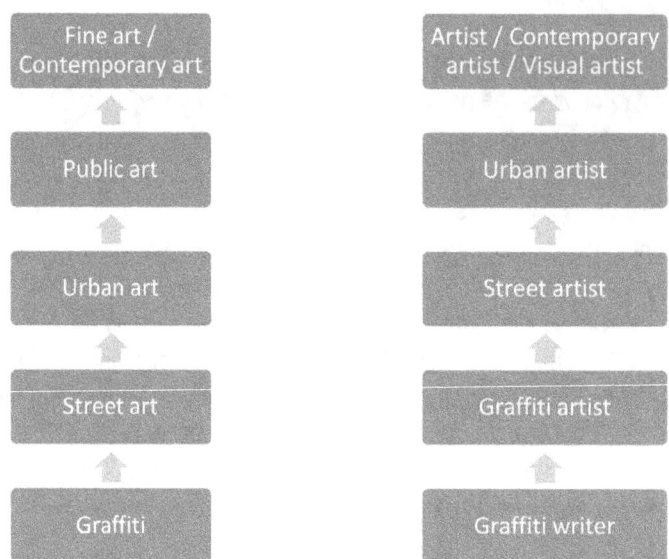

Fig. 1 - Prevailing hierarchies in conceptual frameworks and subjectivities. Copyright Minna Valjakka.

It enables novel sites, agencies, and aesthetics to be appreciated by larger audiences and adds to accessibility. At the same time, commissioned works might have limitations to the aesthetical, artistic, and ideological aims of the practitioners themselves.

The reframing and renaming strategies of artistic and creative practices in urban public space and their (un)conscious implications deserve more (academic) attention. The involvement of various agencies and their position in de/reconstructing the power structures, hierarchies and value constructions (e.g. on commercial, social, symbolic, cultural, and artistic values) need to be taken into account. The intricate value questions underlie any commissions, events, collaborations, and interventions causing heated debates, unequal treatment and even unreasonable accusations. One possible method to examine the ongoing power negotiations and what kind of impact artification actually has on practitioners and researchers is to question the prevailing and dominating hierarchies in both practices and practitioners' professional status (Fig 1).

The linear and reductive understanding of so-called evolution from graffiti to the realm of fine art or contemporary art echoes in the subjectivities and professional roles taken by the practitioners themselves. Both the need to be accepted by the global art world and, possibly, benefit from the exposure and financial profit, encourages the practitioners to follow the path both in self-definitions and practices that might make them globally recognized, as has happened, for instance to Portugese Alexandre Farto (a.k.a. Vhils), French Julian Malland (a.k.a. Seth) and South African Faith47. The pattern of hierarchic progress is especially visible among practitioners deriving from the streets but aiming to reach the acceptance of the art world: while reaching for recognition as artists they tend to replace the concepts of urban art, street art, and graffiti with interventions, site-specific art, and public art. From the perspective of art galleries and curators, such a change can also be a highly positive factor enabling a new position in the art world.

These kinds of conceptual hierarchies aim for artification of the practices in urban public space — and even bringing them into the "white cubes" — and are especially visible among the art institutions and, to some extent, in NPOs and NGOs competing for public funding. The question remains: Does this conceptual framework have an impact on academic discourses, too? What kind of intellectualization processes it might provoke? Do scholars, especially in art studies, employ artification to research projects in order to be academically more accepted, appreciated, and supported?

These linear patterns require more nuanced de-/reconstruction through examining varied agencies from different backgrounds with contradictory intentions. It is essential to acknowledge that the value structures *are not universal*, and vary greatly from one individual to another and are continuously changing. As is well known, the prevalent sentiment shared by many pioneers from the streets, especially those from the old-school graffiti and street art in Euro-American contexts, is that street credibility through unauthorized practices serves as the cornerstone for the other phases in a possible career and as a legitimization of the financial profiting of one's work as art (Fig 2). For many practitioners today, the artistic and aesthetic aims are nonetheless more important than making a statement through, for instance, writing one's name, and the internationally growing public appreciation for art on the streets has shifted for valuating street art, encouraging more people to create it. Hence, the professional roles and subjectivities today have become ever more complex: while for some identification as a graffiti writer is still the core of subjectivity, many prefer alternative roles, even transcending those related to arts and/or creativity *per se* and without clear hierarchic relations (Fig 2).

In addition, in East Asia the genealogies, conceptual frameworks and the evaluation criteria of artistic and creative practices in urban public space do not follow the same logical structures as in Euro-American contexts. For instance, in Japan the strong social norms of proper behavior and the emphasis on aesthetically harmonious urban public space, especially in certain neighborhoods in Tokyo, evoke strong public reaction against contemporary graffiti. Meanwhile, certain forms of commissioned "street art," such as murals, are gradually gaining (limited) acceptance. The discrepancies of the appreciations of artistic and creative practices in different cultural contexts create other forms of pressure for artification of both the practices and professional roles: practitioners aiming for recognition as street artists or artists may find it necessary to conceal their possible background as graffiti writers.

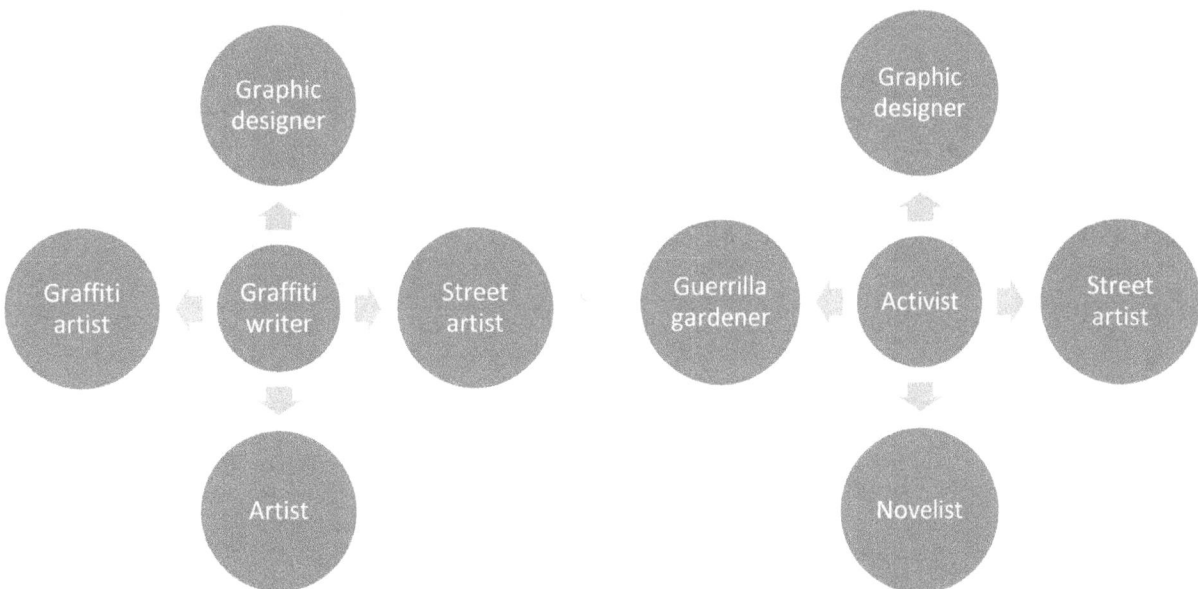

Fig. 2 - One possible example of an alternative understanding in conceptual frameworks and subjectivities. Copyright Minna Valjakka.

Art historical perspective can provide another angle for questioning the need of artification. Since the 1960s, especially avant-garde and experimental artists, such as those involved in the Situationist International, Fluxus, and Japanese Gutai group, among others, aimed for criticizing capitalism, social inequity, and problems caused by urbanization. They have been keen to eschew art world values and reference points by creating radical interventions and participatory projects in urban public space. The questioning of the dichotomy between life and art has been one of the core values among these artists promoted conceptually, for instance, by German artist Joseph Beuys (1974: 48) with his insights on social sculpture aiming to enhance new aesthetic and social consciousness to build "a social organism as a work of art." His broader conceptual take on art did not only aim to erase the dichotomy between art and life but furthermore as to transform art practices to include conversation, collaborations, and shaping the actual world (Beuys, 2004: 9). This tendency has only grown and expanded in terms of new public art practices, especially since the 1990s, in Euro-American art scene, which has brought about novel perceptions and value constructions (see e.g. Lacy, 1996). Following art historian Grant H. Kester's insights, collaborative art practices have an emphasis on exchange and partnership instead of the artist's authorship and aesthetic autonomy. A more nuanced study of these art practices, as Kester (2011: 89) rightfully emphasizes, "can reveal a more complex model of social change and identity, one in which the binary oppositions of divided vs. coherent subjectivity, desiring singularity vs. totalizing collective, liberating distancing vs. stultifying interdependence, are challenged and complicated."

More recently, the conceptual frameworks and values involved have become even more complex and instead of expanding the notion of art to everyday life, there are tendencies to transcend art and the artification processes: instead of labeling their works as urban art or public art, many artists prefer concepts such as interventions, projects, events, and even social studies. This novel process could even be understood as non-artification of art practices and their professional identities: the aim to promote conceptual frameworks, subjectivities, professional roles, and practices beyond art, meaning that they are not merely dependent on the artistic or aesthetic values (Fig. 3).

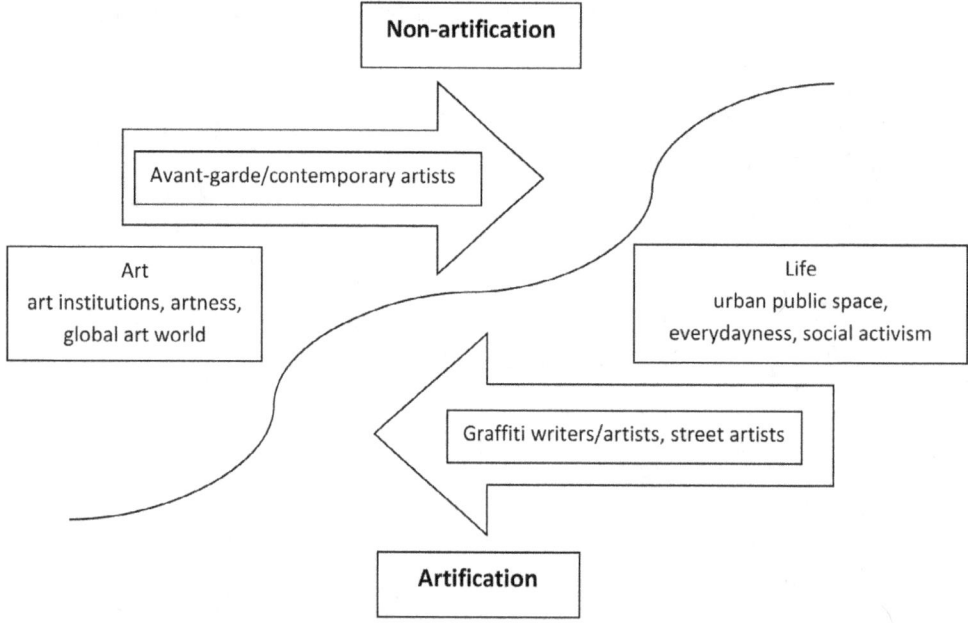

Fig. 3 - The contesting trends of artification and non-artification in practices, values, and discourses. Copyright Minna Valjakka.

To be reductive but rhetorical, a kind of two-way inversion in practices, discourses, values, intentions, and processes has emerged: a movement toward the acceptance by the art institutions foregrounds the practices on the streets. But a movement toward everyday life and employment of urban public space underpins the aims of some of the contemporary artists. These two simultaneous yet contradictory tendencies set an intriguing challenge for our research. How can we do justice to the continuously changing, myriad manifestations, agencies, forms, aesthetics, and intentions across the borders and without forgetting the urbanites who also are actively engaged with urban public space outside of these art discourses?

4. Conclusions: toward more multivalued appreciation

The recent social and political turmoil in cities in East Asia reveal how the authorized city making policies does not always fulfill the everyday needs of urbanites. From this dissatisfaction, the urge for urbanites to develop new artistic and creative practices arises: to facilitate social changes with or *without* the help of established artists. The artistic and creative practices in urban public space today are not limited to art projects initiated and led by professional artists, even though using art and creativity for branding along with NGO-ization of art practices is popular. The multiplication of agencies taking part in reshaping the urban public space to include citizens, activists, designers, educators, professors and/or varied institutions is ever more visible across the globe. Many of them involved in artistic and creative practices in urban public space emphasize process instead of the physical outcome and highlight subjects rather than objects.

Furthermore, either traditional or new forms of artistic and creative practices in cities in East Asia do not always fall under the Western notion of "contemporary art." The forms of creative engagement with the urban public space, such as street furniture, urban knitting, and urban gardening, aim to improve the urban fabric for and by urbanites who do not usually consider themselves as artists or their input as art. We could accept the proposition that everything is art and everyone is an artist, voiced, for instance, by often quoted Joseph Beuys. But what would we actually gain with the aim of the artification of everyday practices? Some of them might be then "accepted" as art and remediated, for example, in digital forms in order to be displayed in art institutions. This kind of institutionalization might benefit their evaluation in terms of collectability, monetary value and/or preservation practices. The physical distancing would, however, separate them from the shared space they aim to build in the city itself and change the ideological framing, too. Moreover, posing value constructions from art world could contradict the perceptions of the urbanites themselves. The major risk of mislabelling includes the probability of transforming the value of the manifestations from social to cultural and even to artistic capital benefitting other institutions more than the people who created them in the first place.

Varied forms of artistic and creative practices are especially visible during social movements. The approaches based on urban art, street art, public art or protest art are beneficial but they fail to grasp the diversity present in protest sites in terms of infrastructure, mediation, and agencies. Average urbanites, without previous experience or training in arts, are joining contemporary artists, art activists, street artists, and graffiti writers to make their concerns heard in relation to local, regional, and global issues, such as social discrepancy, environmental issues, and urban development — by creative actions building up re-imaginations for the future.

As an example, in Hong Kong an unseen wave of creativity by urbanites swept across the city to support the Umbrella Movement in the autumn 2014. Many artists contributed through workshops, lectures, and interventions too, but most of them strongly emphasized the anonymity of their input. They promoted the social rather than artistic values of their works — even by letting the works to be destroyed rather than preserved when the space was cleared by officials. One of the primary examples of non-art intervention was the Lennon Wall Hong Kong, initiated and maintained by a group of local social workers and students, none of claiming the status of an artist. Uncountable number of varied contributions were made by tourists, urbanites, activists, and artists, but majority of them were post-it notes (Fig. 4). Although participation and aesthetics were essential also to the Lennon Wall, it does not fully correspond with current understandings of collaborative art because it was not an art project organized and lead by professional artists. What value would it add to this ephemeral project to artify it, and for instance, to display it in an art museum?

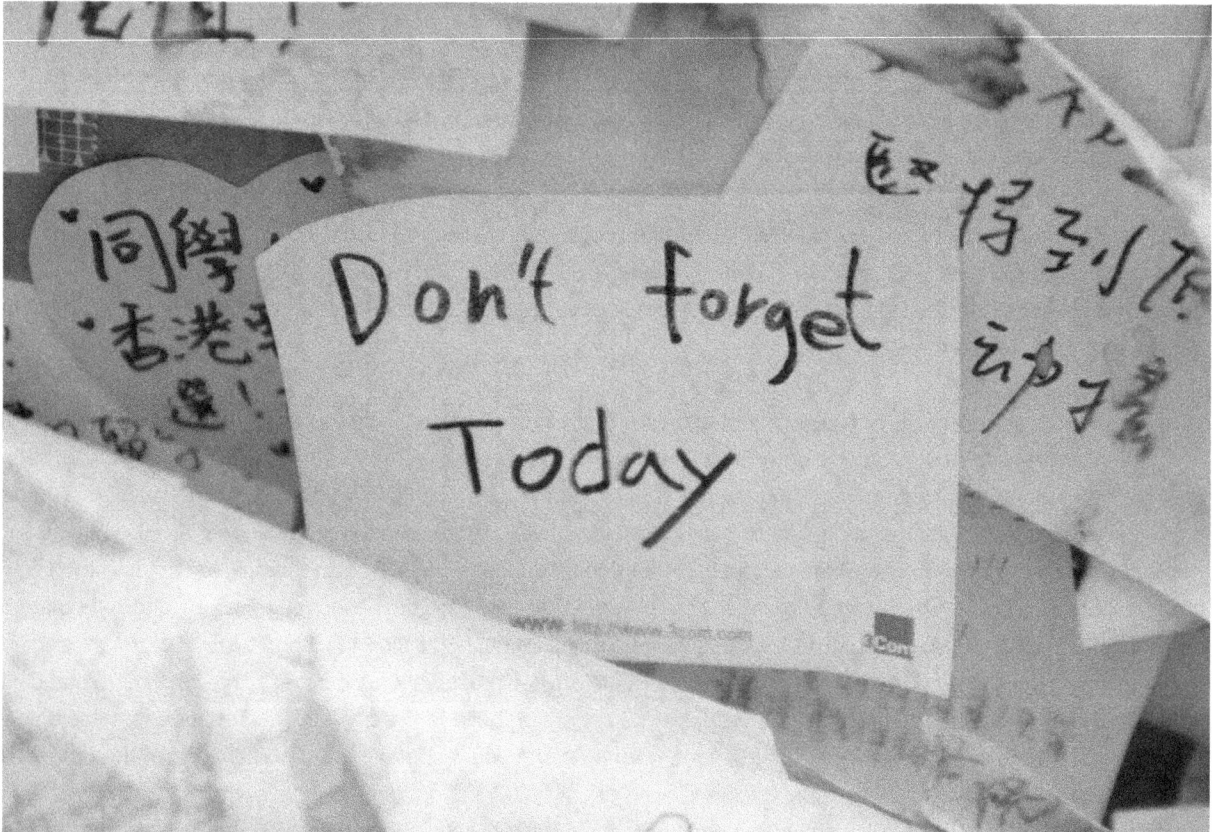

Fig. 4 - One note on Lennon Wall, Admiralty, Hong Kong, November 2014. Photo: Minna Valjakka.

I posit that critical analysis of more versatile practices than those falling under the current notion of 'urban art' is needed in order to transcend the binaries in perceptions as Kester suggests. More detailed understanding of the shifting agencies, conceptual frameworks, power relations, and artification processes will reveal more intricate interrelations of societal changes, art, and creativity. Artification of artistic and creative practices in urban public space does not necessarily add cultural, aesthetical, commercial, social or artistic value to the practices or practitioners themselves. On the contrary, artification may even cause unexpected and unwanted outcomes in terms of misinterpretations and even exploitation of the practices in the benefit of other institutions or official programs.

References

Attoh, K., 2011. What kind of right is the right to the city?, Progress in Human Geography 35, 5, 669–685.

Beyus, J., 1974. I Am Searching for Field Character, in: Tisdall, C. (Ed. and trans.) Art Into Society, Society Into Art, Institute of Contemporary Art, London.

Beuys, J. and Harlan V. (Eds.), 2004. What is Art? Conversation with Joseph Beuys, Clairview Books, Forest Row, UK.

Bonhams website, http://www.bonhams.com/departments/PIC-URB/#/ag1=past&MR1_main_index_key=sale&m1=1 [Accessed 15 January 2017].

Chase, J., Crawford, M., Kalisky, J., (Eds.) 1999. Everyday Urbanism, Monacelli Press, New York.

Clarke, K., 2013. What is the World's Oldest Map?, Cartographic Journal 50, 2, 136-143.

Felshin, N., 1995. But Is It Art? The Spirit of Art as Activism, Bay Press, Seattle.

Harvey, D., 2012. Rebel Cities: From the Right to the City to the Urban Revolution, Verso, London.

HK Walls website, http://hkwalls.org/ [Accessed 8 June 2017].

Hong, S. G., Lee, H. M., 2015. Developing Gamcheon Cultural Village as a tourist destination through co-creation, Service Business 9, 4, 749-769.

Hou, J., 2010. Insurgent Public Space: Guerrilla Urbanism and the Remaking of Contemporary Cities, Routledge, London.

Iveson, K., 2013. Cities within the City: Do-It-Yourself Urbanism and the Right to the City, International Journal of Urban and Regional Research 37, 3, 941-956.

Jelinek, A., 2013. This Is Not Art: Activism and Other 'Not-Art', I.B. Tauris, New York.

Kaur, R., Dave-Mukherji, P. 2015. Introduction, in: Kaur, R., Dave-Mulherji, P. (Eds.), Art and Aesthetics in a Globalizing World, Bloomsbury Academic, New York.

Kester, G. H., 2011. The One and the Many: Contemporary Collaborative Art in a Global Context, Duke University Press, Durham.

Lacy, S. (Ed.), 1996. Mapping the Terrain: New Genre Public Art, Bay Press, Seattle.

Lefebvre, H., 1996. The right to the city, in: Kofman, E., Lebas, E. (Eds.), Writings on cities, Wiley-Blackwell, Cambridge, Mass., 147-159.

Naukkarinen, O., Saito, Y., 2012. Introduction. Contemporary Aesthetics 4, 2012, n.p. http://www.contempaesthetics.org/newvolume/pages/article.php?articleID=634 [Accessed 15 December 2016].

Pinder, D., 2008, Urban Interventions: Art, Politics and Pedagogy, in: International Journal of Urban and Regional Research 32, 730–736. doi:10.1111/j.1468-2427.2008.00810.x

Schmitt, A., Danišík, M., Aydar, E., Şen, E., Ulusoy, İ., Lovera, O., 2014. Identifying the Volcanic Eruption Depicted in a Neolithic Painting at Çatalhöyük, Central Anatolia, Turkey, PLOS, http://dx.doi.org/10.1371/journal.pone.0084711

Seoul Urban art Project's website, http://www.sup-project.com/2012/main.html [Accessed 2 February 2017].

Shapiro, R., Heinich, N., 2012. When is Artification?, in: Contemporary Aesthetics 4,2012, n.p. http://www.contempaesthetics.org/newvolume/pages/article.php?articleID=639 [Accessed 15 December 2016].

Soja, E., 2000. Postmetropolis: Critical Studies of Cities and Regions, Blackwell Publishing, Malden, MA.

Talen, E., 2015. Do-It-Yourself Urbanism: A History, in: Journal of Planning History 14, 2, 135-148.

Thompson, N., 2015. Seeing Power: Art and Activism in the 21st century, Melville House Publishing, Brooklyn, NY.

Valjakka, M., 2015a. Negotiating Spatial Politics: Site-responsiveness in Chinese Urban Art Images, in: China Information 29, 2, 253–281.

Valjakka, M., 2015b. Urban Art Images and the Concerns of Mainlandization in Hong Kong, in: Bracken, G. (Ed.), Asian Cities: Colonial to Global, Amsterdam University Press, Amsterdam, 93-121.

Visser, R., 2010. Cities Surround the Countryside: Urban Aesthetics in Post-Socialist China, Duke University Press, Durham.

Zukin, S., 1995. The Cultures of Cities, Blackwell, Cambridge, MA.

Digital Media & The Urban (Art)

The Embedded Digital Realm in Urban Space

Meltem Şentürk Asıldeveci

PhD Student
Bauhaus-Universität Weimar
Fakultät Architektur und Urbanistik
Vorwerksgasse 3 99423 Weimar-Germany
meltem.sentuerk.asildeveci@uni-weimar.de

Abstract

This research reinterprets urban design theories. Its main aim is to reconsider social structure, which is comprised of individuals and their mobile communication tools. It is inevitable that our mobile society constituted in urban space necessitates a reconsideration of urban identity defined through the cognition and identification of the components of the city. Over the ten years, we've witnessed a perception of urban space and location in which awareness is quite different when individuals use smart phones in wayfinding process or when defining familiar-unfamiliar places.

First part includes a short account of the questionnaire research results. This enables us to interpret the effect of mobile communication devices on individuals' meeting places in urban space. In the second part, the frame of the subject is extended with an example of a sensational mass movement to depict the power of social media. This section based on the Gezi Park demonstrations in Istanbul in 2013, examines the role of social media to identify urban space and redefined identities of urban space. The constant information flow related to particular locations during the Gezi Park demonstrations has created imperishable memories for these places in Istanbul. This research is criticizing the acknowledged images of urban space beyond architectural determinism and asks how the perception of place identities has changed in light of new modes of communication.

Keywords:

Urban identity, urban public space, mobile phones, mobile communication, social media, vested identities

1. Introduction

The objective of this research is to interpret acknowledged urban design theory in light of social structure in urban space which is comprised of individuals and their mobile communication tools. The existence of 'mobile society' in urban space necessitates the reconsideration of the urban identity issue described through cognition and identification of physical and spatial components of urban settings. Hence in the era of wireless connection, physical space and virtual space should be considered together in urban space to define place identities. Shared pictures and texts on social media posted from specific locations are consolidating the identities or enriching the meanings of these places.

In *The Structural Transformations of the Public Sphere* (1962), Jürgen Habermas emphasizes the role of communication in public opinion. However, the means of communication of recent times were unthinkable when Richard Sennett (1974), Jürgen Habermas (1962) or Kevin Lynch (1961) was writing about urban social life and cognitive mapping. This research reviews urban design theory from the perspective of today's mobile communication practices by looking at the impact of social media as one of the most effective channels of perpetual connection with little to no cost and the world to bear witness.

The outcome and earnings of mobile communication possibilities in urban space is conceptualized by 2 examples. One of them is based on a survey conducted in Ankara, Turkey, during 2009 and 2010. It covers the analysis of the responses of several hundred participants to a questionnaire which attempted to identify behavioral changes before and after the advent of the mobile phone. The second subject is based on the recent findings of summer 2013 Gezi Park protests in Istanbul. We all have witnessed the impact of mobile communication possibilities in urban space via social media during mass social movements particularly in the Middle East during the 'Arab Spring'. Gezi Park protests that began in Istanbul and spread throughout the country was one of the examples of mass society movements but it is quite unique because 85 percent of social media posts were sent from within Turkey, whereas in the other examples the majority was sent from abroad [3]. Although the protestors against police violence seem to be lost but Gezi Park protests have resulted with the success of social media. Accordingly, the Gezi Park mass movement itself and how the movement patterns and meeting places constantly defined and redefined through instant shares on social media are the noteworthy issues that shed light on this research.

2. The survey on Meeting Places

This survey is conducted in 2009 and 2010 includes the responses of 630 participants to a questionnaire that attempts to ascertain behavioral changes before and after mobile phone usage. The fundamental question is "How have the meeting places of Ankara are changed in meanings in the mobile phone era". The first section of the survey looks for changes in the cognitive mappings of the citizens of Ankara due to the onset of mobile phone use. The criteria for this survey were; 1) The respondents should have been familiar with the city; 2) The respondents should have experienced the city before and after the advent of mobile phone usage.

According to the answers, the meeting points on the city map were scattered in urban space and they are placed more on streets rather than pointing out nodes as landmarks. An additional extended questionnaire was carried out with denizens of different ages, backgrounds and educational levels aiming to achieve an objective interpretation; including 630 participants in total. The inventory of meeting places in Ankara according to different age groups showed a considerable change. One of the most critical issues of this research was that the specific interior spaces or service points (metro stations, bus stops) were defined as the meeting places by denizens. This shows that the meeting places became the simultaneously scheduled activities, rather than situated /organized activities. The paths (streets or boulevards) in the city center were preferred as meeting places more often according to the questionnaire results (fig.1 and fig.2). After the advent of the mobile phone, meeting places were scattered on these paths. Therefore, it can be interpreted that the meeting places were also perceived in linear form besides point wise. Unlike urban theories which tell us these components of urban structure are ascendant elements for a city to be legible, secondary research (Barlas, A., Şentürk, M., 2012) reveals that these points of references are lose efficiency during cognition mapping processes in the era of mobile information and communication technologies.

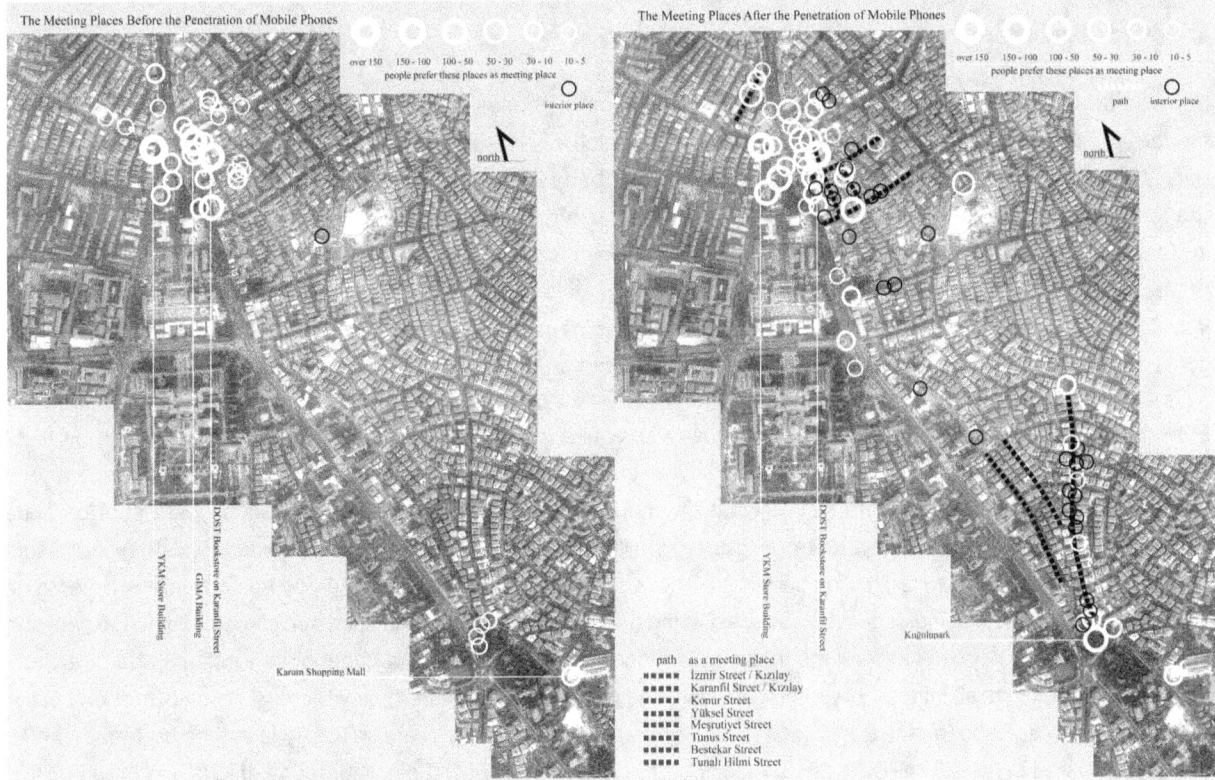

Fig. 1 - Meeting Places before mobile phone
Private archive, Meltem Şentürk Asıldeveci.

Fig. 2 - Meeting Places after mobile phone
Private archive, Meltem Şentürk Asıldeveci.

In order to bring further comment on urban design theories, it is helpful to review what the theory says so far. By the 1960s, the production of flexible environments was increasingly seen in terms of amalgamating the multifunction design principles of modernism with the new media of computers. During the early 1970s a group succeeded in isolating a large number of so-called "patterns" which specify some of the spatial relations necessary to wholeness in the city. The patterns which are defined ranged from the largest urban scale to the smallest scale of building construction (Alexander, Neis, Anninou, King, 1987). Then, Amos Rapoport in "Human Aspects of Urban Form" brought the close relationship between built form and culture to the attention of architects and planners. Urban form is clearly seen as resulting from the interplay of a number of factors such as location, transportation networks, land value and topography (Rapoport, 1977). Mobile technologies breathe a new life into the multi-layered structure and restoration of urban space. As Scott Mc Quire declares, the contemporary city is a media-architecture complex resulting from the proliferation of spatialized media platforms and the production of hybrid spatial ensembles. While this process has been underway at least since the development of technological images in the context of urban "modernization" in the mid-19th century, its full implications are only coming to the fore with the extension of digital networks (McQuire, 2008). The predominant theory of urban identity is largely fed by visually based explanations, supported by interpersonal and inter-communal relations. In this sense, new communication practices and virtual environments of social media embedded into urban structure bring a new approach to the subject of urban design theories as well as the meaning of urban identity.

3. Vested Identities of Urban Public Places

Public places are consolidated by the affordances of smart phones, and question acknowledged urban design theories. The value of the flow of instant information is crucial. It is like spatial knowledge in urban space because the person standing in an urban sphere is connected to everybody and everywhere with his smart phone in addition to the real social composition. Such that, in the previous years we have observed a determinative role of social media in demonstrations in Egypt and Tunisia; we experienced it in Istanbul at the Gezi Park protests too. The Gezi Park protests arose from disputed urban development plans, which had little public input to remove Taksim Gezi Park, the last significant green space in the center of Istanbul, and replace it with a shopping mall. The protest and its effect on social media increased exponentially with the police intervention.

29th of May 2013, was the first day of the police intervention in Gezi Park and thus the beginning of the protests in Istanbul. According to the New York University Social Media and Political Participation (SMaPP) Department, 7,328,937 Tweeter messages were sent on that day and 18,835,909 protest-related messages were sent on June 1. Hashtag direngeziparki is used more or less four million times during Gezi Park protests. Turkish Twitter users increased from 1.8 million to ten million people [1]. These statistics show that people rely on social media in order to be informed about what is going on in urban space. During the Protests, participants used social media to define safe and unsafe places and they transformed the meanings of locations. Via Twittter and Facebook messages, the protestors declared a mosque as an infirmary, a hotel lobby as a shelter, a café as an emergency battery charging spot and made these places to be used in that way. In 2017, the number of smart phone users in Turkey is estimated to reach 40.5 million compared to just 16 million in 2013. Along comes the importance of the collaboration of ICTs and urban design practices in order to breathe new life into the debate of successful cities.

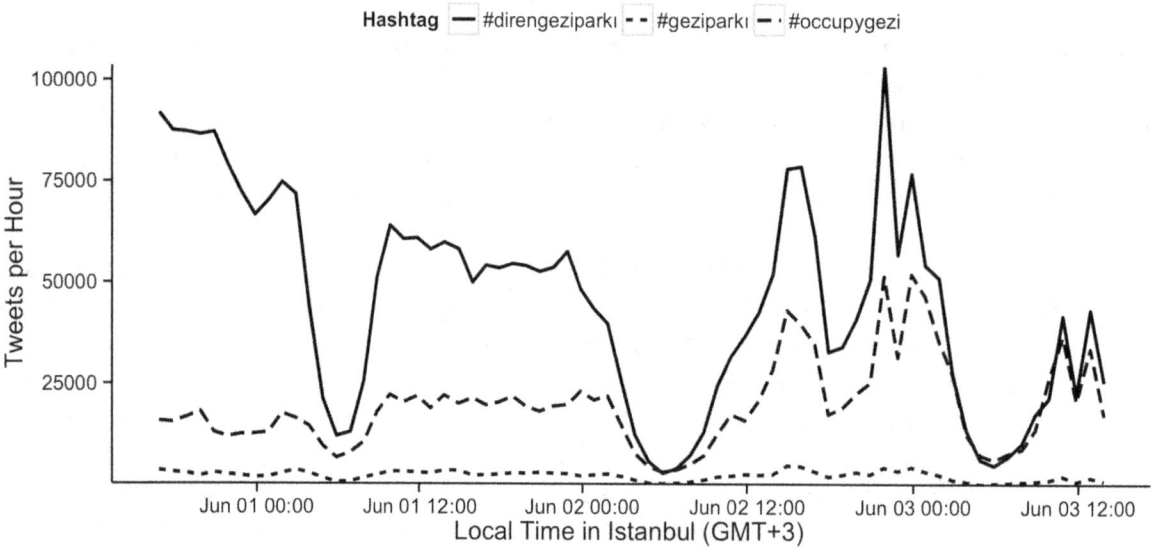

Fig. 3 - The density of hashtags in the Twitter messages during Gezi Park Demonstrations, https://www.technopat.net/2013/06/04/gezi-parki-ve-sosyal-medya-etkisi/ (04.06.2016).

Spontaneous and reflexively growing crowd of Gezi Park movement raise many questions in the fields of urban design, urban sociology, and architecture. The architect Murat Çetin (2013) says that Gezi Park is a real architecture and urban design laboratory for all of us. As suitable to the atmosphere of the post-modern era virtually started on social media, digital space turns into a concrete, physical, archaic and primitive image and converted to one basic land struggle at the 21st century at the heart of Istanbul. Çetin,M (2013) explains that the self-organized urban space and the urban space network is formed during Gezi Park protests (camping tents, common service tents, soup kitchen, infirmaries, free chairs, etc.) [2]. Susan Buck-Morss called Gezi Park protests and similar kinds of mass movements as "global crowd". She argues that the diplomacy of global crowd has created its own street art, political performances, common cultures, tweets and etc. According to the research of New York University's Social Media and Political Participation Department (SMaPP), the Gezi Park protests should not be compared to the other movements such as Occupy Wall Street and Arab Spring, it is unique because 85 percent of the posts were sent from Turkey whereas the majority was sent from foreign countries in other examples and because social media was used as a driving force as argued above [3].

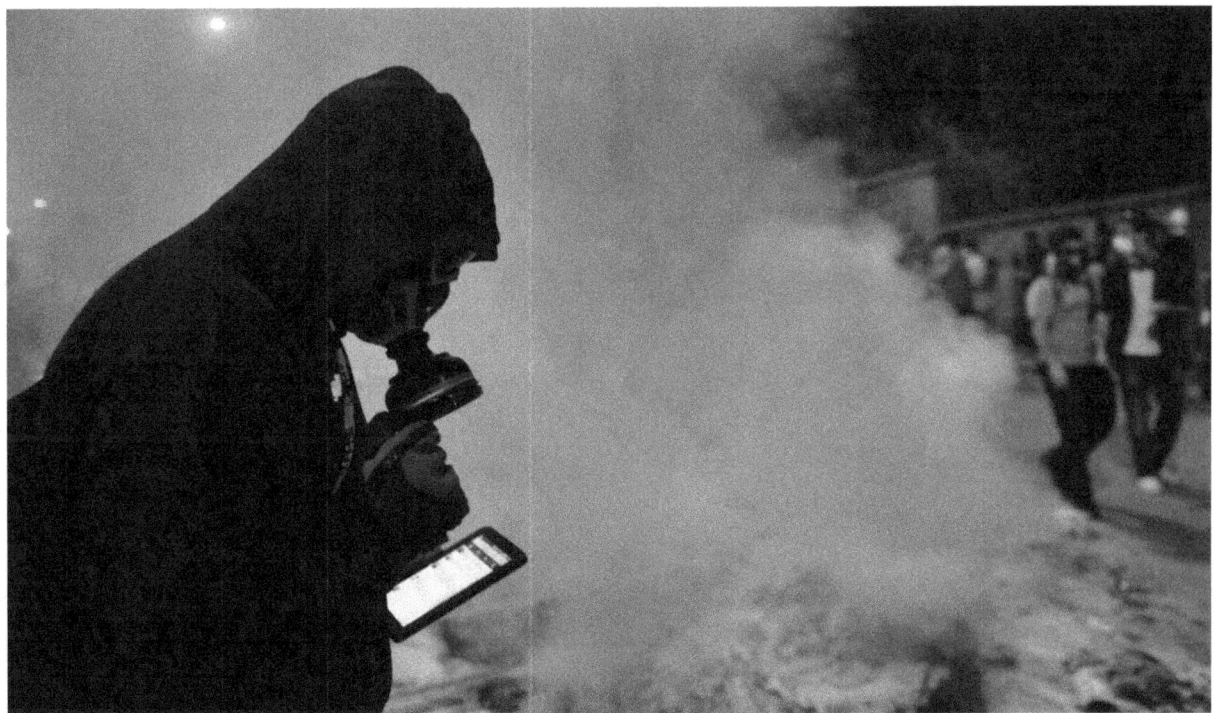

Fig. 4 - Social Media, http://www.huffingtonpost.com/2013/06/09/turkey-social-media-smartphones-occupy-gezi-protests_n_3411542.html (18.01.2017).

3. Conclusion

My aim is to illuminate both everyday practices in urban spheres and the reliability of current urban design theories. In this way, a new theoretical explanation of urban public place and urban social life is described by the role of mobile communication technologies in everyday life. Constant information flow related to particular locations during the Gezi Park demonstrations has created imperishable memories for these places in the city of Istanbul. The power of social media has ensured these memories of particular places in Istanbul are known worldwide.

What happens during the Gezi Park protests are extreme but the protests were crucial example to prove possibilities of establishing common platforms of sharing place memories, building collective memory, artistic and intellectual productivity, consequently increasing the diversity of place identities. Among the redefined places in Gezi Park and around it, I mention two of them: *yeryüzü sofraları* (translation: dinner table of the earth surface) and *park forumları* (translation: forum of the parks). These are the examples of created places of Gezi Park demonstrations. Yeryüzü sofraları are the tables are set up on the Istiklal Street along with an approach embracing everybody and open to everyone. The food was served and shared by the protestors. The reputation of them spread very fast with the hashtag #YeryüzüSofraları on Twitter and started to settle in different cities right after Istiklal Street.

Yeryüzü Sofraları was another unique creation like other places that brought Gezi Park Protests to the city. Following Gezi Park Demonstrations Ramadan started. These tables are established on the Istiklal Street along with an approach embracing everybody and open to everyone. The reputation of the *Yeryüzü Sofraları* spread very fast with the hashtag #YeryüzüSofraları on Twitter and started to settle in different cities right after Istiklal Street.

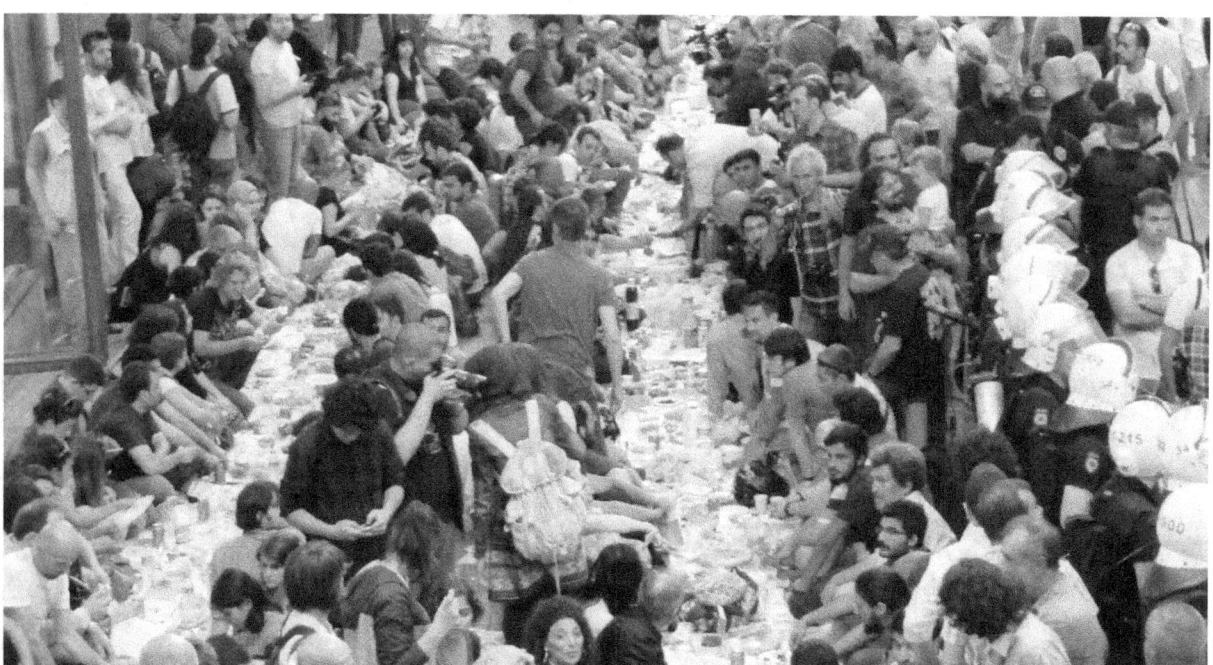

Fig. 5 – Yeryüzü sofraları at Istiklal Street, Istanbul, https://onedio.com/haber/ramazan-a-bes-kala-yeryuzu-sofralarinin-tum-bilinmeyenleri-527040 (18.01.2017).

Another creative example of collective memory is the Park forumları. After the Gezi Park camp was cleared by riot police on June 15, protesters began to meet in other parks all around Turkey and organized public forums to discuss ways forward for the protests. *Park Forumları* were a free platform of speech. These unique formations of urban space were one of the most important bi-products of Gezi Park protests which are created in the synergy of protestors.

Learning from the collaboration, communication and organizational skills in the Gezi Park protests, we can argue that the mobile communication practices in urban space over a very long period of time can leave permanent marks on the city. The presence of real encounters in physical space is essential but urban connoisseurs should not underestimate the effect of mobile communication possibilities on random meetings and location awareness. We must think about urban public place through technical, habitual, fluxional notions with all aspects in order to conceptualize urban design theories and place identities.

References

Alexander, C., Neis, H., Anninou, A., King, I., 1987. A New Theory of Urban Design, Oxford University Press, New York.

Appleyard, D., 1970. Styles and Methods of Structuring a City, ProQuest Information and Learning Company

Appleyard, D., 1981. Livable Streets, Berkeley, Ca., University of California Press

Barlas, M.A., 2006. Urban streets and urban rituals, Ankara: METU Faculty of Architecture Printing Workshop.

Barlas, A., Şentürk, M., 2012. In Research For Urban Identity In The Mobile Phone Era, in: Abend, P., Haupts T., Müller, C. (Eds.), Medialität der Nähe, Situationen – Praktiken – Diskurse, Transcript Verlag, Bielefeld, pp.161-175.

Habermas, J., 1962. The Structural Transformation of the Public Sphere, An Inquiry into a Category of Bourgeois Society, Translation, (1989) Massachusetts Institute of Technology, The MIT Press, Cambridge, Massachusetts

Jacobs, A.B., Appleyard, D., 2007. Toward an Urban Design Manifesto from a Journal of American Planning Association (1987), in: Larice, M., Macdonald, E. (Eds.), The Urban Design Reader, Routledge, Milton Park,Abington, Oxon OX14 4RN, pp.107.

Lynch, K., 1961. The Image of the City, Cambridge, Mass., The MIT Press.

McQuire, S., 2008. The Media City: Media, Architecture and Urban Space. London, Sage Publications.

Rapoport, A., 1977. Human Aspects of Urban Form, Towards a Man – Environmental Approach to Urban Form and Design, Pergamon Press.

Sennett, R., 1974. The Fall of Public Man, New York: W.W. Norton & Co.

Wall E., Waterman, T., 2010. Basics Landscape Architecture 01: Urban Design, Switzerland, AVA Publishing.

[1] https://www.technopat.net/2013/06/04/gezi-parki-ve-sosyal-medya-etkisi/, Accessed on 04.06.2016

[2]http://muratcetin-architect.blogspot.com.tr/2013_10_01_archive.html, Written by Dr. Murat Çetin, Accessed on 12.05.2016

[3]http://bianet.org/bianet/siyaset/150986-gezi-dayanismasi-kuresel-eylemlerdeki-paylasimin-sembolu , Accessed on 04.06.2016

[4]https://www.statista.com/statistics/467181/forecast-of-smartphone-users-in-turkey/, Accessed on 04.06.2016

Acknowledgements

I would like to express my special thanks to all of the scholars of Urban Art: Creating the Urban with Art Conference, especially to Prof. Dr. Ilaria Hoppe. I would like to express my deepest gratitude to my supervisor Prof. Dr. Frank Eckardt. Many thanks to my lovely family. I gratefully acknowledge my sister Melda Şentürk and Soleil Sabalja for their invaluable support and critiques.

Above all, I respect and pay my gratitude to the Gezi Park defenders who did not hesitate to give their lives for the sake of nature, peace, democracy and human right. Future generations should recognize unity and solidarity shown during Gezi Park Demonstrations in 2013.

Notes on the Archive:
About Street Art, QR Codes and Digital Archiving Practices

Katja Glaser

Independent Researcher
Graduated at the DFG Research Training Group 'Locating Media' at the University of Siegen
Website: www.locatingstreetart.com
E-mail: katja.glaser@gmx.net

Abstract

My paper focuses on one specific case study, a QR code project by Berlin based artist Sweza: Graffyard. This, in turn, constitutes the starting point of my further reflection on digital archiving practices, with special attention to the concept of location and placement. My approach implies the questioning of both time and space as well as Graffyard's archive architecture. As will be shown, Graffyard not only functions as a hybrid, "real-virtual archive", as the artist himself states (Sweza, 2012), but exposes its inherent logics and processes. In that way, it both alludes to the topic of ephemerality – street art is generally known for – and addresses broader questions regarding digital archives, the availability of data, digital art history, the production of memory and the consolidation of a street art canon. Graffyard elaborates on these topics in a playful-experimental way and makes them reflexive in the medium of art. My paper emphasizes that it is more and more important to also reflect on what is missing in our digital archives and what kind of 'connecting practices' are involved. This, inevitably, demands taking into account the investigation of data monopolies, platform politics, algorithms and net critique in general.

Keywords:

Street Art, QR Codes, Digital Archiving Practices, Net Critique, Digital Art History

1. 'Getting Up': About Street Art and Zombies

Berlin based artist Sweza uses QR codes to preserve graffiti or street art for posterity by photographing it before it got removed. After the pieces have been cleaned off by the local authorities or building owners he places a QR code in the exact location which resolves to an image of the original (fig. 1, 2).[1] "In that way a mobile phone with a QR code reader can be used to travel back in time"[2]. Sweza states: "By scanning these codes individual graffiti or street art pieces got reanimated and 'get up' as zombies. That is why you can also call them 'graffiti-zombies'." (Sweza, 2012: 52 sec ff. [transl. KG]) And this, at least on the first sight, might be obvious – because if you read in the QR code with your smartphone, respectively your QR code reader, the image of the disappeared graffiti appears on the screen of your mobile smartphone device. This means that it has been digitally reanimated.

2. The Archive

In the following, nevertheless, I want to elaborate a little bit more on the discourse of the archive. Discussing this topic, one of the main challenges or problems will be that the archive not only points to both an institution and a concept – which means it both addresses a specific place and a method (Ebeling and Günzel, 2009: 10), – but rather that it alludes to a complex, overflowing and therefore almost unmanageable phenomenon. While historians use the archive for historiography, others, in return, question its generative effects (Ernst, 2009). Cultural scientists, like Aleida Assmann (2006, 2009) for instance, question the archive as the place of our cultural or collective memory – an idea which can be linked with Boris Groys understanding of the archive as a "machine for the production of memory" (Groys, 2009: 140-141 [transl. KG]). Groys states that on the one hand, the archive is associated with the idea of completion. This means that it should collect and represent everything that is outside of the archive. On the other hand, "archive things" (ibid.), as Groys names them, generally *do* have a different destiny than all the profane things outside of the archive. 'Archive things' are considered valuable and worth keeping in a safe place whereas the mortality of the profane things outside of the archive is generally accepted. Therefore, a fundamental difference between the things inside and outside of the archive has to be highlighted – a difference in regard to value, destiny, ephemerality, destruction, and death (ibid.: 141).

In the same way archives (pretend to) endeavor for objectivity, in the same way they are ideologically (pre)structured. They decide what is visible and preserved in a culture, and what is not, and therefore decide what remains hidden from both present and future societies. "Archives precede historiography, which is their effect", Ebeling and Günzel (2009: 14 [transl. KG]) claim in the introduction of the "Archiveology". This shows that the archive, as a mediator between the visible and the invisible, the included and the excluded, the remembered (or memorable) and the forgotten has become a central category within cultural studies. Its ongoing dissolution and metaphorical extension to different ways of collecting, storing, saving and remembering – nevertheless, or precisely because of that – asks for further differentiations (Ernst, 2009: 184). Since the emergence of new media technologies and digital archiving practices, this demand has gained in impact, relevance and complexity. Today, the archive should no longer be considered as the place of historical storage, but, following Wolfgang Ernst (2009: 186), of availability, accessibility and actualization.

3. 'Lighting up the Dark'

However, at this point let me come back to *Graffyard*. I'm questioning: What happens in this mobile smartphone box – it is *truly* possible to travel back in time, as Sweza states on his website: "In that way a mobile phone with a QR code reader can be used to travel back in time"[3]. In addition, what happens to street art – is it 'ghosting around' –, and if so, where? And moreover, will it finally 'get up' as a virtual zombie? So let us open the black box to the graveyard of graffiti.

Ephemerality is an issue within the street art scene, Sweza states (2012: 35 sec ff.). For him it is interesting to see the process of 'decomposition', when pieces take on different shapes and, in the end, disappear forever (ibid.). Sweza plays with this fact by "superimposing this 'real-virtual archive'" (ibid. [transl. KG]). Given that both the form and the content of his archive have 'real-virtual' reference points, it is not only constituted, but permanently processed on the intersection between 'the physical' and the 'digital'. Within this constellation the two opposite layers are interconnected with each other by means of a QR code which synchronizes the process of disappearing and 'getting up' – respectively 'rising up from the dead' – of aforementioned street art and graffiti pieces. The QR code, consequently, presents itself as a mediator within a network of complex sociotechnical relationships that interconnects both layers in a significant way: it separates by linking and links by separating. Sweza's QR codes, consequently, must be understood as pictorial signs that do not only include, but also refer to their own backside. This shows that Sweza's *Graffyard* renounces any determined 'either-or', a characteristic that brings us back to the metaphor of the temporary street art zombie which can also be located in an undetermined space-time, somewhere 'in between', on the intersection of life and death.

It is interesting to note here that *Graffyard* not only reflects on the topic of ephemerality, but rather depends on it as well. Thus, not only the found street art and graffiti pieces are ephemeral, their 'graveyard' is ephemeral as well. The intermediate stage between life and death, passing away and getting up, destruction and (temporary) revitalization is not only artistically addressed, but also inscribed into the project. The functionality of the hybrid, time-spatial interplay of *Graffyard* is decisively dependent on the life span of the QR codes. The pasted codes, on the long run, do not guarantee a long-term remembrance or survival of the street art and graffiti pieces, rather they contribute to a sudden, selective, unexpected and zombie-like appearance of their digital copies. *Graffyard*, consequently, must be understood as a self-reflexive project, which does not confront the fast moving time outside of the archive with a certain 'place of protection' or 'stability' (Stäheli, 2002). It rather refers to its own archiving logic and exhibits its inherent processes.

In sum, *Graffyard* is an archive, attached to, or even augmenting urban space, that is both locative, situational and self-reflexive and offers limited access to its own archival documents. It is produced and permanently re-actualized in the process of its reanimation. Consequently, we might possibly understand *Graffyard* as some kind of hybrid memory black box that is characterized by qualities of situativeness, selectiveness, temporality, subjectivity and incompleteness.

4. The Logic of the Archive

This, in return, makes clear that *Graffyard* must be dependent on preliminary research and preparation. Even though Sweza, apparently seems to somehow undermine the 'traditional' understanding of (urban art) aesthetics – by mainly adding tags to his archive instead of decorative street art and graffiti pieces – he, nevertheless, is not able to lever out the logic of the archive. Thus, every single 'import', 'add' or 'upload' marks a difference, which separates documents worth archiving from documents not worth archiving. Individual tags as well as street art and graffiti pieces are always privileged in comparison to others that have no access to the archive. This amply demonstrates that every archive contains a border which separates the internal from the external, the archive from the non-archive, the closed from the open, the included from the excluded, and in the end, the preserved from the non-preserved (Fohrmann, 2002: 20-21). "No archive without outside," Derrida states (ibid., with reference to Derrida [transl. KG]). Sweza's selection, whether conscious or not, must therefore always be understood as a first interpretation that determines which works will be remembered and which ones will not. This shows that the archive, as the place to remember, is closely linked to the logic of exclusion, ignorance and oblivion.

So let me finally close with a series of questions. Given the fact that ephemerality determines Sweza's project in a significant way and, on the long run, contributes to cut the recently outlined interplay between 'the physical' and 'the digital' I am asking: Does Sweza, in the end, offer the possibility of a final oblivion? Alternatively, what happens to the said graffiti and street art pieces once the digital lid of the archive is snap shut? Will they be offered a last resting place, and thus, confront death; or are they condemned to an eternal life inside a non-accessible, digital web space whose gates will be closed forever? (see also Warnke, 2002: 270).

5. The Internet as an Archive and (Art Historical) Storage Medium

This question, on the one hand, leads to the questioning of the internet as a digital archive and art historical storage medium, on the other hand, the addressing of associated potentials and impositions. As will be shown, the outlined discourse draws attention to the conditions in which cultural heritage and knowledge is made accessible. Given the fact that culture is the result of its storage media, then cultural memory turns out to be the effect of an archive whose basic operations constantly change with new media innovations (Ernst, 2009: 178). Nevertheless, the idea of the internet as storage medium fosters some misunderstandings, because archive material is not only stored but also published (Ebeling and Günzel, 2009, with reference to Assmann, 2009).

However, it can be assumed that Sweza never intended to create an archive in the proper sense of the word. Rather, he exposes its inherent logics, processes and dynamics and provides a meta comment on digital archiving practices in general. By not selecting pieces that go hand in hand with the common taste or criteria of the art system, he adds another level of reflection and unveils the fictional qualities of the archive. By revaluating tags, which are otherwise underestimated, marginalized, displaced and unwanted, he reveals the selectivity of the archive and its inherent ambiguity. In this way, his project complies with other works of contemporary art. In her article *Anarchy in the Archive* (2009) Monika Rieger points to a similar perspective. She states that the majority of artists do not associate the archive with a safe storage room and the possibility of an identical reconstruction of the past. Rather, they focus on its framework and do not spend too much time on analyzing its content. (ibid.: 266) Sweza's project follows this genealogy. With his work, the dynamic conception of the archive becomes evident, addressing the dialectic between remembering and forgetting. This idea can be associated with the increasingly important question – or problematic – of digital archiving and storage practices in general. Sweza addresses these topics in a playful and experimental way, making them reflexive in the medium of art. Following Aleida Assmann it could be stated that art unveils that culture does not remember anymore (Rieger, 2009, with reference to Assmann, 1999: 371); or, in other words, that the storage capacity of our cultural archives has exceeded the amount that can be retranslated into our human memory (Rieger, 2009, with reference to Assmann, 2006: 94 ff.). At the same time, she indicates that the selection criteria of our cultural memory have become unclear (ibid.). This fact, in particular, can be observed in the context of street art festivals. Here, it is especially worth questioning *if* and *in what ways* our cultural memory and related media practices of documenting, archiving and storing have already contributed to establish – and permanently reprocess – some kind of international street art canon (Glaser, 2015).

6. 'Doing the Archive' and the Changing Accessibility of Cultural Heritage, Goods and Knowledge

Within this context, further questions can be raised. One might possibly think of Google's *Street Art Project,*[4] which was founded in 2014 and meant to archive street art worldwide. Apart from all the advantages of an easily accessible, digital archive in high-resolution, it remains to be questioned what this kind of archive furthermore entails. In his study on digital archiving, Jeff Rothenburg states: "Digital documents last forever – or 5 years, whichever comes first" (Warnke, 2002: 276, with reference to Rothenburg, 1999). Moreover, he adds: "There is – at present, no way to guarantee the preservation of digital information" (ibid., with reference to Rothenburg 1999). At the same time, Martin Warnke indicates that digital archives only endure as long as they are permanently in use (ibid.: 280). This means that data, in regular intervals, have to be stored to new media and converted into new formats, in order to impede death (ibid.: 276). Due to the fact that internet packages are fitted with a mechanism of self-destruction (ibid.: 272), the internet has proved to be inappropriate as an archive, Warnke states (ibid.). What is not on the servers anymore is not accessible; the well-known *error 404* occurs (ibid.). French artist MTO was one of the first artists who explicitly addressed this topic,[5] while at the same time criticizing Google's practices of surveillance and censorship, which are also associated with their archive project.

If one assumes that technical standards and software technologies will further improve, the archive, eventually, will not only be addressable as a 3-, but as a n-dimensional space (Ernst, 2009: 200). This would offer new search options and organizing tools (ibid.). For instance, one could easily be able to search melodies with melodies, images with images, etc. (ibid.). *Google Photos*[6] is one example, which points into this direction. Here, photos are algorithmically sorted and categorized. Google, most likely, uses this as a playground to improve its own face and object recognition software (Hernandez, 2015). This makes evident that, in the context of digital archiving practices, it is increasingly important to also question the supposedly 'free' infrastructures on which our digital archives are based, considering especially the fact that they are offered by multinational companies like Google. Berlin based curator Lutz Henke supports this idea by also voicing some concerns regarding the Google *Street Art Project*. He questions what kind of algorithms are working in the background and if they, sooner or later, will tell us what kind of images generate the highest advertising impact, and in the end, most of the money (Henke, 2015). The questions of who owns and controls images and what for, as well as who establishes and handles data monopolies, is, at present, one of the greatest sociopolitical challenges, Henke states (ibid.).

7. Conclusion

As my paper has shown, in the future it will be extremely important to also reflect on what is missing in our digital archives (Ernst, 2002: 29) and what kind of 'connecting practices' are involved. On the one hand, this implies the questioning of archive architectures and their inherent processes and mechanisms of selection, which separate documents worth archiving from documents not worth archiving (Fohrmann, 2002: 21-22; Stäheli, 2002: 74) and, in the end, favor the consolidation of a street art canon. On the other hand, this implies the questioning of associated practices, which are often based on commercial interests.

Against this background, it seems to be crucially important to no longer understand the internet as a simple tool or storage medium, but as an inseparable part of our political, economic, social and cultural life (Lovink, 2012: 94). Multinational companies like Google – much like the internet in general – do not offer a free infrastructure. Rather, the whole cultural, political, economic and educational landscape is strongly influenced by its networking structures, its algorithms and mechanisms of coordination (ibid.: 199). Debates about spatial appropriation, advertising, institutionalization, domestication, censorship, privacy as well as the questioning of hierarchies – which in the context of today's street art are still tied to the framework of the physical city – have to be transferred to the nets (Glaser, 2015). The current but decisive challenge will be to critically question familiar conventions, mechanisms of control and exclusion within existing – most possibly centralized – network infrastructures. The nets and its central nodes are places of decision making, which inevitably display the current infrastructures of power (Glaser, 2015; Lovink, 2012; Lovink and Rasch, 2013). Consequently, we are no longer in charge to simply 'reclaim the city', but to 'reclaim the internet' (Glaser, 2015).

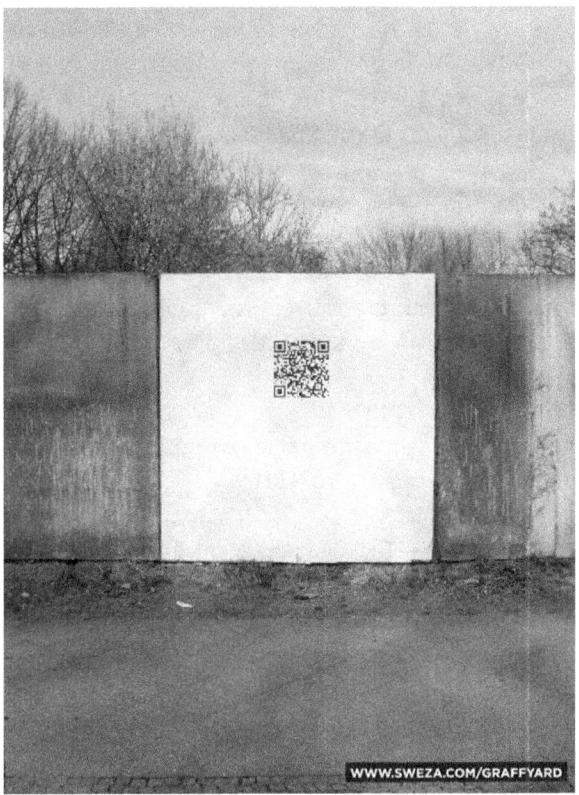

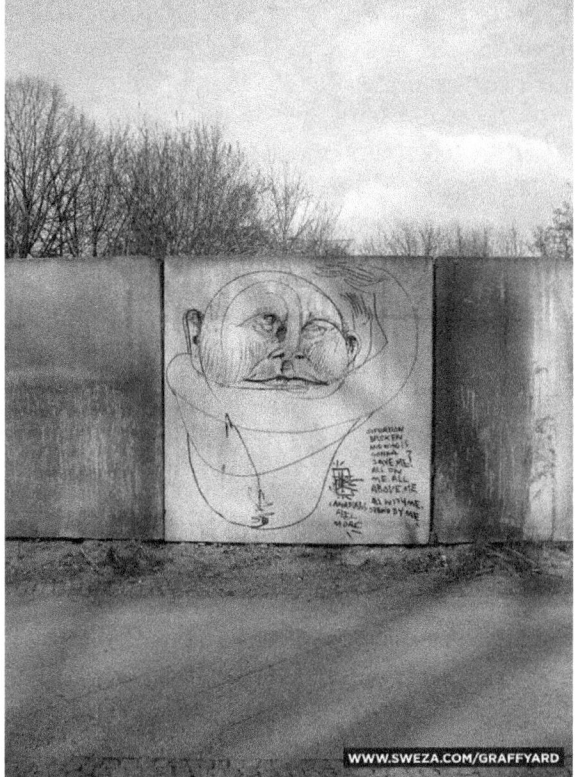

Fig. 1 - website picture from 2014, website relaunch in 2016; photo: © Sweza.

Fig. 2 - website picture from 2014, website relaunch in 2016; photo: © Sweza.

Endnotes

1 - See www.sweza.com/graffyard (accessed 30.07.2013, website relaunch in 2016).

2 - www.sweza.com/graffyard (accessed 30.07.2013, website relaunch in 2016).

3 - www.sweza.com/graffyard (accessed 30.07.2013, website relaunch in 2016).

4 - www.streetart.withgoogle.com/de as well as www.google.com/culturalinstitute/project-/street-art (accessed 22.04.2015).

5 - The documentation of the mural is accessible online at www.facebook.com/media/set/?set=a.10152768696 761723.1073741871.195423476722&type=1 (accessed 22.04.2015); for further information see also Levy (2015).

6 - www.google.com/photos/about/ (accessed 08.12.2016).

References

Assmann, A., 1999. Erinnerungsräume. Formen und Wandlungen des kulturellen Gedächtnisses, C.H. Beck, Munich.

Assmann, A., 2006. Die Furie des Verschwindens. Christian Boltanskis Archive des Vergessens, in: Beil, R. (Ed.), Christian Boltanski. Zeit, Hatje-Cantz, Ostfildern, 89-97.

Assmann, A., 2009. Archive im Wandel der Mediengeschichte, in: Ebeling, K, Günzel, S. (Eds.), Archivologie. Theorien des Archivs in Philosophie, Medien und Künsten, Kadmos, Berlin, 165-176.

Derrida, J., 1997. Dem Archiv verschrieben. Eine Freud'sche Impression, Brinkmann und Bose, Berlin.

Ebeling, K., Günzel, S. (Eds.), 2009. Archivologie. Theorien des Archivs in Philosophie, Medien und Künsten, Kadmos, Berlin.

Ernst, W., 2009. Das Archiv als Gedächtnisort, in: Ebeling, K, Günzel, S. (Eds.), Archivologie. Theorien des Archivs in Philosophie, Medien und Künsten, Kadmos, Berlin, 177-200.

Fohrmann, J., 2002. 'Archivprozesse' oder Über den Umgang mit der Erforschung von 'Archiv'. Einleitung, in: Pompe, H., Scholz, L. (Eds.), Archivprozesse. Die Kommunikation der Aufbewahrung, Dumont, Cologne, 19-26.

Glaser, K., 2015. The 'Place to Be' for Street Art Nowaday is no Longer the Street, it's the Internet, in: Soares Neves, P., de Freitas Simões, D. V. (Eds.), Street Art & Urban Creativity Scientific Journal 1, 2, 6-13.

Groys, B., 2009. Der submediale Raum des Archivs, in Ebeling, K., Günzel, S. (Eds.), Archivologie. Theorien des Archivs in Philosophie, Medien und Künsten, Kadmos, Berlin, 139-152.

Henke, L., 2015. Digitales Feigenblatt. Google archiviert Street Art, in: Monopol. Magazin für Kunst und Leben, www.monopol-magazin.de/Google-archiviert-Streetart (accessed 22.04.2015).

Hernandez, D., 2015. The New Google Photos App Is Disturbingly Good at Data Mining Your Photos, www.fusion.net/story/142326/the-new-google-photos-app-is-disturbingly-good-at-data-mining-your-photos (accessed 13.07.2015).

Levy, R., 2015. MTO Paints ,We Live on Google Earth', a new Piece in Gaeta for Memorie Urbane, www.streetartnews.net/2015/04/mto-paints-we-live-on-google-earth-new.html, (accessed 22.04.2015).

Lovink, G., 2012. Das halbwegs Soziale. Eine Kritik der Vernetzungskultur, transcript, Bielefeld.

Lovink, G., Rasch, M. (Eds.), 2013. Unlike Us Reader. Social Media Monopolies and Their Alternatives, Institute of Network Cultures, Amsterdam, 31-49.

Rieger, M., 2009. Anarchie im Archiv. Vom Künstler als Sammler, in Ebeling, K., Günzel. S. (Eds.), Archivologie. Theorien des Archivs in Philosophie, Medien und Künsten, Kadmos, Berlin, 253-269.

Rothenburg, J., 1999. Avoiding Technological Quicksand. Finding a Viable Technical Foundation, Washington. Council on Library and Information Ressources, https://www.clir.org/pubs/reports/reports/rothenberg/pub77.pdf (accessed 14.07.2015).

Rushmore, RJ, 2013. Viral Art. How the Internet Has Shaped Street Art and Graffiti, www.viralart.vandalog.com/read/ (accessed 17.07.2014).

Stäheli, U., 2002. Die Wiederholbarkeit des Populären. Archivierung und das Populäre, in: Pompe, H., Scholz, L. (Eds.), Archivprozesse. Die Kommunikation der Aufbewahrung, Dumont, Cologne, 73-83.

Sweza, 2011. Deutsche Welle, Interactive Street Art by Sweza, www.youtube.com/watch?v=X5wmsHX-9dU (accessed 30.07.2013).

Sweza, 2012. ZDFkultur, Kunst und QR, https://www.youtube.com/watch?v=MhSJTAlzPvg, (accessed 30.07.2013).

Warnke, M., 2002. Digitale Archive, in Pompe, H., Scholz, L. (Eds.), Archivprozesse. Die Kommunikation der Aufbewahrung, Dumont, Köln, 269-281.

Spatial and Media Connectivity in Urban Media Art

Annette Urban

Abstract

In order to investigate the preconditions of urban media art – in the context of the recent convergence of real and virtual space – it makes sense to focus on art projects and exhibitions that use connectivity as a model for interlaced (not separated) urban media space. Artists intertwine the flows of data and mobility, and reconnect these supposedly immaterial networks to an urban terrain. By comparing urban art projects and exhibitions from the 1990s to some today, this paper shows that similar issues were relevant before the advent of mobile media technology. Moreover, the dialectics of de- and reterritorialization are a valuable analytical tool for urban media art in general.

Keywords:

urban media art, real and data space, connectivity, deterritorialization, reterritorialization, mobility, locative media, locative arts, Lynn Hershman, rude_architecture, Mark Shepard, M+M, Marc Lee, *Connected Cities, Hacking the City*

Urban Media Art, Its Relation to Street Art and Their Dependence on Real and Virtual Space

Besides its strong reliance on urban surfaces and their materiality, street art today is deeply marked by the convergence of real and virtual space. While it is still possible to stroll past street art in urban sceneries – and this remains one of its key characteristics – we have to acknowledge that "most viewers of street art experience it online" (Blanché, 2015: 36).[1] This includes the possibility of uploading geotagged images of dispersed street art pieces, thus transforming the old model of urban flânerie into a kind of scavenger hunt (Blanché, 2015: 37), but also of parallelizing the experience of getting lost in dedifferentiated urban spaces with the disorientation of web surfing or even the loss of any sense of locality. The general hybridization of virtual and real space is a central concern for artists working within and with the city because the city itself is becoming smart and loosening its roots in physical space (Bourdin et al., 2014). However, simultaneously the concept of the "smart city" promises to reconcile the two supposedly antagonistic spheres of urban and media space. This tension grows even more acute when urban artists do not choose spray cans or stencils but new media as their means; these media can bridge distances, compensate for on-site experience, and therefore partake in the general process of obliteration of space. On the other hand, many of them have changed into location-aware technologies, thus generating some sort of net locality (Gordon et al., 2011).

The two related dialectics outlined above can be better understood as processes of dis- and relocation, or of de- and reterritorialization;[2] as fundamental tensions, they underlie every kind of what I call "urban media art" and — as shall be shown — are made productive in some of its convincing examples. I shall focus on exhibitions and works that clearly have their origins in "public art," but undermine the problems of art under public and curatorial mandate with strategies of cultural-digital hacking, thus coming close to the unauthorized tactics of street art. And instead of using the term "urban art" for "street art" that finds its way into museum spaces (Blanché, 2015: 38),[3] I propose a new concept of "urban media art" that provides for the fundamental dialectics outlined above and shares with street art an interest in ambulatory, nodal spaces constituted by traversal and intersections (Hoppe, 2009). In order to explore the specific preconditions for this kind of urban media art, I shall examine a telling phenomenon that is exceptional in the wide spectrum of public art exhibitions. This kind of exhibition has been established as a promising branch of contemporary art even and precisely at a time when the relevance of urban space as public space was declining (and this correlation persists). Apart from long-term projects such as the *Skulptur Projekte* Münster, numerous new exhibitions are launched every summer, such as the exhibition series *Playing the City* (2009–2011) organized by the Schirn Kunsthalle Frankfurt. It can readily serve as an example of the recent reconceptualization of site-related practices through performance art. By contrast, the pervasion of urban space by new media, as indicated by the subtitle of the exhibition *Sensing place. Mediatising the urban landscape* at the House of Electronic Arts at Basel in 2012 (Buschauer and Himmelsbach, 2013), is often delegated to institutions specialized in new media and digital art.[4]

Some exhibition formats or singular projects have nevertheless experimented with conceptually correlating the urban and the media sphere: one way of doing so can be described as an exploration of the common connectivity characteristic of decentralized urban spaces and media networks. To this extent, I accept the vagueness of concepts such as "network" and "connectivity" in order to make their overlapping usages productive in the various discourses concerned. In such art projects, spatial patterns considered deficient with regard to the ideal city core gain relevance because of the interconnection between physical mobility and mobile communication. Even transit spaces, once the epitome of non-places, can paradoxically engender site-related practices encouraged by a heightened awareness for the aesthetics of infrastructure both in terms of transportation and communication technology.[5] My perspective is in keeping with recent research by Regine Buschauer (2010) and others who want to overcome the separation of the historiographies of media and mobility. They prefer to focus on the interplay of "mobile communications, physical mobility and the city" and pay attention to "the locatedness of mobilities" (Sheller and Urry, 2006: 3). Accordingly, I shall single out artistic examples that interlace the flows of data and mobility. This has two important consequences: it helps to make comparisons between brand new and older new media art with respect to the fundamental dialectic of dis- and relocation and to overcome a narrow, technically determined understanding of locative media.

1. Connected – Telematic Spaces and Bodies

The common connectivity of urban and media spaces is often already stressed by the mottos of exhibitions and their accompanying posters and covers, particularly in the case of those examples that I have chosen from the Ruhr region and its characteristic agglomeration of 53 towns and cities. The idea of using this kind of (traffic) infrastructure in public art projects resonates in exhibitions such as *A 40 – die Schönheit der großen Straße* and *Emscherkunst,* which focuses respectively on a main traffic artery and a river running through this territory; the river is in the process of being restored to its natural state. Moreover, in the same context, namely the context of the European Capital of Culture *Ruhr.2010*, Sabine Maria Schmidt from the Folkwang Museum Essen launched the project *Hacking the City*. It suggested the parallelization of urban spaces with spaces of communication by dedicating both of them to strategies of hacking. Even in 1999, during the heyday of net art and before the advent of location-aware media, the exhibition *Connected Cities* at the Lehmbruck Museum Duisburg started to launch "processes of art in the urban network," which was meant in a double sense. It was the aim of the exhibition, curated by Söke Dinkla, and of many of the participating artists to interweave such post-industrial agglomerations like the Ruhr area and their nodal urban spaces without a center with networked data space. This leads to double connectivity that is more specific, even site specific in a new manner, although the whole exhibition *Connected Cities* remained within the institutional framework of public art, launched by a museum and partly situated in its indoor spaces.

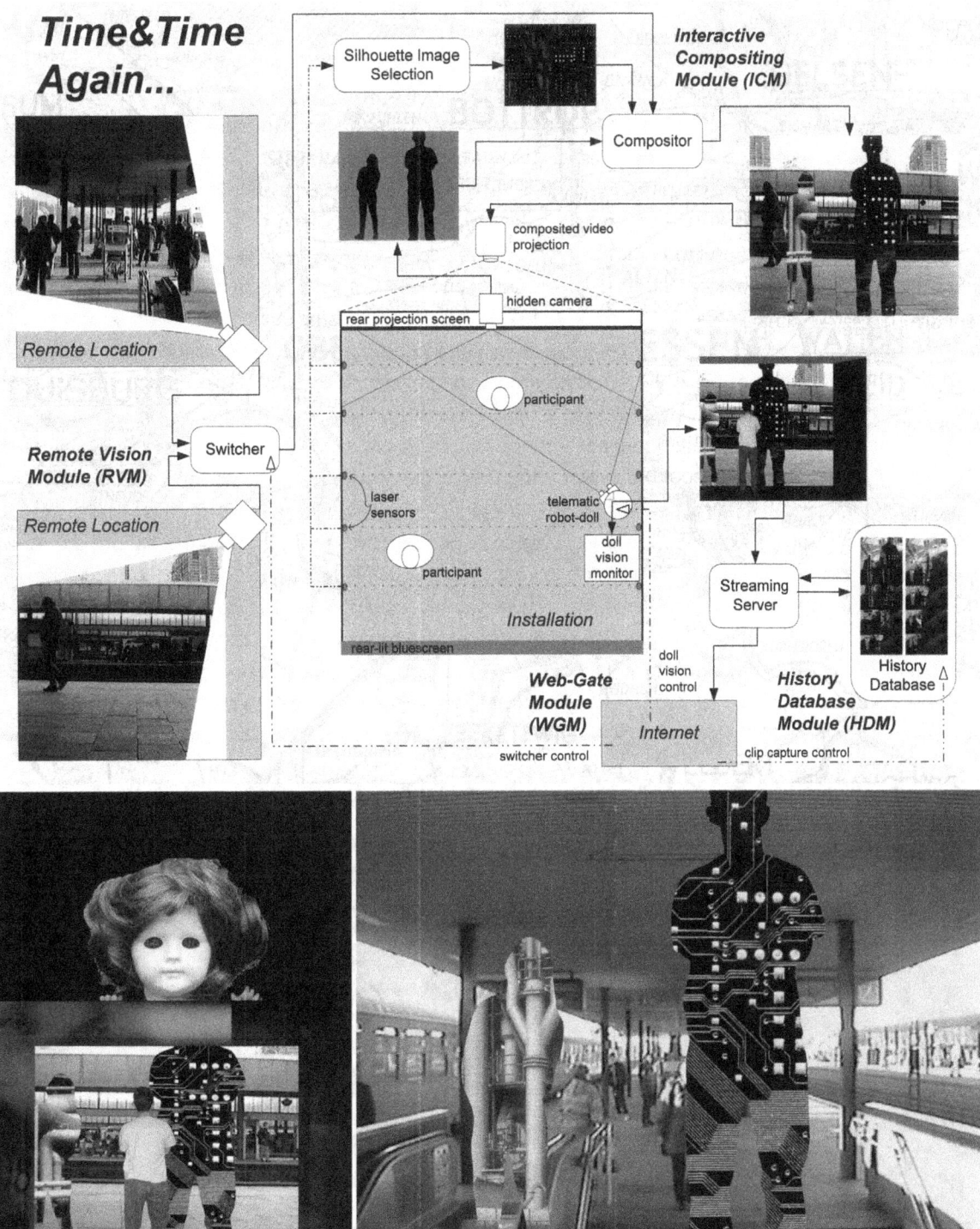

Fig. 1 - Lynn Hershman and Fabian Wagmister: *Time & Time Again*, 1999, telecommunicative installation, internet project and robotic doll, in the context of the exhibition *Connected Cities,* 1999.

Let me focus more closely on the contribution by net art pioneer Lynn Hershman in cooperation with Fabian Wagmister because their networked installation *Time & Time Again* (fig. 1) interconnects the supposedly autonomous detached sphere of the museum with urban and web space. It puts into perspective the paradigm of virtual space as a separated sphere of its own as it was prevalent in the 1990s. By means of a bluebox process, the silhouettes of visitors at the Lehmbruck Museum who were filmed by a camera behind a rear projection screen were inserted as 2D-graphics into live images transmitted from surveillance cameras at the train station (Dinkla, 1999: 134–144). The electronic separation and mixture of images intensified an experience of dislocation in the dark placeless museum space: a feeling of being transported to another place or even of the unreal tele-presence of being at two places at once. On the other hand, the realistic impact of the familiar train station and the live stream heightened the consciousness of the here and now: deterritorialization reverts to a sort of resituating. In addition, the human silhouettes were filled in with emblematic images delivered by a history database presenting connective structures of all kinds such as tubes and circuits. Depending on their position in the room, the visitors could change this content. They thus somehow navigated through the history of the Ruhr region with images amalgamating the old infrastructure of heavy industry and the new one of communication, flanked by an aspect of technoid bodies as the patterns of connectivity turned into arteries of organisms. The involvement of museum visitors was crossed with a second interactive feature engaging an online audience and reinforcing the affinity with gaming. This interface with the web possessed a humanoid form with a robotic puppet surveying the exhibition space. Her eyes could be controlled telematically from the web, thus producing another multi-layered projection of the real visitors in front of their avatar-like data bodies within the composite picture of the remote train station. In the hybrid space of this networked installation, the museum turns into an arena of a corporal skipping backward and forward through past, present, and future, merging urban mobility, actual movement and web activities, while data traffic is governed by gazes that oscillate between surveillance and game control. This fragile balance of activation and subjugation has been later pursued in locative games such as those of Blast Theory, which make use of the implementation of GPS into smart phones in order to root online games in urban real spaces.

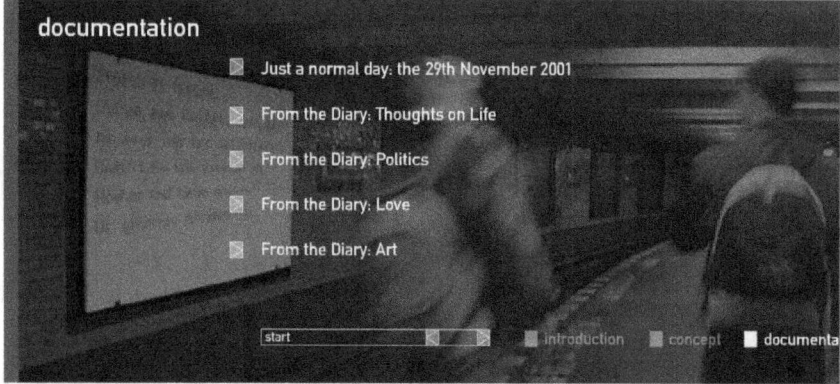

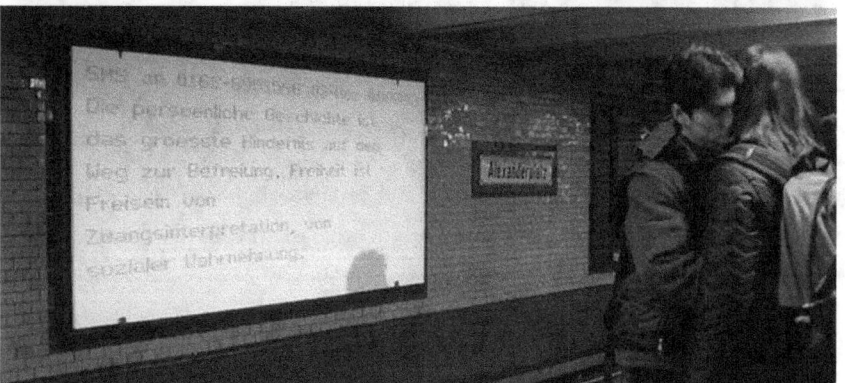

Fig. 2 - rude_architecture (Friedrich von Borries, Gesa Glück, Tobias Neumann): *urban_diary*, Berlin U Alexanderplatz, 2001–2002, sms-diary in public space, two projection screens.

2. Converging the Flows of Mobility and Communication

While Hershman's installation stages the ghostly presence of bodies mobilized in between real and virtual spaces, it has not yet directly converged data flows of communication with flows of mobility as they depart from the train station. Such transit spaces are often seen as antagonistic, i.e. as spaces of non-communication in accordance with Marc Augé's characterization of non-places, that regulate behavior in a non-personal way and therefore create lonely users (Augé, 2000). Numerous art projects try to break up these situations of non-communication. They even reinterpret surveillance cameras, which Lev Manovich mentions as one of the three key elements responsible for the merging of data and real space (Manovich, 2006), as partners in a game that—in contrast to the observational regime in *Time & Time Again*—stresses much more the idea of reciprocity and togetherness. This was the case with Chess for *CCTV Operators*, the contribution of Mediengruppe Bitnik to the exhibition *Hacking the City* in 2010 (Schmidt, 2011: 25–39). Other projects confront the non-communicative character of transit spaces with the simultaneous but closed communication taking place within these spaces via mobile media without addressing what is physically close. This reinforces the indifference among people lacking a sense of community during their daily routine of commuting.

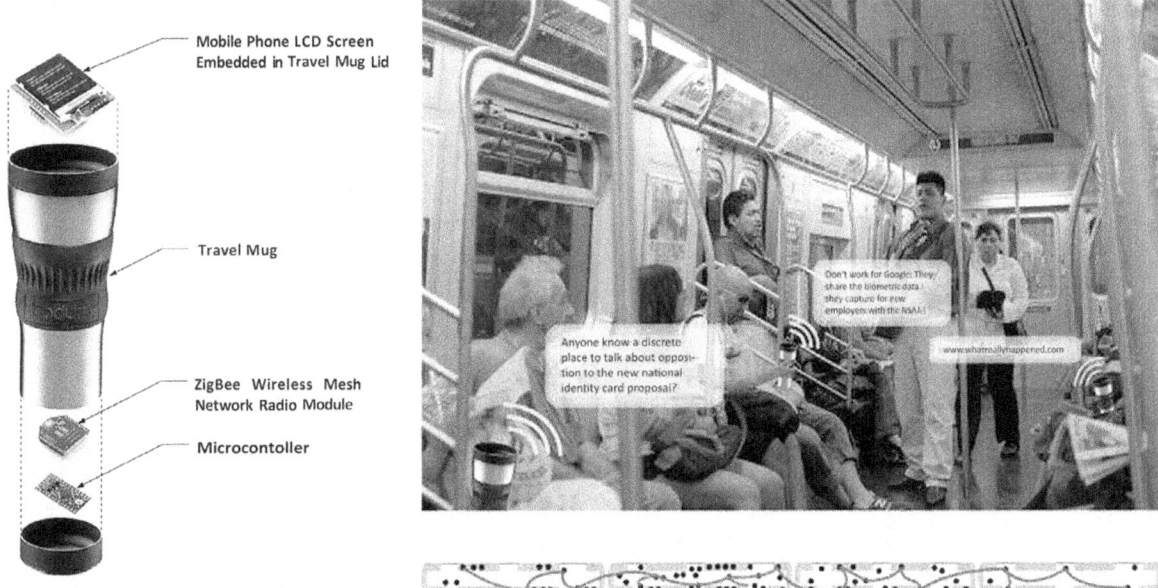

Fig. 3 - Mark Shepard i.a.: *Ad-hoc Dark (Roast) Network Travel Mug* (Concept Sketches), 2010, part of *Sentient City Survival Kit*, 2010, Video documentation, 5:15 min., project website http://survival.sentientcity.net.

This situation was significantly altered by a project realized by the collective rude_architecture in Berlin in 2001–02. It short-circuited the small personal screens of mobile media with the big advertising screens installed in public transportation systems. In this way, *urban_diary* (fig. 2) somehow extends the idea of writing on urban walls, which is at the heart of graffiti and street art, to electronic billboards by opening them for all short private messages in flux. These texts were now readable for everyone around and written in the awareness and with the intention that they would have been made public (Blume, 2004: 39–40).[6] Much like anonymous graffiti, they therefore oscillated between private diary and public utterance. The project explored the site specificity of spaces of mobility in multiple ways: using a 24-hour delay, text messages could be sent out at a precise moment addressed to oneself or to another person who would be there at exactly the same time the next day. The project reflects the time economy and rhythms specific for these transfer points in the network of subway routes. The monotonous regular use of space even inspired some participants to write mini-serials of ongoing text messages. While it was not a rare thing for singular messages to display the stereotypical communication amplified by all kinds of social media, the continuous linear reception of the *urban_diary* in situ caused a clash of messages which strongly varied in style and content. This corresponded perfectly with the heterogeneity of commuters and their contingent communities, thus underlining the media-site specificity of the project.

Urban_diary still restricts itself to place-bound screens in order to make public a collective hypertext mirroring the distracted thoughts of waiting commuters and tries to spread the online communication over to the silent mass on site. A more recent project is able to make immediate use of the connectivity of mobile media. It raises, in a sense, the concepts of urban creativity and bricolage to the next technological level of a city's infrastructure, which today is increasingly interwoven with the mobile devices of urbanites themselves; the project even freely offers the necessary circuit diagram and source code. The *Ad-hoc Dark (Roast) Network Travel Mug* (2010) is part of the *Sentient City Survival Kit* (Shepard, 2010; Buschauer and Himmelsbach, 2013: 108–112),[7] which Mark Shepard first presented completely at the *ISEA2010 Ruhr* and realized in the public transportation system of New York City. This prototype amalgamates the coffee-to-go cup with the second essential of the morning commuter: It embeds a mobile phone screen in the lid of the mug, together with a small wireless mesh network radio module designed for close range. This kind of network is established among all passengers in one subway train equipped with such a mug, who can thus send messages to the mugs near them by lifting their own up as if to drink (fig. 3). Confined to the immediate vicinity and therefore limited, the network at the same time expands flexibly: it is based on mobile media riding through the subway system of a whole city; mesh networks and related mobile ad-hoc networks are continuously self-generating without any infrastructure. This mug is meant to offer an alternative in the near future of the *Sentient City* "where all network traffic is monitored by smart filters, where access privileges are dynamically granted and denied based on the fly of your credit card transaction history, and where bandwidth is a function of your market capitalization" (Shepard, 2010: 116). In this case, the smart city reveals its dystopian dimension while the "dark network" becomes an emancipatory space of grassroots activism.

The contingent community of daily commuters with their smart phones, which are normally used for distraction or extended work, is reinterpreted as a set of micro-cells in a liberated counter-web. This infrastructureless web thrives parasitically based on the old material-intensive infrastructure of metropolitan transportation. Its dislocating effect is balanced by a locatedness of mobility that starts with the common focal points that the uncontrolled exchanged messages have in the interests shared by citizens of the same city. In addition, it is intensified as the nodes of this web are somehow humanized. We thus have both an aspect of embodiment and an object-turn, which has been qualified as a further stage of locative arts. With this object-turn, according to Marc Tuters, the artistic strategies move away from an absolute concept of proximity as implicated in the GPS technology: they now privilege a relational understanding of nearness (Tuters, 2011), which comes close to my idea of connectedness.

3. Net-Based Orientation and the City – Hacking Google Maps

So far, we have seen how a common connectivity of media and urban space can engender a new site relatedness of urban media art. In the projects from Berlin and New York, it was the constant flow of job mobility within the megastructure of urban transportation that was interlocked with electronic communication supporting the working world as well as recreation. My last two examples envision the tools of net-based orientation itself as a correlate of today's city structures on a regional and global scale. In the media-based performance *Call Sciopero* (fig. 4), which was part of the exhibition *Hacking the City* at Essen, orientation and mobility primarily serve as methods of investigation and additionally evoke an explicitly political idea of mobilization. With this project, the duo M+M (Marc Weis, Martin De Mattia) experimented with hacking or recoding standard web-based cartography in order to write an alternative version of the history of the Ruhr region. First, their research about the area's neuralgic points was done with help of Google Maps (Hoffmann, 2011), locating not only the well-known spots of the heritage of the industrial era such as the Villa Krupp, but also—more difficult to detect—the head offices of recent regional players such as the WAZ media group, Evonik Industries and the ALDI discounter whose billionaire founders live nearby; they thus retraced hidden power coordinates. Then M+M wove this network by following their self-created heritage route using a navigation system. They drove up in front of these headquarters in a Fiat 600, thus re-enacting a famous scene in Michelangelo Antonioni's movie *The Red Desert* (1964). Whereas their strike call went largely unnoticed in situ, the idea was to complementarily implement videos of these performances back into Google Maps and link them to the relevant company address. The viral potential of web contents would have met the old idea of mobilizing the working class via megaphone if the control mechanisms of Google Maps had not expectedly prevented the unauthorized videos. Thus, both attempts to mobilize and communicate proved futile and reflected on the limitations of political impact today. Nevertheless, this emblematic scene from an old movie shed light on the combative past as a forgotten or even repressed tradition of the region and on the fact that it is lacking completely today. At first glance, restaging a fragment from *The Red Desert* with historical props, the original film monologue, partly in Italian but within an altogether different context, caused a deep disconnection from place and public. However, this displacement again found its counterpart in a relocation: the movie scene acquired a new realism in the banal surroundings of contemporary head offices and underwent a significant form of embodiment.

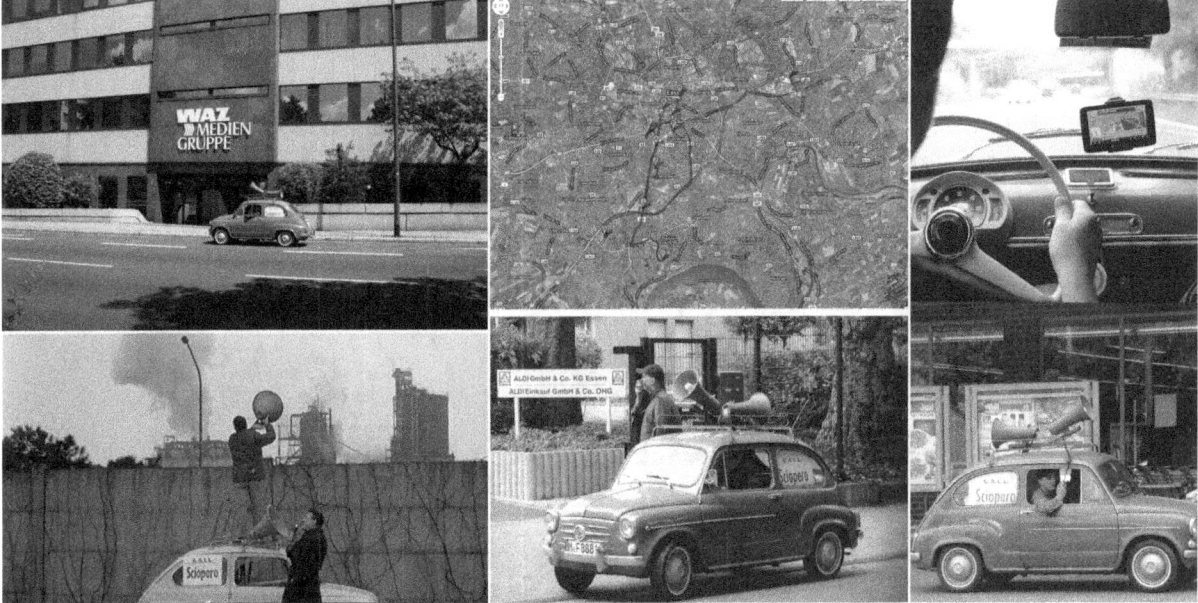

Fig. 4 - M+M (Marc Weis, Martin De Mattia): *Call Sciopero,* 2010, actions in public places, reconstructed Fiat 600, megaphones, two performers, Essen, 16th of July – 25th of September 2010, in the context of the exhibition *Hacking the City*, 2010 and film still from *The Red Desert/Il deserto rosso* (IT/F 1964, D.: Michelangelo Antonioni) – bottom left.

Conclusion: The Geospatial Web and the Return of VR

As *Call Sciopero* shows, this kind of relocation is not specifically reserved for locative media and locative arts. Similarly, the many-to-many paradigm of the latest forms of online communication can be anticipated by older media as we have seen with *urban_diary*. Their linkage to nodal spaces—such as city agglomerations but also transit spaces of metropolitan transport that can also function as sites—offers telling models for the convergence of media and urban space. A last example is intended to check the thesis that today the virtual is inseparably rooted in physical space. In his media installation *10 000 Moving Cities* (fig. 5), Marc Lee extracts user-generated web content from social media—photos, video clips, and verbal commentaries concerning specific cities (Lutz and Weibel, 2015: 4, 29). They are projected in real time onto empty silhouettes of high-rise buildings, creating a virtual city that can be traversed with a head-mounted display. At the bottom of this display, Google Maps is inserted and used as a navigation tool for choosing another city and uploading new content. Unlike locative media, the geo-coded net contents are not used in this case for annotating real space. Instead, the data sphere is again staged as a virtual space of its own cut off from the (factual) surroundings of the participant. Nevertheless, the simulated world receives feedback from the real one: after all, online navigation with a map is the standard tool that we use today for orientation in real topographies. Moreover, Marc Lee's installation takes account of the fact that the new guiding model of the internet turns out to be geography. Instead of a "'wasteland of unfiltered data' (Stoll, 1995)," it presents us with a "physically contextualized map of information" (Gordon and Silva, 2011: 7). *10 000 Moving Cities* thus examines whether geo-indicated contents detached from the experience of real space can nevertheless evoke some kind of site-related experience. With its offer to select one of 10,000 cities and abruptly switch from one to another, however, this kind of mobility has little in common with that of sedentary inhabitants, but rather reminds us of frequent travellers, tourists or even mere internet surfers. From this point of view, the geospatial web (Varnelis and Friedberg, 2008: 32–35) tends to take priority over the immediate physical environment and—in spite of all aspects of relocation—privileges a life predominantly transferred to the virtual sphere.

Thanks to the artists for permission to publish illustrations of their work, to Katharina Boje for her assistance with the bibliography and to Donald Goodwin for proofreading the English text.

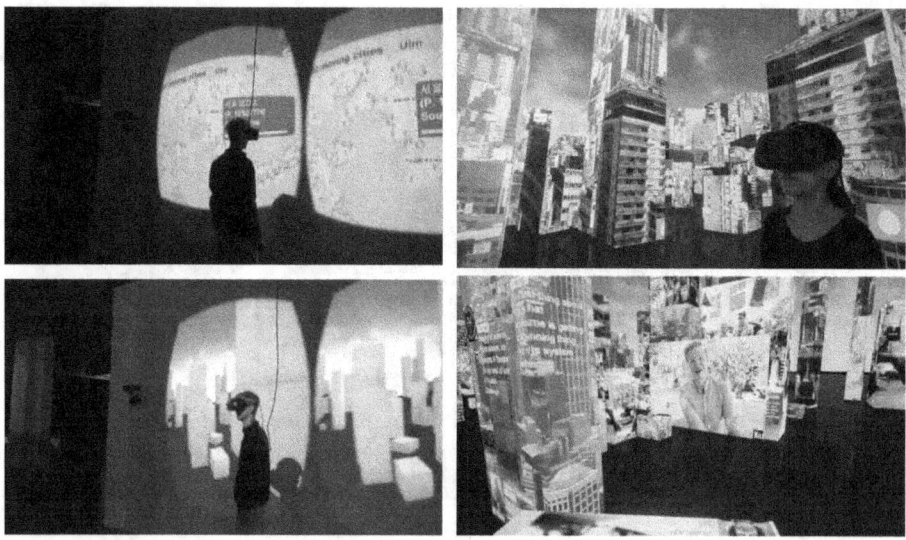

Fig. 5 - Marc Lee: *10 000 Moving Cities,* Version 3, 2015, interactive installation based on internet- and telepresence, room 5x 5x 4m, oculus rift-glasses, 4 kinect-sensors, http://marclee.io/en/10-000-moving-cities-same-but-different-vr.

Endnotes

1 - See also Katja Glaser's article in this volume.

2 - The theoretical impact of this de- and reterritorialization will be elaborated in an upcoming research project by the author.

3 - See for example the Museum of Urban and Contemporary Art founded at Munich in 2016 and the Museum for Urban Contemporary Art opening at Berlin in 2017.

4 - The *Skulptur Projekte* 2017 however promise to unite a focus on the body and on performance with digitalization.

5 - See for the focus on media infrastructures Parks, 2015.

6 - See also http://gesaglueck.de/diary/index.html [Accessed: 14/2/2017].

7 - See also http://survival.sentientcity.net/ [Accessed: 14/2/2017].

References

Augé, M., 2000. Non-Places. Introduction to an Anthropology of Supermodernity, Verso, London.

Blanché, U., 2015. Street Art and Related Terms – Discussion and Working Definition, SAUC-Journal V1 N1, 32–38.

Blume, T., 2004. Urbaner Medienaktivismus, in: Id., Langenbrinck, G. (Eds.), Dot.City. Relationaler Urbanismus und Neue Medien, Jovis, Berlin, 37–61.

Bourdin, A., Eckardt, F., Wood, A., 2014. Die ortlose Stadt. Über die Virtualisierung des Urbanen, Transcript, Bielefeld.

Buschauer, R., Himmelsbach, S. (Eds.), 2013. Exhibition catalogue. Sensing place. Mediatising the Urban Landscape, House of Electronic Arts, Merian, Basel.

Buschauer, R., 2010. Einleitung, in: Id., Mobile Räume. Medien- und diskursgeschichtliche Studien zur Telekommunikation, Transcript, Bielefeld, 9–18.

Dinkla, S. (Ed.), 1999. Exhibition catalogue. Connected Cities. Processes of Art in the Urban Network, Wilhelm-Lehmbruck-Museum, Hatje-Cantz, Ostfildern-Ruit.

Gordon, E., de Souza e Silva, A., 2011. Net locality. Why Location Matters in a Networked World, Wiley- Blackwell, Chichester.

Hoffmann, A., 2011. M+M: *Call Sciopero*, in: Schmidt, 2011, 111–115.

Hoppe, I., 2009. Street Art und "Die Kunst im öffentlichen Raum," kunsttexte.de, online available at http://edoc.hu-berlin.de/kunsttexte/2009-1/hoppe-ilaria-6/PDF/hoppe.pdf [Accessed: 14/2/2017].

Lutz, J., Weibel, P. (Eds.), 2015. Exhibition catalogue. Infosphäre. Das neue Kunstereignis im digitalen Zeitalter, ZKM Lichthof Karlsruhe, Zentrum für Kunst und Medientechnologie, Karlsruhe.

Manovich, L., 2006. The Poetics of Urban Media Surfaces, in: First Monday, Special Issue, 4, Urban Screens. Discovering the Potential of Outdoor Screens for Urban Society, unnumbered, online available at http://www.firstmonday.dk/ojs/index.php/fm/article/view/1545/1460 [Accessed: 14/2/2017].

Parks, L. (Ed.), 2015. Signal Traffic. Critical Studies of Media Infrastructures, Univ. of Illinois Press, Urbana, Ill.

Schmidt, S. M. (Ed.), 2011. Exhibition catalogue. Hacking the City. Interventions in Public and Communicative Spaces, Museum Folkwang, Folkwang/Steidl, Göttingen.

Sheller, M., Urry, J., 2006. Introduction. Mobile Cities, Urban Mobilities, in: Id. (Eds.), Mobile Technologies of the City, Routledge, New York, 1–17.

Shepard, M., 2010. Near-future Urban Archaeology. The Sentient City Survival Kit, in: Seijdel, J. (Ed.), Beyond Privacy. New Perspectives on the Public and Private Domains, NAI Publications, Rotterdam, 110–118.

Tuters, M., 2011. Forget Psychogeography. The Object-Turn in Locative Media. Paper presented at the Conference Media in Transition 7: Unstable Platforms. The Promise and Peril of Transition, Massachusetts Institute of Technology, Cambridge, May 13–15.

Varnelis, K., Friedberg, A., 2008. Place. The Networking of Public Space, in: Id. (Ed.), Networked Publics, MIT Press, Cambridge, Mass., 15–43.

http://gesaglueck.de/diary/index.html [Accessed: 14/2/2017]

http://survival.sentientcity.net/ [Accessed: 14/2/2017]

Affect & Performance

Art of serenity.
Aesthetic function of humor in Street Art

Agnieszka Gralińska-Toborek

University of Lodz, Institute of Philosophy.

ul. Lindleya 3/5, 90-131 Łódź, Poland

grala@filozof.uni.lodz.pl

Abstract

"That which allows us to see the trivial within the officially important and the important within the officially meaningless is comic and stimulates laughter" (Marquard, 1989: 54). There is no doubt that many Street Art activities, small interventions in the existing public order, play just such a role—disrupting the hierarchy of importance, reversing official relations for a while. Thus, Street Art evades serious tasks attributed to the arts and in a perverse way reaches its objectives. Sometimes the goal is only pure enjoyment, but quite often also an attempt to release and remove bad emotions through laughter. Even the most socially and politically engaged Street Art usually wins when laughter is its only weapon. Without preaching and imposing a new order, it uncovers what we do not want or fear to see in public spaces. Ludic, naive, childishly simple forms of Street Art confound critics and art curators, disarm viewers, and transform strained expectation into nothing (Kant, 2007: 161). Perhaps that is why Street Art thrives in places of the most serious conflicts and tensions.

Keywords:

Street Art, Odo Marquard, Humor, comical, Aesthetic values

Introduction

In 2014, a blogger who writes about city art asked me to make a short statement explaining what Street Art is for me. The blog is called *Artique* and the statement I gave was as follows:

> "I am a theorist of art, so Street Art poses the biggest challenge for me. And up till now, with a great deal of pleasure – I have been losing against this type of art. You cannot create a definition, distinguish genres, trends and approaches or their representatives; it is impossible to create a trendy theory or to agree on common views. Street Art is for me the best proof of the unbridled instinct of creativity that defies all educational methods and attempts at institutionalising. (...) I appreciate this kind of Street Art, in which I see spontaneity, sense of humor, insolence, diversity, unpretentiousness, respect for technique and which doesn't preach." (Korzeniewski, 2014)

After two years of further research (Gralińska-Toborek and Kazimierska-Jerzyk, 2014), I still agree more or less with what I said then, though the issue of institutionalization of Street Art is raising my doubts more and more. However, I wish to present this feature which is difficult to name and which I tried to capture using some of the before-mentioned terms. In my opinion of a theorist of art, what distinguishes Street Art from mainstream art is serenity.

1. Serenity [Heiterkeit]

This term can be attributed to philosophical considerations on *Aesthetics and Anaesthetics* of Odo Marquard. Perceiving in philosophy a critique of reality, "passionate, sad and bitter knowledge" (Marquard, 1989: 48), he seeks in art a sanctuary for serenity. But not always, especially in the twentieth century, art has been serene. There is no doubt that the avant-garde, by becoming philosophy and art critique in one, and striving to merge with the reality, sided with seriousness. "If seriousness comes into power, it banishes serenity" (Marquard 1989: 48), and there, where art is "forbidden this serenity through critique, it emigrates to a specific area that in a compensatory manner (...) protects the serenity (...), to comic art, the realm of humor and laughter." (Marquard, 1989: 53) I do not want to suggest here that Street Art was in principle the art based on the aesthetic category of humor, I just want to show its aspect of serenity, which we—theorists—increasingly often try to banish from this type of art, imposing seriousness.

1.1. Something trivial in something important

Many examples of more or less known Street Art works are based on the principle of humor, which Marquard aptly described:

> "what stimulates laughter is that which allows to see something trivial in something officially recognised as important and to see something important in something officially meaningless" (Marquard, 1989: 54)

How many road signs have already been made into stories from the life of black stick figures? Especially prohibitory traffic signs have become a field for joyful and mocking activities, probably because of their most categorical original meaning and the ease of transformation of this simple form. The works of Jenkins, Clet or Dan Witz make you laugh because they change that which is important, functional, and creates order into something trivial. At the same time, they turn something straightforward and anesthetic for us into an ambiguous, narrative representation, which has no function apart from this particular one—to disarm functionality and seriousness. It is also very important for the signs to remain in their original place and continue to bear the marks of their original function in order for the humor to work. We can be amused by continually found on the internet photographs or collected, specially made, signs or reproductions of those signs that can be purchased like any merchandise in a gift shop. In this case, though, the comic aspect of surprise does not exist; there is no direct experience of this humor. This means it does not meet the principle of incongruity, "it is the perception of something incongruous—something that violates our mental patterns and expectations" (Morreal, 2012). This happens when, for example, the artist nicknamed Roadsworth transforms road lines and pedestrian cross walks into ornamental vines or zippers. Of course we can talk about a subversive action, deregulation, and criticism of overwhelming attempts to organize the reality according to rules that are imposed on us externally. However, the first and primary reaction of the passer-by—the recipient—is disbelief and then a smile. The transformed prohibitory or mandatory traffic sign becomes for us something trivial. Art is not able to lift the prohibition, but can make it shortly powerless.

> "His intention was to disrupt the regulated code of the city streets not to cause harm, but instead to play with the images, to re-employ them in such a way as to communicate something abstract and humorous rather than something regulative, cold and calculative." (Murray, 2014: 62).

This statement provides us with an important clue. The artist perceives something that is important to us (backed by the law), which has an unambiguous meaning, only as an image. Seeing the image—the form—he transforms it with the use of his imagination and allows us to see the play of images. This way, he frees the original image and us, viewers, from seriousness. At least for a moment. In addition, admittedly, seeing such a sign turned into a story, we wonder if it is still in force as a prohibition.

1.2 Something important in something trivial

Returning to Marquard's definition of humor, we must remember about the reverse method—about seeing something important in something trivial. Street Artists, like children, have the uncanny ability of noticing small things and turning them into something meaningful, important or interesting. A stone, a gap in the wall, or a simple electrical box becomes something exciting and full of potential. That is how Street Artists work creating works that are often called interventions. Of course, transforming a tuft of grass into hair and a gutter into an elephant's trunk does not constitute an important change. It does not undermine anything or claim to save the world, and that is where the selflessness of the aesthetic experience of humor lies. This is only a flitting moment of attention being drawn by something trivial, something that was completely excluded from our life and worldview. Laughter is inclusive in its nature by including what has been repressed by our mind, excluded from rationality. Therefore, when the artist in a comical way makes a trivial, damaged or degraded object stand out, through laughter we embrace it; welcome it back to the world.

2. Infantilization

Street Art does not have to be complicated, sophisticated, and professional. It often seems childish, almost infantile, and in the context of anonymity still existing in Street Art, it is often difficult to distinguish what is the work of an adult and what was made by a child's hand. Light-heartedness and childishness are part of the serenity of Street Art. The very activity—guerilla, illegal—may be considered immature and frivolous. If the democratic nature of this type of art lies in the fact that "anyone can do it" (Young, 2014: 27), this relieves the democracy from the burden of maturity. Of course, we can call it infantile, although it must be noted that this word is usually used not to define the natural childishness, but retrogression of what had been mature. For a long time, at least from the beginning of the twentieth century, artists have stopped being treated deadly serious:

> "Were art to redeem man, it could do so only by saving him from the seriousness of life and restoring him to an unexpected boyishness (…) All modern art begins to appear comprehensible and in a way great when it is interpreted as an attempt to instill youthfulness into an ancient world." (Ortega y Gasset, 1968: 50)

Of course, over time the avant-garde became more serious due to its theoretical and critical attitude, which is the phenomenon of banishing the serenity of art that I will mention further. Marquard argues that nowadays in the era of accelerated pace; we all become childish through detachment from the world (Marquard, 1991: 75–76). As in the case of children, we increasingly lack personal experience and only make use of the experience of hearsay, we live based on fiction and illusions. Perhaps Street Art with its risks and illegality is just return to the world, a search for our own experience?

3. Game

Ortega y Gasset meant the avant-garde when he said:

> "Other styles must be interpreted in connection with dramatic social or political movements or with profound religious philosophical currents. The new style only asks to be linked to the triumph of sports and games. It is of the kind and origin with them." (Ortega y Gasset, 1968: 50–51)

Even today, after more than 90 years (first published in 1925), this quote can be used to analyze Street Art. Especially, I would like to recall 3D images evoking a playful gaiety or anamorphoses painted with the use of the traditional technique. Illusions of space that nowadays become tourist attractions are primarily there to surprise, and hence entertain. What is humor if not the way we perceive these representations? Perhaps the definition of laughter presented by Immanuel Kant best explains it "Laughter is an all action arising from a strained expectation being suddenly reduced to nothing" (Kant, 2007: 161). If from a certain distance, we see precipices, waterfalls, or multi-level dungeons opening up before us, we are surprised. Our surprise is associated with tension. Approaching closer, we see that this is only a painting. The wait turns into nothing, but is followed by ludic fun. Like other play activities, it sometimes takes the form that would not be mistaken for serious activity (Morreal, 2012). The viewer ceases to be just a passive observer, but is caught up in the game, becomes its participant. The viewer usually enters the painting as another element of illusion, adopting unnatural poses, pretending, cheating. 3D paintings are perhaps the fulfilment of the theory of art as a game presented by Hans-Georg Gadamer:

> "The attraction of a game, the fascination it exerts, consists precisely in the fact that the game masters the players. (…) The real subject of the game (…) is not the player but instead the game itself. What holds the player in its spell, draws him into play, and keeps him there is the game itself." (Gadamer, 2004: 106)

Gadamer points out that the game is a representation that actually presents itself. Illusion of space presents itself as a trick, and the participant that "makes it real" is only another element. What's more, the participant of the anamorphosis presents it for others, for people photographing this person, for its inactive recipients. This person agrees to this game for a while, pretending to be someone else, leaving the usual role of observer to present this trick to others. In fact, the person's behavior is justified only by this illusion perceived by the viewer set in the right place. Others, unaware passers-by, may laugh not because they recognize the trick, but because of the surprise caused by an odd behavior of a stranger. This is its ludic nature—the participant goes beyond the conventions of behavior in the public space, co-creating the quasi-reality, is subjected to its rules, and serves the illusion. Moreover, as Gadamer points out, participation in the game "is experienced subjectively as relaxation" (Gadamer, 2004: 105). Fun brings pleasure, although in this case it is burdened by a big dose of risk connected with breaking the established form of behavior.

4. Laughter brings relief

> "Humorous is or has to be something which we cannot cope with – in a cruel or nice way (…) in this temporary situation of lack of burden, we enjoy the privilege of taking on the status of powerlessness." (Marquard, 1989: 55)

Usually, economic and political crises evoke ironic defense mechanisms. Everywhere where a crisis is growing, humorous commentary also appears on walls. Political humor has the longest tradition in Western civilization, as well as political graffiti.

> "Political humor has something of a folk nature, and the same story will appear in different guises with different characters but the same point over the years. It is a testimony of certain enduring features of politics to continue to the object of ridicule or aggressive humor." (Schutz, 1977:26)

Whether in Athens or Palestine, Belfast, Istanbul or Cairo, you can always find mocking and humorous works among politically engaged works of Street Art. Those are often caricatured presentations of politicians that is why they can be read as funny only in the local and time context. Political allusions, usually difficult to grasp clearly, save us expenditures necessary for real collision with official relations (Marquard, 1989: 55). The fight with the use of images and inscriptions, or jokes, has no chance of victory in the political reality, but it gives instantaneous relief, by putting it temporarily upside down. Throwing flowers instead of stones will not cause a sudden change, but in the future, when this change occurs, in historical and cultural reflections, those images will become its main symbol.

During the rule of martial law in the 1980s in Poland, apart from the strictly political underground opposition, a strong youth guerilla movement developed. The most spectacular were happenings organized by students participating in the underground anarchic movement called *Orange Alternative*. In places where authorities painted over political inscriptions, clear patches of fresh paint remained. On those patches, representatives of *Orange Alternative* painted the dwarfs.

"Twice Major and his friends were arrested while painting dwarfs. During one of these times Major while detained at a police station in Łódź, proclaimed (…) artistic manifesto of the so-called "dialectic painting" in reference to his own graffiti art. "The Thesis is the [anti-regime] Slogan, the Anti-thesis is the Spot and the Synthesis is the Dwarf" - he announced, furthermore defining himself to be the greatest successor in the Hegel and Marx tradition. - „Quantity evolves into Quality – the more Dwarfs there are, the better it is." (orangealternativemuseum.pl)

Happenings of *Orange Alternative* were full of absurd actions. To this day, many participants of this movement, and even scholars, claim that it was the alternative movement, not the political opposition that dismantled the communist system in Poland. Street images won the war for the memory, especially since they became the source of a new wave of graffiti and Street Art in free Poland. In those difficult times for the Poles, humorous inscriptions and images, though ephemeral, allowed to maintain at least some serenity.

Conclusion

The art critique is dangerous for serenity of art, because critics blame it for escape

"from that absolutely serious task which - (…) it must not shrink: from the alleged and total duty to turn sad relations into better ones, the best ones, hence seek to contribute to the improvement of the world." (Marquard, 1989: 51)

The critique wishes to call art back to seriousness, make it accountable, drive out the spirit of serenity with a distrustful question what its relationship to this absolute task is (Marquard, 1989: 51). Indeed, a large part of Street Art manifests its commitment to improving the world and itself becomes its critique. If Street Art does so in a witty way, we are dealing with irony and satire. Artists taking the satirical attitude consistently and uncompromisingly fight with what they deem wrong. Ironists from a distance and with a sense of their own superiority negatively relate to the objects of their criticism. Apart from them, there are also more serene ones in Street Art, those that can be called humorists. Polish novelist Boleslaw Prus described this attitude as follows:

"A humorist, in a grand style, does not try to gain anything, does not convert anyone and does not submit to anyone, instead watches everyone and everything with indulgent calm. A humorist, in a grand style, does not recognise any dogma, does not think that something is necessary or impossible, just probable..." (Prus, 1890).

The main objective of a humorist is to evoke our smile, which is a manifestation of acceptance. Even if the artist is trying to be rather a humorist than a satirist, often art specialists or public space experts, seeing in this art a rebellion, which they cannot take up themselves, strip it off its serenity. We need a really great sense of humor and compassion for the world to escape propaganda or critique meeting the requirements of art. We should remember, that analysis is the most deadly thing for humor. I can't say that I have found in serenity the essence of Street Art. Unfortunately, serenity remains only a small part of Street Art, which we should enjoy, at the same time being careful not to frighten and chase it away.

Translated by Marta Koniarek

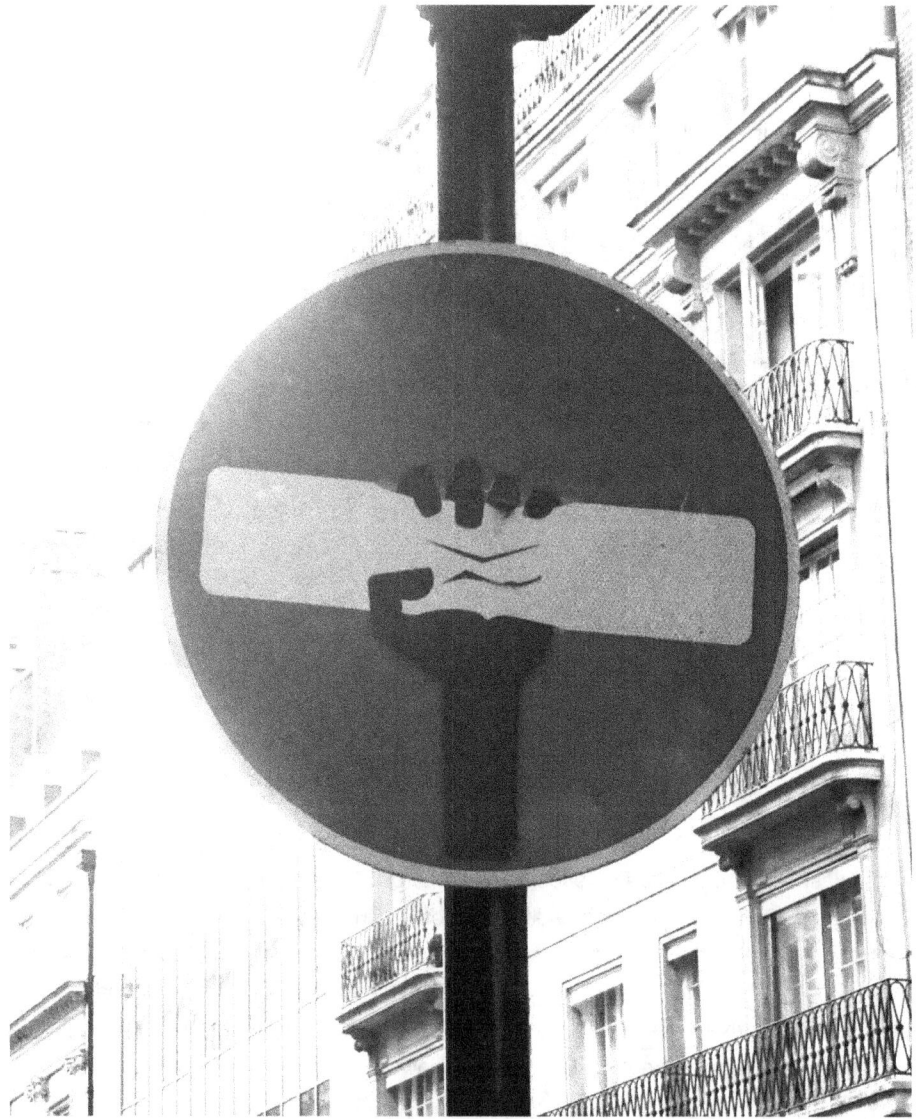

Fig. 1 - Clet, London, 2017, photo: A.G.-T.

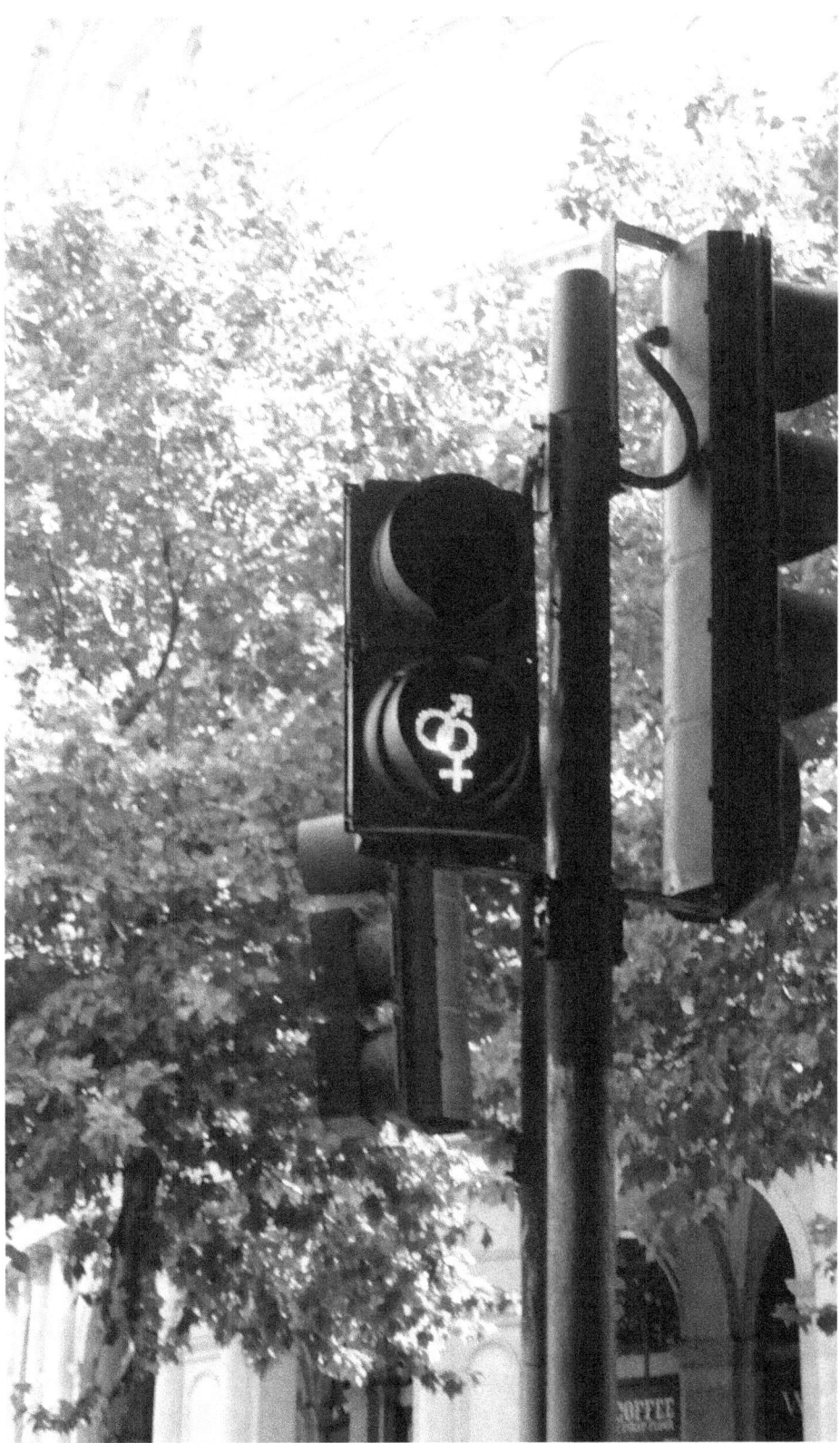

Fig. 2 - author unknown, London 2017, photo: A.G.-T.

References

1982-1983 Dwarf graffiti on the walls of the Polish cities during Marshall Law, http://www. orangealternativemuseum.pl/#dwarfs-under-martial-law, [Accessed: 28.01.2017]

Gadamer, H.-G., 1960 (2004). Truth and Method, Continuum, London, New York.

Gralinska-Toborek, A., Kazimierska-Jerzyk, W., 2014. Experience of Art. in Urban space. Urban Forms Gallery 2011-2013, Urban Forms, Lodz.

Kant, I., 1790 (2007). Critique of Judgment, Oxford University Press, New York.

Korzeniewski, K., 2014. Street Art – Czym Jest? http://www.artique.pl/street-art-czym-jest/5/, [Accessed: 26.01.2017].

Marquard, O., 1989. Aesthetica und Anaesthetica. Philosophische Überlegungen, Ferdinand Schöning, Paderborn.

Marquard, O., 1991. In Defense of Accidental. Philosophical Studies, Oxford University Press, New York Oxford.

Morreal, J., 2012, *Philosophy of Humor, in: Stanford Encyclopedia of Philosophy,* https://plato.stanford.edu/entries/humor/ [Accessed: 26.01.2017].

Murray, K., 2014. Rethinking Political Subjectivity in the Urban Context through the Lens of Graffiti and Street Art, in: Lisbon Street Art & Urban Creativity. 2014 International Conference, Pedro Soares Neves (ed.), Urbancreativity.org, Lisbon.

Ortega y Gasset, J., 1925 (1968). The Dehumanization of Art, and Other Essays on Art, Culture, and Literature, Princeton University Press, Princeton, New Jersey.

Schutz, Ch. E., 1977. Political Humor form Aristophanes to Sam Ervin, Associated University Presses, New Jersey.

Young, A., 2014. Street Art, Public City: Law, Crime and the Urban Imagination, Routledge, London.

Street Art as Process and Performance: The Subversive Streetness of Video-Documentation

Susan Hansen

Middlesex University, London

Abstract

This paper offers an initial response to the common framing of street art and graffiti as a form of creative expression that does not always translate well when removed from its indigenous urban context and placed in institutional gallery space. This framing is grounded in the apparent lack of correspondence between decontextualized works of urban art and the site-specific signification of street art and graffiti in situ, which invokes a phenomenologically powerful element of risk by recalling a dynamic creative performance. As RJ Rushmore notes, work on the street "is a kind of documentation of [...] a performance. Writers have to climb fences, repel down buildings, and break the law in highly visible places without being seen" (Rushmore, 2017). Accordingly, this paper argues for a greater priority to be given to a mode of displaying work in gallery space that more effectively conveys this vital element of illicit performativity—artists' video-documentation of their creative process as performance. Four artists' videos are described here as case studies that illustrate the subversive promise of this alternative approach to the rendering of street art in institutional contexts. Such documents are seldom subject to scholarly analysis nor displayed as works in their own right in formal art spaces, perhaps as they are not marketable in the same way as physical paintings or prints, however more recently artists' videos have been included in some museum shows as additional cultural artefacts or supplements to more conventional works of urban art.

1. Introduction

The process through which [street] artists produce their [...] artefacts is customarily considered [...] to be as important an element of the overall practice as its resultant residual remains [...] the ephemeral performance [is] paramount, a more vital, efficacious element of the aesthetic than the final image in itself. (Schacter, 2015: 204)

It is common for graffiti and street art to be defined as fundamentally both an act and an aesthetic, with reference to some kind of dynamic creative performance as the powerful source of the resultant work. However, the institutionalized display of urban art has been critiqued for its inability to effectively capture this vital and foundational creative act (Chang, 2013). Indeed, Riggle (2010: 254) notes that "what is exhibited in the museum is at most a vestige of street art [and that] the experience of seeing street art in designated art spaces [...] invariably feels dead and inauthentic." Less trenchant critics concur that, at the very least, displacing work from the street to the gallery diminishes its aesthetic power and can fundamentally alter its meaning (e. g. Young, 2015; Chang, 2013).

The currently dominant forms of institutionalised exhibition and display of urban art—in the form of sellable reproductions, limited edition prints, or other versions of work that may or may not have existed in some form, on city walls—have been dismissed by some critics as being "inauthentic"—and as falling short of capturing the "streetness" of street art (Riggle, 2010).[1] Indeed, there are a number of distinctive aspects of this streetness that appear difficult—if not impossible—to (re)capture in formal gallery space. Foremost amongst these is the status of the artwork, by its very presentation as such in a "respectable" institutional space, as a complete and contained object, worthy of conservation and appreciation—and thus as no longer a dynamic (and often illicit) element in ephemeral dialogue with an abject and unpredictable urban environment. MacDowall has argued that a defining feature of street art (when in situ) is that it is "permanently unfinished," and that, accordingly, works of street art should not be considered as the singular product of individual artists, but rather as, "unstable and permanently unfinished object[s], subject to both material decay and erasure and to semantic refashioning as the artworks and urban fabric change" (MacDowall, 2014: 36).

Despite these charges of inauthenticity in representation, and of the absence of streetness in contemporary urban art exhibitions, gallery shows featuring urban art remain popular and well-attended, perhaps in part as they appear to contain a residue of connection to the phenomenology of risk and the "wild" creative energy of work from the street. The question that remains, is then, how else could we represent street art in gallery space? Might there be a mode of exhibition that is less vulnerable to accusations of inauthenticity and lack of streetness? That is, is there a form of display or documentation that could operate to "bring this work (back) to life" and that might capture more effectively its distinctive, if ephemeral, phenomenological conditions of production (and destruction)?

2. Video-documentation as performance

Artists' and writers' video-documentation of both their creative process and the life of their works on the street are ideal resources for (re)activating the streetness of street art and graffiti. Rather than presenting street art as framed and finished works of urban art, such films operate as performative documents that animate the usually risky, invisible, and ephemeral conditions of production of street art, or what Schacter (2015: 204) has called "a sense of corporal illicitness"—offering a rare insight into the dynamism of these works in urban situ.

Street artists' process videos are not (just) documents that reveal an original process of authentic creation. It may be argued that street art, as an ephemeral, performative art form, needs documentation as proof that it existed; and conversely, that this documentation (whether in the form of photographic stills of the kind often disseminated on social media, or in the form of moving images) in turn needs the original creative act to have occurred, and the original artwork to have existed (however momentarily) as an ontological anchor of its indexicality (Auslander, 1999). However, the power of artists' process videos does not derive merely from their function as an indexical access point to past events in-the-world. Indeed, the creative performances they depict may or may not have even happened in actuality or real-time.

Artists' video-documents should thus be regarded as performances in their own right. That is, their authority is not merely ontological and documentary, though this is certainly part of their power. Rather, their aesthetic impact is fundamentally phenomenological. They offer us presence in absentia—we do not need have to have witnessed the original events they depict in order to share in their aesthetic experience. Such illicit creative acts are unlikely to have had any public audience in any case, as they are usually carried out furtively, under cover of darkness (or at least, this is how we have been encouraged to imagine the creation of street art).

---

1 - Mural festivals have been similarly critiqued. Here work is painted on city walls, but the conditions of production (with the permission of authorities, painting openly by day, rather than secretly by night) are accused of not being 'spontaneous' or involving any risk to the artist.

Four artists' videos are discussed here in order to illustrate the potential of this form of documentation-as-performance to (re)animate graffiti and street art in gallery space. It should be noted that the selection of just four artists' videos represents only a partial overview of the wide range of available artists' video-documentation in circulation, particularly online. For instance, Brooklyn Street Art (which has a readership of two million) provides regular links to the growing body of street art videos, as part of its popular Film Friday feature. The decision to discuss just this restricted sample of videos here is primarily based on a desire to cover a few examples in depth, rather than to gloss many examples in précis, so as to initiate a preliminary discussion of some provocative elements of artists' documentation-as-performance and process-based art.

The videos selected as case studies for discussion are: NUG's (2009) *Territorial Pissings*; BLU's (2008) *Muto*; MOBSTR's (2016) *Progressions*; and MOMO's (2005) *Manhattan Tag.* These each invoke key aspects of the streetness of graffiti and street art, including its visceral and heightened "wild" performativity; its reputation as an abject and grotesque form of territory marking, and as an index of imminent "social breakdown" – yet also as a signifier of impending gentrification and social displacement; its capacity to spontaneously engage citizens in urban play and/or politics; and the teeming socio-visual life of city walls when viewed over time.

BLU and MOMO's video work have been previously covered in a number of high profile publications (e.g., Riggle, 2010; Young, 2014) and are, as such, perhaps almost obligatory inclusions in any review of artists' video-documentation. However, these artists' videos are ordinarily referred to as a supplemental index to their physical, street-based work, and are less commonly discussed as primary works in their own right. Thus, it seems justifiable to take a closer look at these pieces on their own merits, as performative documents that powerfully animate the life of these artists' work on the street. NUG's work has a similarly high profile as a controversial work of graffiti/video art, but this is the case primarily in Nordic contexts – here a wider dissemination, and more detailed discussion may prove fruitful, particularly as this work so powerfully conveys an element of the wild phenomenology and corporal illicitness of graffiti that eludes gallery space.[2] Finally, it should be noted that MOBSTR's work is included in this review despite the fact that it does not technically qualify as video art, as his Progressions are currently only accessible as an unfolding online series of time-lapse photographs. The inclusion of MOBSTR's work here reflects the multi-modal play of contemporary viewers' interactions with street art, between urban and virtual space.

The sequence of works discussed is not chronological. Rather the order of discussion reflects a curatorial intention to cover a diverse range of potential aesthetic and affective responses, from the chaotically and disruptively performative (NUG) to the grotesque and abject (BLU) to the playful and inclusive (MOBSTR and MOMO) and a variety of temporal modes – from the apparent "real time" of NUG's urgent performance to the radical compression of time found in BLU and MOBSTR's work. This order also reflects the differential priority placed by these artists on the role/presence and engagement of the urban citizen, which in turn effects the positioning of the viewer. The aesthetic impact of these artists' videos offers us a diversity of forms of presence in absentia, some apparently veridical, and some radically impossible, in actuality.

---

2 - My thanks to Jacob Kimvall and Erik Hannerz for bringing this work to my attention.

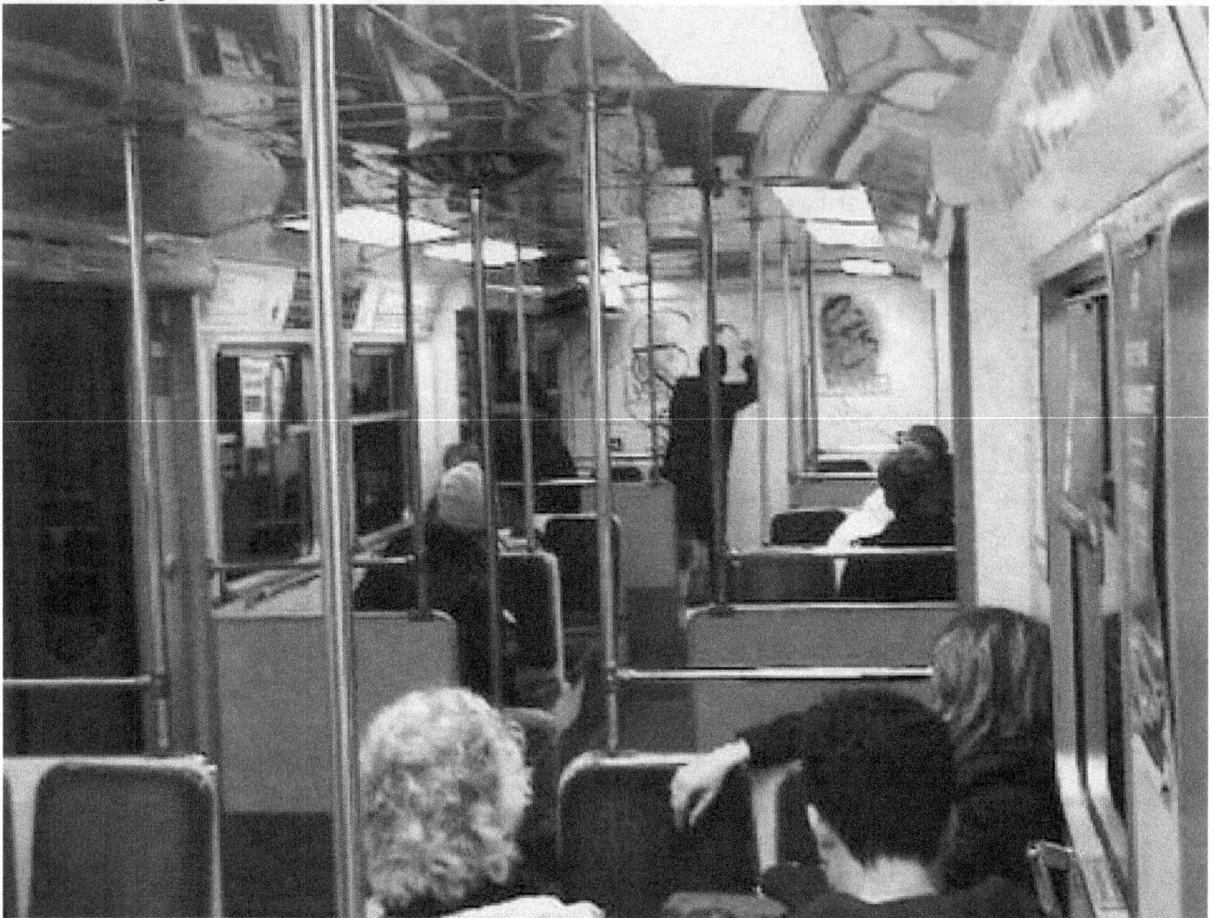

Fig. 1 - Territorial Pissings photo: ©NUG 2009.

Territorial Pissings (2009) by Swedish urban artist NUG is a video-installation that generated considerable controversy in Stockholm when it was released. *Territorial Pissings* was displayed at the Market Art Fair in Stockholm alongside precious antiques. The Market Art Fair is a prestigious Nordic fair for contemporary art and represents leading galleries from Sweden, Norway, Denmark, Iceland and Finland. After viewing the work, Lena Adelsohn Liljeroth, the Swedish Minister for Culture, declared that it was, "incredibly provocative. Graffiti is illegal by its very nature. This is not art" (Svantesson, 2009 cited in Kimvall, 2013). Her statement spurred a heated public debate of the status of the work as art, and in consequence, *Territorial Pissings* was removed from the art fair.

Territorial Pissings is a black and white video, with a shaky frame implying a handheld documentary camera-in-action. The film's black and white monochrome is also an important element of its (gritty) "reality effect." As Erickson (1999: 98) has noted:

> There is a sense of mere utility in black-and-white, which points to the idea that documentation is really only a supplement to a performance… of which the (film) is primarily a reminder.

The video shows a hooded figure inside a subway car engaged in frenzied abandoned spray painting of the carriage before smashing a window and diving out of the train onto the platform. This video appears to document a wanton and uncontrollable act of graffiti-as-vandalism—and this is certainly how the Swedish Minister for Culture responded to it. However, the passengers sitting in the carriage remain calm, and seem disinterested in the abject visual carnage being inflicted on the interior walls of the train. In contrast to the dampened affect of the passengers, who are present, but somehow absent and unaffected by the scene, the actions of the artist appear particularly frantic and chaotic, but also fundamentally dislocated from the quotidian urban reality of the oblivious passengers.

Territorial Pissings makes unambiguous reference to the discourse of graffiti as a form of abject territorial marking. Such aesthetic socio-moral judgements are based on long-held associations between graffiti and criminal activity, as a visible index of social deprivation and urban decay, and as a form of abjection and territory marking akin to public urination, as dirt or filth, or "matter out of place." (Douglas, 2002: 36) NUG's video constructs this creative practice as a form of visceral vandalism—a high energy and intensely performative act, offering viewers a sense of the heightened "wild" phenomenology of graffiti, and perhaps also a reminder of the importance of the attributes we value in more respectable art historical moments such as Action Painting—that is, painting as an energetic, instinctual and dynamic act and a form of "unfettered personal expression" (Encyclopaedia Britannica, 2016).

As Kimvall (2013) notes, despite its documentary aesthetic, and clear affective and political impact, NUG's video is ultimately a film produced by an art school graduate, and exhibited at Sweden's most prestigious art fair. *Territorial Pissings* very effectively indexes and animates the act of graffiti writing—with all of its criminalised associations, as demonstrated by the reaction of the cultural minister, and the consequent withdrawal of the work from the art fair.

4. BLU
MUTO (2008)

Italian urban artist BLU's animated short film *Muto* (2008) expresses a similar abject frenetic energy to NUG's *Territorial Pissings*, however this is not achieved by capturing the artist-in-motion. Rather, *Muto* is a moving image/animation, based on BLU's photographs of his paintings in urban space, meticulously reassembled as film. This film is one of a series of animated films produced by BLU. These are available as a collection in BLU's (2010) *Sketch Note-book*.

The beings depicted in *Muto* are grotesque, abject, and abased. BLU's writhing figures consume themselves in increasingly violent transformations: they recede into the wall only to re-emerge as new bodies, intent on an endless movement through derelict urban spaces, in a relentless cycle of destruction and regeneration. They appear disturbingly complicit in their own fate—one figure removes its own head to hand it to a larger being, who immediately consumes it. Kristeva (1982) notes that the horror of the abject is located in its signification of the "symptoms of social breakdown." And indeed, this cycle of consumption echoes the voracious appetites of late modern consumerism, and the vulnerability of urban environments, and ordinary urban citizens, to being swallowed alive by the inevitable march of gentrification.

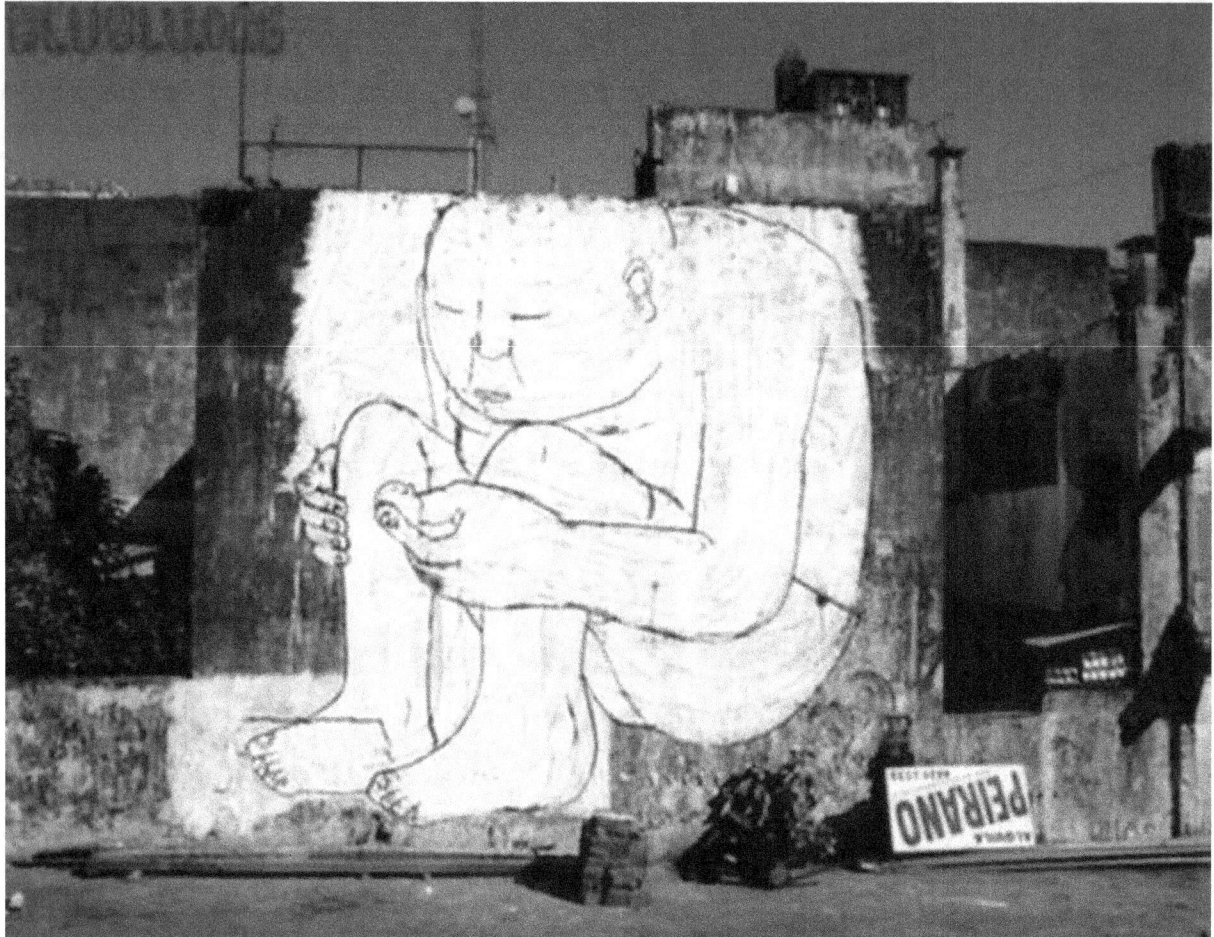

Fig. 2 - *Muto*, photo: ©BLU 2008.

Muto is not a "cleaned up" animation, nor a polished end product. Even though BLU is absent from the frame, he retains an authorial creative presence by capturing traces of the process of producing the paintings that together comprise this film. Indeed, the traces of former versions of the painted figures are clearly visible on the walls they move across and through. They recall the act(s) of illicit painting that produced these apparently living beings. A churning stream of greyish white paint trails in their wake, tracing the palimpsest of their passage—both a partial erasure and a constant reminder of the active work of the artist as painter. These dimensional traces have the effect of softening the surface of the wall, like knife marks hollowed in butter, endowing these ordinarily grey and impassive surfaces with seething, teeming, abject life.

As with *Territorial Pissings*, ordinary urban inhabitants are also present in *Muto*. However, due to BLU's time-lapse photography, these figures are only present in momentary flashes across the screen—the slowed temporality of BLU's animated beings is somehow out of kilter with the 'real time' speed of the city, whose citizens zoom past the scene, unaware that the paintings being executed are moving in their own time. Like the passengers in NUG's film, BLU's pedestrians appear barely present—detached from the more vital energy of the work on the wall.

Muto offers the viewer a temporary escape from the alienating pace of urban existence, by offering an alternative temporal experience of the city. (Chang, 2013: 227) In doing so, BLU brings the walls to life, and shows street art as something that is mobile rather than static, "permanently unfinished" and open to erasure, rather than complete and contained. (MacDowall, 2014: 36; Riggle, 2010: 255)

5. MOBSTR
PROGRESSIONS (2016)

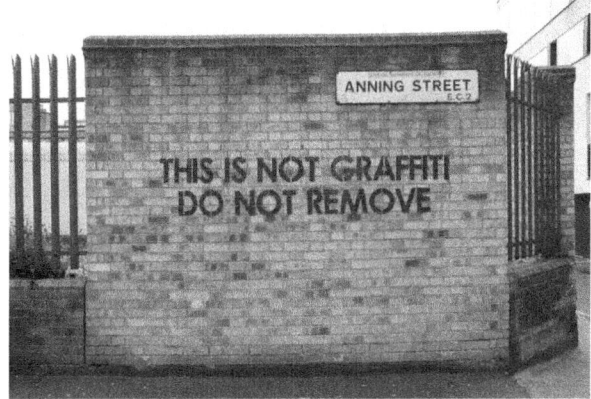 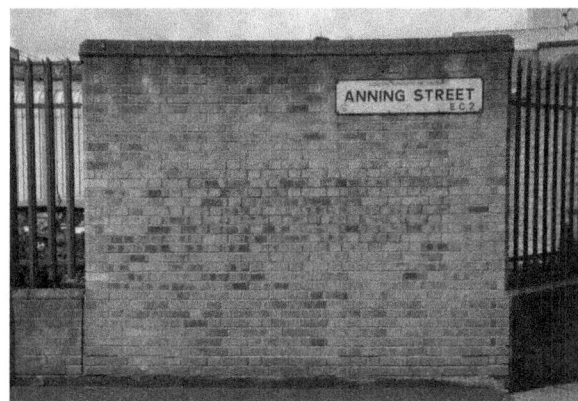

Fig. 3 - Progressions, photo: ©MOBSTR 2016.

MOBSTR's (2016) *Progressions*, like BLU's (2008) *Muto*, utilise time-lapse or repeat photography to animate the life of a wall, through recording a series of discrete paintings photographically, then reassembling the photographs as a consecutive series. However, MOBSTR's work is distinct from BLU's in that it involves a degree of collaborative authorship and play. The urban citizens in MOBSTR's work are not detached and alienated, but are often active interlocutors, leaving their own marks on the wall in response to MOBSTR's provocations. More recently, MOBSTR's *Progressions* have also involved virtual urban citizens as collaborative authors via his execution of a series of physical amendments to his work suggested by his social media following. The interactivity inherent to MOBSTR's work animates the multi-modal play of contemporary viewers' interactions with work on the street, in a democratic form of visual dialogue that melds urban and virtual spheres of action.

Unlike NUG's more abstract visceral spray painting, and BLU's representational figures, MOBSTR works primarily with text. His *Progressions* engage in interaction with the local authorities responsible for buffing—or painting over—illegal work on city walls. The evolving painting is thus effectively co-authored. *Progressions* offers the viewer an insight into an animated dialogue between the artist and those responsible for removing his work. This would ordinarily only be witnessed by local passersby, but by photographing each change made to the work on the wall (and uploading these to his website) MOBSTR stitches time together to animate these often witty exchanges—that may in real time have occurred days, or even weeks later. His work operates as a series of cheeky taunts designed to elicit a visual response from non-artist others. Like BLU, MOBSTR's work highlights destruction as generative, but MOBSTR's *Progressions* does not present destruction as abject or grotesque, but rather as a form of urban play through palimpsest—a crucial element in appreciating street art "in the wild" as a form of democratic "dialogue between the city and the people." (Petri, 2015: 27)

6. MOMO
MANHATTAN TAG (2005)

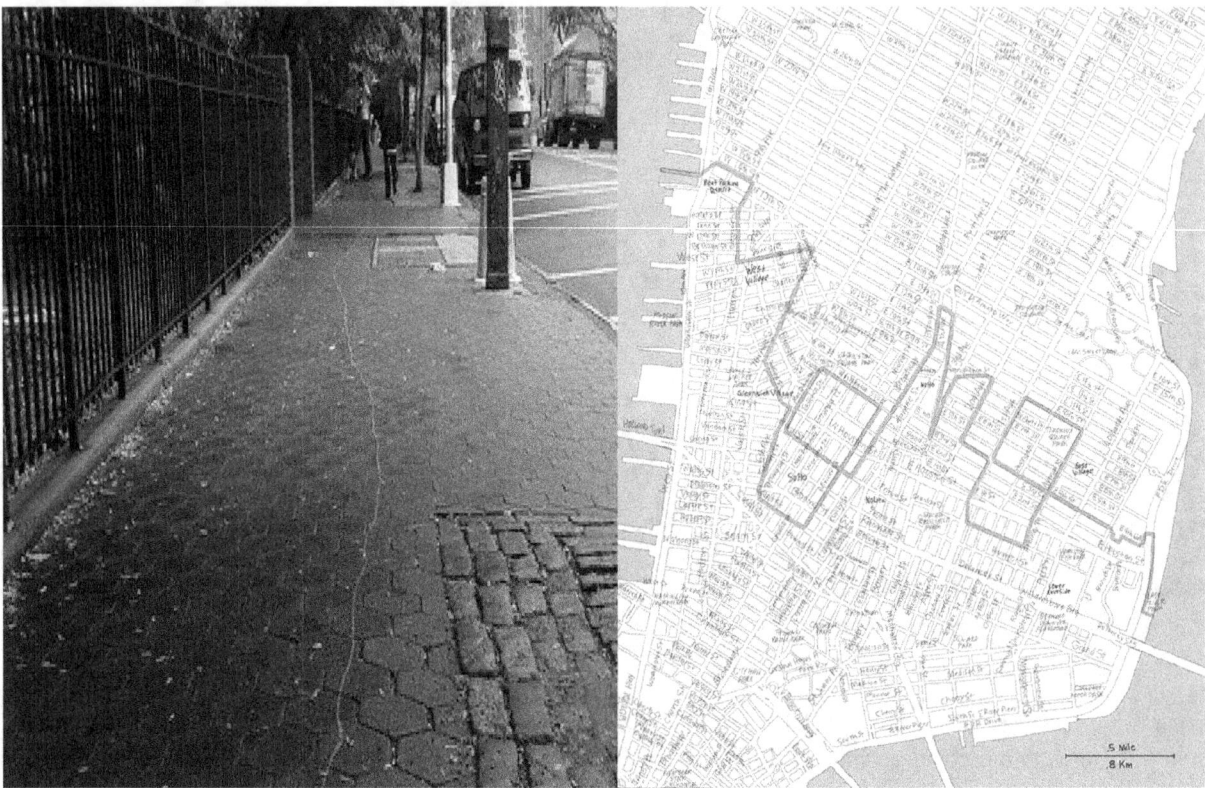

Fig. 4 - Manhattan Tag, photo: ©MOMO 2005.

MOMO's process video of the creation of his *Manhattan Tag* (2005) shows a continuously dripping line of paint that leaves a thin orange trail running along the sidewalk. He repainted this trail in 2011, as the first version had all but worn off under the constant abrasion of pedestrian footfall. Viewed from the sidewalk, the scale of the work is deceptively modest, and seems almost accidental, like the trail left unwittingly by a leaking container, that only incidentally tracks the movement of its unaware carrier.

However, as MOMO's *Manhattan Tag* video shows, if followed, this modest line seems unending—weaving around corners and out of sight. Cartographically, this apparently minimal work also exists on a more massive (non-human) scale (Abarca, 2016). A map displayed on MOMO's website reveals the form taken by this apparently inconsequential line: it forms a giant tag of MOMO's name, spanning the entire breadth of Manhattan island. As Young (2014) notes, the viewer's discovery of MOMO's map transforms this unassuming trickle of paint into an artwork too enormous to apprehend in its totality, although it may be traversed by foot, and simultaneously mapped as a virtual tag by activating the geo-location apps on our almost embodied smart phones.[3]

---

3 - Manhattan Tag is among the world's largest artworks. In scale, it is larger than Robert Smithson's Spiral Jetty, Michael Heizer's Double Negative, and James Turrell's Roden Crater (Riggle, 2010).

Like MOBSTR's *Progressions*, MOMO's *Manhattan Tag* shows the production of a form of urban art that invites participation in situ. It offers a seemingly minimal aesthetic intervention, but one that when apprehended in its full signifying intent, may transform the viewer's sense of scale and being in the city. The contrast between the thin line of the paint that is immediately available to the senses, and the massive scale of the tag formed by the totality of the line, may be an initially confronting experience as it is not something that we can fully apprehend from our restricted view from the street (or, rather from the street presence in absentia offered by MOMO's process video). MOMO's map provides the viewer with the key to the puzzle posed by his wavering and seemingly inexhaustible thin line of paint. Riggle argues that this offers the viewer a sublime release from the initial overwhelming scale, and seeming lack of purpose or pattern, to the work. As he notes, "it is sweetly ironic that the biggest tag in the world is designed to be invisible in its entirety." (Riggle, 2010: 58)

7. Conclusion

These artists' videos provide for a mode of exhibition that compellingly conveys the ephemeral phenomenological conditions of production of work on the street. Video-documentation (both in real time, and over time) is a vibrant form of urban art that is arguably less likely to be met with the accusations of inauthenticity and lack of streetness that characterize the critical reception of street art as static works in gallery space. Artists' video-documentation may more effectively capture the streetness and illicit corporal performativity of the creation of work on the street and the inherent capacity of such work to arrest and engage onlookers. The aesthetic impact of these artists' videos offers us presence in absentia, which positions the viewer as both inside/outside gallery space.

A powerful aspect of the liminal presence afforded to the viewer by such video-documentation is the phenomenological experience of enchantment – an aesthetic response ordinarily restricted to our unanticipated encounters with work on the street. Young (2014: 45) argues that street art and graffiti may offer unexpected opportunities for ethical engagement as it arrests our otherwise fluid motion through urban space, which may in turn create productive fissures in our ordinary ways of seeing, and being with others, in the city. Conceived as a "tangle in the smooth spaces of the city out of which comes the potential for enchantment," these moments of arrest need not necessarily involve visual pleasure, but may instead be experienced as troubling, unsettling or *unheimlich*. Indeed, these videos together provoke a diversity of positive and negative affective responses, identifications and disidentifications – moments of vicariously seeing and viscerally experiencing other possible ways of being in the city that may fall outside of viewers' conventional expectations and realms of experience. Arguably, such moments of enchantment, even in absentia, may provide unexpected points of potential connection with others, and a sense of attachment within a potentially dehumanizing urban space. In this sense, artists' videos may afford the conditions of possibility for viewers to experience the forms of ethical engagement normally associated with our accidental encounters with work on the street.

These performative forms of documentation thus have the subversive potential to "bring work (back) to life" in gallery space, not just as artefacts or supplements to sellable works, but as powerful works of urban art in their own right, which serve also to remind us of the critical outsider stance, always unfinished energy, and participatory democratic nature, of work on the street. However, as yet, this is currently not a form of work adopted as a primary mode of exhibition by many galleries, for artists' video-documentation is – along with performance art and street art itself – a "per se non-sellable form of art" and a "consumer critical art form that criticizes the role of an art object as a consumer product" (Blanché 2016).

Although not considered in the process videos included here, the photographic documentation of the entire lifecycle of work in urban situ may also offer a means to translate the transitory nature of such work in otherwise protected gallery space. By documenting the gradual decay in situ of street art and graffiti (e.g. Hansen and Flynn, 2015) we may highlight the defining ephemerality of work in the streets, which is, unlike work in gallery-space, subject to environmental degradation and decay, as it is constantly exposed to the elements. For instance, SWOON's paste up work depicts destruction as inevitable and beautiful. Rather than simply animating the more stereotypically masculine adrenaline-fuelled conditions of production of street art, SWOON's work attunes us to the ephemerality and fragile lifecycle of work on the street. This, too, is part of what is not ordinarily captured in either white cube contexts or street art festivals, where the work featured is pristine and protected from the elements, and from being buffed by authorities or written over by others. Indeed, Riggle (2010) argues that, for a work to count as street art, the "artist must willingly expose their work to the risks of defacement, destruction, theft, alteration and appropriation; in short, [they] must be committed to ephemerality."

References

Abarca, J. (2016) From street art to murals: what have we lost? Street Art & Urban Creativity Journal, 2 (2), 60-67.

Auslander, P. (2006). The Performativity of Performance Documentation, Performing Arts Journal: A Journal of Performance and Art 84, 1–10.

Barthes, R. (1977). Image, Music, Text, Fontana, London.

Blanché, U. (2016) Banksy. Urban Art in a Material World, Tectum, Marburg.

BLU (2010). Sketch Note-Book, available at: http://www.blublu.org (accessed June 2017).

Chang, V. (2013). Animating the City: Street Art, BLU and the Poetics of Visual Encounter, Animation: An Interdisciplinary Journal 8(3), 215–233.

Debord, G. (1983). Society of the Spectacle, Black and Red, Detroit.

De Certeau, M. (1988). Walking in the City, in: Rendall, S. (trans.), The Practice of Everyday Life, University of California Press, Berkeley.

Derrida, J. (1993) Le Toucher: Touch/To Touch Him. Paragraph: A Journal of Modern Critical Theory 16(2), 122–57.

Erickson, J. (1999). Goldberg variations: Performing distinctions, Performing Arts Journal: A Journal of Performance and Art 21 (3).

Jones, A. (1997). 'Presence' in Absentia: Experiencing performance as documentation, Art Journal 56 (4), 11–18.

Kimvall, J. (2013). Scandinavian Zero Tolerance on Graffiti, in Bertuzzo, E. T. et al. (Eds.) Kontrolle öffentlicher Räume. Unterstützen Unterdrücken Unterhalten Unterwandern, LIT Verlag, Berlin,102–117.

Kristeva, J. (1982). Powers of Horror: An Essay on Abjection, Trans. L. Roudiez, Columbia University Press, New York.

MOBSTR (2016). Progressions, available at: http://www.mobstr.org/ (accessed June 2017).

MOMO (2005). Manhattan Tag, available at: http://momoshowpalace.com/a-tag-the-width-of-manhattan/ (accessed June 2017).

NUG (2009). Territorial Pissings, available at: https://vimeo.com/25811133 (accessed June 2017).

Petri, J. (2015). The Artistic Turn in Graffiti Practice: Szwedzki Vs Mona Tusz, Art Inquiry: Recherches sur les arts, vol. XVII, 371–387.

Rancière, J. (2009). The Emancipated Spectator, Verso, London.

Rancière, J (2004). The Politics of Aesthetics, Continuum, London.

Riggle, N. (2010). Street Art: The Transfiguration of the Commonplaces, The Journal of Aesthetics and Art Criticism 68 (3), 243–257.

Rushmore, R. J. (2017). All Big Letters, available at: http://exhibits.haverford.edu/allbigletters (accessed June 2017).

Sacks, H. (1995) Lectures on Conversation. Volumes I and II. Cambridge: Blackwell.

Schacter, R. (2015). The Invisible Performance/the Invisible Masterpiece: Visibility, Concealment, and Commitment in Graffiti and Street Art, in: Flynn, A., Tinius, J. (Eds.), Anthropology, Theatre, and Development: The Transformative Potential of Performance, Palgrave Macmillan, London, pp. 203–223.

Schegloff, E. (1995) Introduction. In Sacks, H. (1995) Lectures on Conversation. Volumes I and II. Cambridge: Blackwell.

Young, A. (2014). Street Art, Public City: Law, Crime and the Urban Imagination, Routledge, London.

RE/viewing Jerusalem:
Political Art Interventions in Occupied East Jerusalem

Elisabeth R. Friedman

Associate Professor, Art History & Visual Culture, School of Art, Illinois State University

CVA 203E, Campus Box 5620, Normal, IL 61790-5620, USA

efriedm@ilstu.edu

Alia Rayyan

DFG Graduiertenkolleg »Kulturen der Kritik« (Cultures of Critique), Culture science department

Leuphana Universität Lüneburg, Scharnhorststraße 1, 21335 Lüneburg

rayyan@leuphana.de

Abstract

This collaborative essay emerges from the authors' ongoing dialogue about the political potential of participatory urban art interventions in the contemporary context of occupied East Jerusalem. Although contemporary Western discourses of participatory art offer productive starting points for thinking about the role of art as a means of political engagement, they do not adequately address the ongoing colonial situation that shapes life in occupied East Jerusalem. This essay calls attention to the gaps between the prevailing art-world discourses of participation and community engagement, and the realities of life in occupied Jerusalem. To find methods adequate to these unique local circumstances, critical reflection upon common methodology is required in order to rethink dominant paradigms. This essay examines an art walk titled *RE/viewing Jerusalem* (2015-16), one of several participatory, community-based art projects initiated during Alia Rayyan's tenure as Director of Al Hoash Gallery—Palestinian Art Court in Jerusalem. The authors ask how political engagement might be imagined and practiced through art in the context of the ongoing Israeli military occupation of the city. *RE/viewing Jerusalem* was an aesthetic and performative strategy of counter-occupation in a contested and highly politicized space. The authors demonstrate the ways in which *RE/viewing Jerusalem* reflected upon Western urban art intervention practices and translated them to the specifics of the local situation in Israeli-occupied Jerusalem. The goal of *RE/viewing Jerusalem* is shown to be twofold: to decolonize both thought and space. In other words, the projects seeks both to intervene in Western discourses about political art, and to resist the occupation through the collective activation of public space.

Keywords
Decolonization, social practice art, urban interventions, occupied, Jerusalem, Palestine, activism

1 Introduction

This collaborative essay emerges from the authors' ongoing dialogue about the political potential of participatory urban art interventions in the contemporary context of occupied East Jerusalem. Although contemporary Western discourses of participatory art offer productive starting points for thinking about the role of art as a means of political engagement, they do not adequately address the ongoing colonial situation that shapes life in occupied East Jerusalem. In this essay, we aim to call attention to the gaps between the prevailing art-world discourses of participation and community engagement and the realities of life in occupied Jerusalem.

We take as our starting point an art walk titled *RE/viewing Jerusalem* (2015-16), one of several participatory, community-based art projects initiated during Alia Rayyan's tenure as director of Al Hoash Gallery—Palestinian Art Court in Jerusalem. Through an analysis of this urban intervention, we ask how political engagement might be imagined and practiced through art in the context of the ongoing Israeli military occupation of the city. *RE/viewing Jerusalem* was an aesthetic and performative strategy of counter-occupation in a contested and highly politicized space.

2 Life in Occupied Jerusalem

The Israeli occupation operates through the sophisticated manipulation of spaces and bodies, and seeks to create a sense of fatalism and inevitability for those subject to it. Although the harsh effects of the occupation are felt throughout occupied Palestine, residents of East Jerusalem face unique challenges as a minority in the city. They are increasingly being forced out of their shrinking neighborhoods as settlers illegally appropriate their homes; their basic right to reside in Jerusalem is precarious—dependent on the possession of residency permits that may be abruptly revoked by the Israeli authorities—and they are cut off from even the semblance of Palestinian autonomy that exists in parts of the West Bank. The duration and severity of the occupation has caused community members and social associations in Jerusalem to respond to such conditions with a high level of skepticism, a fearful resistance to change, and a reluctance to challenge the current system. This situation illustrates the theories of Franz Fanon (1964), who described how colonialism becomes internalized in the very bodies of suppressed peoples. The repressive circumstances of colonialism influence and restrict both bodies and psyches; colonized subjects learn to stay within the limited borders imposed by the system. This is evident in the fact that Jerusalemites tend to restrict themselves to private spaces—the only places where they can feel free and secure (although even that security is increasingly under threat by settlers). The experience of fear and insecurity in public spaces is enormous and has of course increased throughout the years of occupation and the ongoing cycles of violence in the streets. What role can art play in responding to this situation, and what forms might creative responses take?

3.1 *RE/viewing Jerusalem*

In the first edition of *RE/viewing Jerusalem*, which took place in 2015, groups of local residents and visitors followed a route through Jerusalem's Old City and into the East Jerusalem neighborhood of Al Zahra, stopping at various art "stations"—mundane or forgotten places that had been subtly transformed into sites of urban art—a parking lot, a flower shop, a community garden, an ancient abandoned covered bazaar that was once a thriving vegetable market in the Old City. Along the way, participants encountered traces of a suppressed history, glimpses of possibility in the present, and new visions of the future. None of the art stations in *RE/viewing Jerusalem* presented work that was explicitly political in any conventional sense, yet each offered participants new ways to occupy public space—something that is in itself a political act in Palestinian Jerusalem.

3.2 Social practice and the debates of participatory art

Before we turn to the specifics of *RE/viewing Jerusalem*, it is important to contextualize it within the broader field of participatory social art practices that inform urban interventions, as well as to consider the contemporary debates concerning its ethics, aesthetics, and politics. Since the 1990s, contemporary artists have become increasingly interested in collaborating with various "non-art world" publics. The artists associated with these practices are

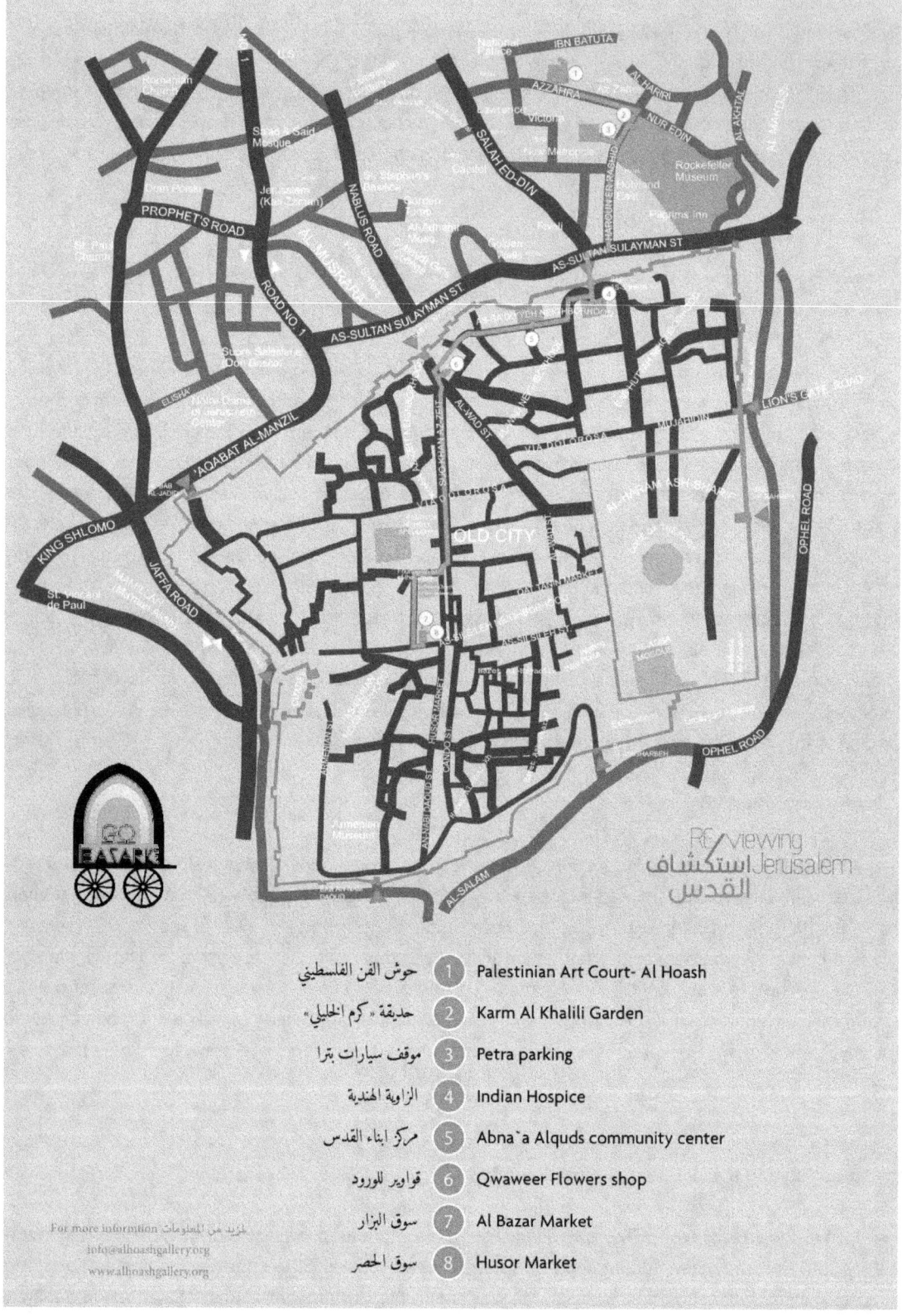

حوش الفن الفلسطيني	1	Palestinian Art Court- Al Hoash
حديقة «كرم الخليلي»	2	Karm Al Khalili Garden
موقف سيارات بترا	3	Petra parking
الزاوية الهندية	4	Indian Hospice
مركز ابناء القدس	5	Abna`a Alquds community center
قواوير للورود	6	Qwaweer Flowers shop
سوق البزار	7	Al Bazar Market
سوق الحصر	8	Husor Market

For more information المزيد من المعلومات
info@alhoashgallery.org
www.alhoashgallery.org

Fig. 1 - *RE/viewing Jerusalem* art walk map, 2015.

frequently driven by a desire to address social injustices, and they view the participation of the public as an ethical imperative (Bishop, 2012). A diverse array of participatory, community-based, socially-oriented art projects is referred to today as "social practice." As Bishop (2012) observes, such practices are often based in everyday social forms such as talking, eating, gardening or walking; sometimes they are discursive rather than visual, engaging the public through publications, workshops or lectures. These contemporary practices may offer new and at times confounding notions of art, but they are the legacy of a century of avant-gardist assault on the boundaries between art and life.

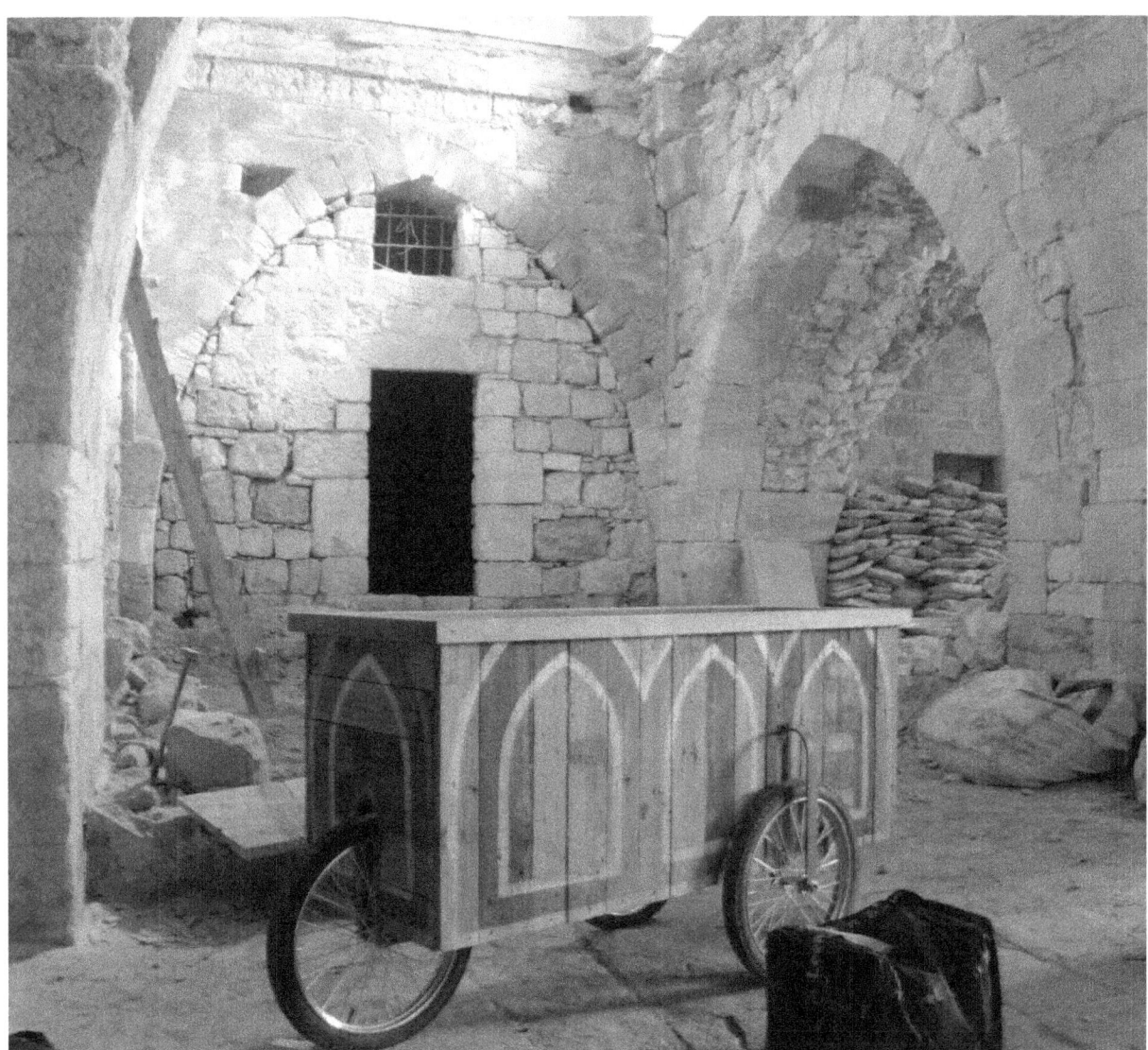

Fig. 2 - A cart specially designed by Al Hoash for *RE/viewing Jerusalem*, in the style of the traditional carts used to transport goods through the narrow alleyways of the Old City. The cart is painted with colorful arches, reflecting the architecture of the old bazaar. Photo by Ahed Izhiman and Majd Zughayer.

Although they may not meet the demands of the commercial art market, participatory social practices have become well integrated into the contemporary artworld: they fit readily into the rapidly expanding public arenas of biennial culture and are welcomed by museums eager to provide interactive experiences for their visitors. However, such practices are not without controversy. Many forms of "social practice"—particularly so-called community art projects—have been sanctioned and funded by various states agencies as non-threatening forms of "social work"—what political theorist Oliver Marchart (2002) referred to as "privatist version[s] of public welfare." Art critic Claire Bishop (2012) notes that that in seeking to establish a critical distance from the neoliberal new world order "collaborative practice is perceived to offer an automatic counter-model of social unity, regardless of its actual politics." She calls attention to the risks of perceiving all works of collaborative social practice as equally significant "artistic gestures of resistance." While Bishop may at times seem intent on protecting a space for aesthetic critique, her insistence on criticality is also an insistence on politics. Both Bishop and Marchart are wary of a social practice in which art is instrumentalized to co-opt underprivileged communities into the existing neoliberal order, rather than to challenge the assumptions on which that order is founded. While their critiques do have validity, they are principally aimed at the discourse of Western political art and its implication in or appropriation by neoliberal capitalism. However, contemporary art may no longer be adequately defined in the terms of a "western tradition." At its best, art is a complex and contradictory set of practices—and if globalization may be said to impose a degree of cultural sameness, art introduces a source of alterity that confounds such a reductive formulation. Artists and art worlds in many colonial and post-colonial contexts increasingly refute the distinction between the local and the global, the West and "the rest." Such is the case in Palestine, where the traditional dichotomies that structure Western political art discourse (social vs. political, individual vs. community, local vs. global, aesthetics vs. ethics) do not make sense in the context of an ongoing colonial occupation. There are significant differences between the accommodation to capitalism/neoliberalism that Marchart and Bishop identify in some Western artistic practices and participatory social practices in the Palestinian context. To borrow Achille Mbembe's (2015) timely phrase, it may be necessary to "decolonize knowledge" (in this case, the discourse of political art) as well as to decolonize Palestinian territory. Such an approach unites the psychic and spatial dimensions of the occupation, and connects the logic of capitalism to the logic of the occupation.

3.3 The twin logics of capitalism and occupation

In The New Spirit of Capitalism (2007), Boltanski and Chiapello update Max Weber's notion of the "spirit of capitalism" to explain the contradictions of capitalism today and how the system works to overcome them. Weber's vital—and still relevant—insight was that the capitalist system cannot operate without the complicity or co-optation of most of its subjects. As Boltanski and Chiapello observe, this system successfully defies its own contradictions by sustaining a dialectic between capitalism and its "critique." Capitalism typically overcomes the crises it generates by neutralizing "critique"—stealing the thunder of its critics by ostensibly answering some of their challenges while diverting attention from other grievances that are left unremedied or even exacerbated.

Such a dialectic also informs the logic of occupation. Marchart, Bishop and Boltanski emphasize the danger that art—even in the anti-capitalist (non-commercial or commodity forms) that characterize much social practice - may be coopted into the capitalist system, thus losing its critical force and effectively becoming disarmed. In the Palestinian context, what Boltanski terms „neutralisation of critique" takes the form of a very real fear that any expression of critique will be neutralized—either through its violent elimination or through integration into the very system of occupation that it seeks to oppose. To some degree, this dialectic touches all forms of critiques within a totalizing system. But what makes art different from other forms of social/political critique is its capacity to sustain contradiction—to hold opposites in tension and thus to offer a different dialectical movement. As such, art offers a unique space of possibility—a place to imagine and visualize alternate realities.

4.1 Making "place" in East Jerusalem

We are currently seeing an increasing turn towards participatory and performative practices in Palestinian art. How might such practices begin to unravel the intertwined logics of capitalism and occupation? In *RE/viewing Jerusalem*, a precondition for transferring artistic practices of place-making to Palestinian Jerusalem—and a major difference from its counterparts in Europe—was the decision to avoid those public spaces already defined and claimed by the state, but instead to discover (together with the artists and the community) new approaches to making space accessible for public use and engagement. In Jerusalem, permissions issued by the Israeli municipality are required for any public activity in East Jerusalem. As any sort of public gathering tends to be qualified as political activity, requests for permits to assemble are usually denied. The lack of public infrastructure and public spaces in East Jerusalem—in comparison to the expansive public spaces and rich resources of West Jerusalem—complicates all attempts to design public engagement beyond the traditional format of the street festival. In addition, public spaces in East Jerusalem are subject to intense surveillance by the Israeli army or police. These spaces have become increasingly unsafe, as soldiers injure and kill Palestinian residents with impunity in the name of vague and frequently unfounded claims of self-defense. Because most Palestinians do not feel safe to gather in public space, it was imperative for Al Hoash to develop a creative and subversive approach to place making in East Jerusalem.

4.2 Space and Place

Michel de Certeau (2011) draws an important distinction between place and space. Place, according to de Certeau, refers to the "locational instantiation of what is considered to be customary, proper and even pre-established" (Pannell, 2006). Space, on the other hand, has none of this stability but instead is composed of the "intersections of mobile elements," which are ambiguous and often in conflict (Warner, 2002). Space may be abstracted and viewed objectively, but place must be activated by bodies, by walking—it must be experienced subjectively. Space is produced while place is risked or activated in practice. Space signifies an abstract representation of knowledge about the world, while place represents the actions or practices by which this knowledge is produced, affirmed or transformed. Al Hoash realized that in order to elicit public engagement, it needed to turn hidden and forgotten "unofficial" spaces into places.

4.3 Transforming space into place

The Israeli occupation of East Jerusalem has created a widespread sense of political depression and apathy amongst Palestinian residents. Activism is blocked and "a disintegration of politics results in isolation, frustration, anomie and forgetfulness" (McLennan, 2012). Al Hoash's task was to find a spark to revive the community—to disrupt the passivity of residents of Palestinian Jerusalem. They approached this challenge by identifying new kinds of spaces in East Jerusalem—spaces that could be defined and opened by participatory art interventions. The goal of *RE/viewing Jerusalem*, to use de Certeau's formulation, was for artists and the public to join forces in activating hidden and forgotten spaces and transform them into embodied places.

The Al Hoash team became location scouts, making the rounds of community centers, shops, hotels, or forgotten/abandoned public buildings in their search for such potential places. They invited artists from Palestine and abroad to participate in a residency. These artists formed a temporary collective to jointly create art interventions in the selected semi-public spaces. Over a period of three weeks, this collective took over the Al Hoash Gallery and discovered the surrounding area, meeting with community members and discussing possible topics for the selected "art stations."

Ownership of the process was given to the artists in order to dissolve the hierarchy of the classical curatorial and institutional set up. After much discussion with community members, local organizations, and time spent observing the daily routines of life between the Old City and the Zahra Street neighborhood, the artists selected the central themes of silence and repose for their project—a form of response and resistance to the stress and turmoil that comprises daily life in East Jerusalem.

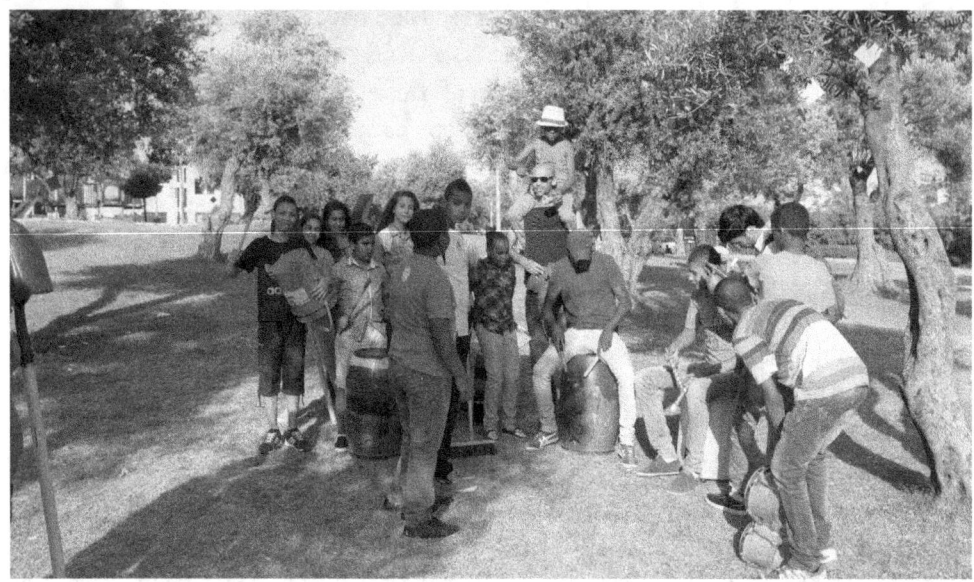

Fig. 3 - Making use of the only public park in Palestinian Jerusalem. Photo by Ahed Izhiman and Majd Zughayer.

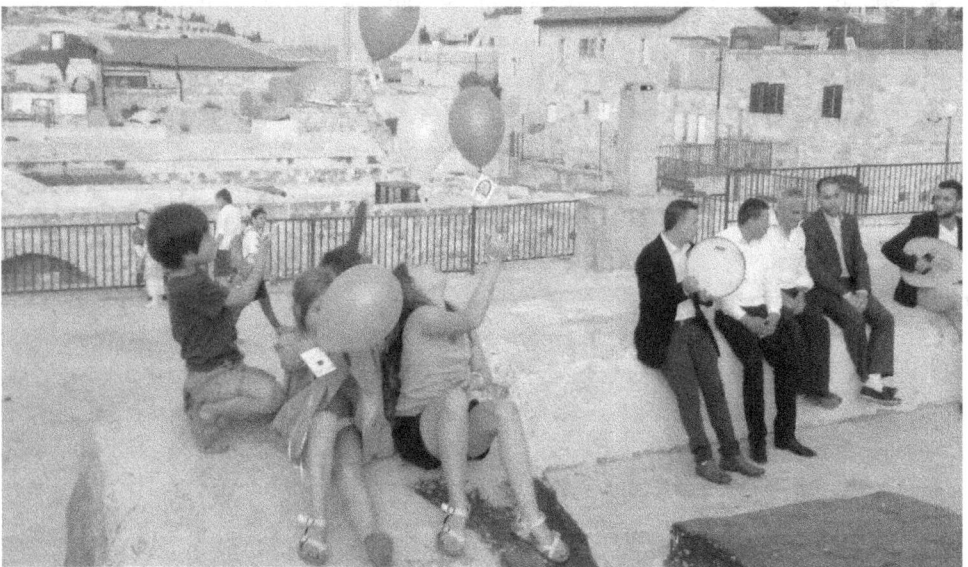

Fig. 4 - *RE/viewing Jerusalem*, 2015. Photo: Ahed Izhiman and Majd Zughayer.

5.1 *RE/viewing Jerusalem*: **a new way of looking**
In a city that attracts tourists to its religions processions and rituals (the route along the stations of the cross, the Via Dolorosa, being the most well-known) but restricts their exposure to the injustices of the occupation, the "art stations" subverted such practices and addressed the contemporary daily life of Palestinian residents. Yet this was not done in the tragic mode of political victimization but in a creative and life-giving spirit.

Each art station offered a new vision or surprising alteration—the route led participants between al Zahra Street and the Suf Market in the Old City and varied from an encounter with "urban furniture" to a pause in a forgotten dead-end street next to a public garden, an art intervention in the community center Ibna Al Quds, to a music performance in an abandoned, semi-ruined former vegetable market in the bazaar.

The artists cleaned up and reclaimed this old bazaar (the Al Bazar Market) and it became a central location on the walk. During the tours, participants of were led from one station to the next and provided with an introduction to the space, its background, and its connection to the art intervention. None of the artists used the spaces simply as exotic background for their own work but instead involved the participants in activating each new place and making it their own. (Each station had its very particular set up, the specific details cannot all be described in the scope of this essay.) One intervention exemplifies the multilayered thoughts behind the project. The Qwaweer Flower shop next to the Damascus Gate in the Old City was one of the middle stations of the tour. Participants were invited to enter the shop, but at this station they found no art installation present. Instead, they were asked to pick up a small flowerpot and carry it through Suq al Seit until they reached the final station—the rooftop of the reclaimed bazaar overlooking the Old City. There participants placed their flowerpots in a prepared wooden frame, thus creating a living roof garden and activating this space through their collective installation. What began as an alternative tour through the city turned into a performative demonstration—one that played with and subverted a dominant tourist cliché in the Old City: the carrying of religious symbols. The participants now became artists. This simple yet powerful activity turned out to be one of the most successful aspects of *RE/viewing Jerusalem*. It attracted the attention of neighboring Palestinian shop owners and residents who became interested in learning about and participating in future versions of the project.

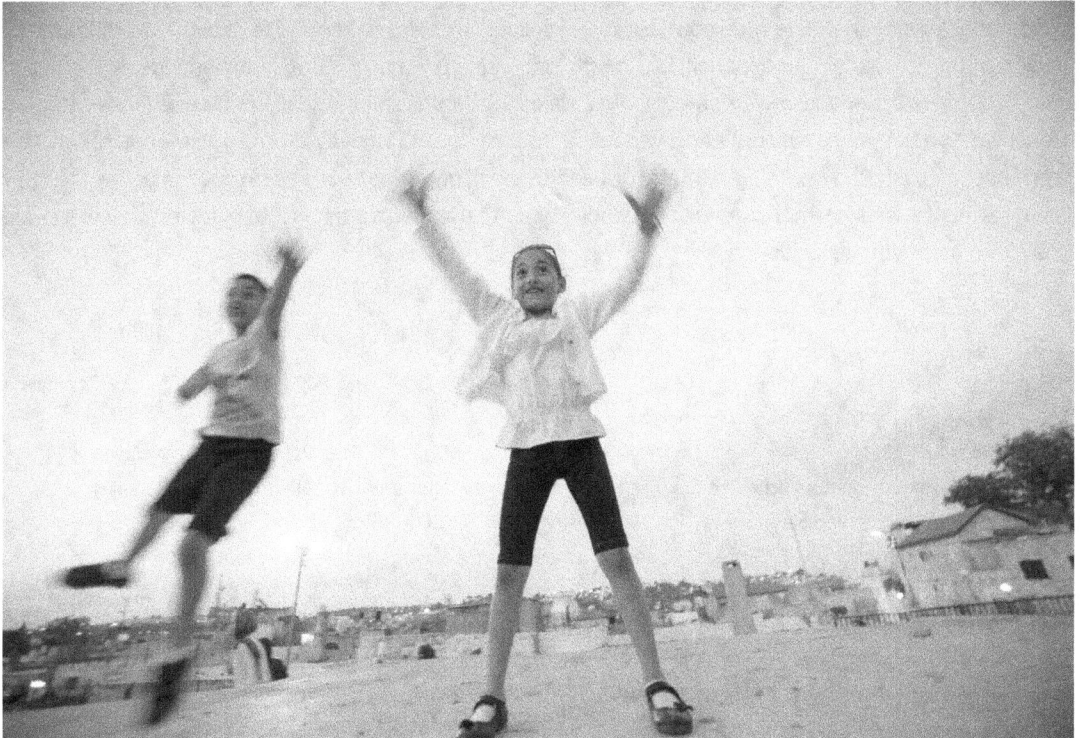

Fig. 5 - *RE/viewing Jerusalem*, 2015. Photo: Ahed Izhiman and Majd Zughayer.

5.2 Challenging expectations

Half a year later, Alia Rayyan discussed this event with a group of German *RE/viewing Jerusalem* participants during a lecture at the University of Lueneburg in December 2015. Many of those present expressed the discomfort they had felt carrying the flowerpot through the Old City. Perhaps these visitors had arrived with predetermined ideas and expectations of Jerusalem that were disrupted by the intervention and the resulting blurring of roles between participant and artist. Interestingly, the local participants did not feel that estrangement but experienced the "flower procession" as an unusually liberating act of performing in a familiar place—a claiming of ownership. The tour was repeated six times and successfully attracted a local audience. This act of place-making in Jerusalem—a subtle gesture of political resistance—engaged the local community on a different level than it did some of the participants. Perhaps it more effectively blurred the boundaries between art and life for those who live under occupation.

6 Conclusion

Placemaking interventions such as *RE/viewing Jerusalem* will not bring the occupation to an end. But art is not an endeavor to be judged by measurable concrete outcomes—as Bishop and Marchart emphasize in their critique of the instrumentalization of art. Yet artistic practices may provide a spark for change when they react with other existing elements. These effects simply cannot be known in advance—or they may be belated. While such local practices of urban intervention are necessarily influenced by the recent wave of participatory art interventions taking place in the Western world, we need to continue the search for methods that speak to the specific circumstances of Palestinians living under occupation in Jerusalem. To find methods adequate to these unique local circumstances, we need not only critical reflection upon common methodology but also a means to disconnect (even if only partially) from dominant paradigms (McLennan, 2012). *RE/viewing Jerusalem* reflects upon Western urban art intervention practices and seeks to translate them to the specifics of the local situation in Israeli-occupied Jerusalem. Its goal is to decolonize both thought and space: to intervene in Western discourses about political art, and to resist the occupation through the collective activation of public space. The experience of participation is very much a bodily experience, a sharing of public spaces and collective experiences with other bodies. Palestinians understand that the most effective form of resistance is to activate places in unexpected and overlooked spaces, and to occupy them—to embody them. This cannot be currently accomplished by winning territory, or even by building new structures or public spaces, but *RE/viewing Jerusalem* has successfully demonstrated the capacity of art to transform spaces into places, and to generate new possibilities for an art of counter-occupation.

References

Fanon, F., 1964. The Wretched of the Earth. Trans. C. Farrington. Grove Weidenfield Press, New York, NY.

Bishop, C., 2012. Artificial hells: participatory art and the politics of spectatorship. Verso Press, London and New York.

Marchart, O., 2002. Art, Space and the Public Sphere(s), pre_public journal (01-2002). http://transversal.at/transversal/0102 (accessed 16 March 2016).

Mbembe, A., 2015. Decolonizing knowledge and the question of the archive. Public lecture. http://wiser.wits.ac.za/system/files/Achille%20Mbembe%20-%20Decolonizing%20Knowledge%20and%20the%20Question%20of%20the%20Archive.pdf (accessed 6 June 2016).

Boltanski, L., Chiapello, E., 2007. The New Spirit of Capitalism. Trans. Eliot, G. Verso Press, New York.

De Certeau, M., 2011. The Practice of Everyday Life. Trans. Steve Rendall. University of California Press, Berkeley, CA.

Pannell, S. N., 2006. From the poetics of place to the politics of space: redefining cultural landscapes on damer, maluku tenggara, in: Fox, J, (Ed.), The poetic power of place: comparative perspectives on austronesian ideas of locality. Australian National University Press, Acton.

Warner, M., 2002. Publics and counterpublics, Quarterly Journal of Speech 88, 4, 413-425.

McLennan, G., 2012. Postcolonial critique and the idea of sociology, Working Paper 02-12, University of Bristol, 10.

Territories

Street Art and the Nature of the City[1]

Peter Bengtsen

Department of Arts and Cultural Sciences, Division of Art History & Visual Studies,
Lund University, Hämtställe 30, 22100 Lund, Sweden
peter.bengtsen@kultur.lu.se
https://lu.academia.edu/PeterBengtsen

Abstract

Since the beginning of the 21st century, street art has become an increasingly prolific part of the urban landscape. Concurrently, street art has received growing attention from scholars from a number of disciplines such as art history, sociology and philosophy. One important point of discussion in academic literature has been the role that the street as a site plays in the viewer's interpretation of artworks and how the artworks may in turn influence the viewers' perception and use of urban public space. This chapter expands the established notion that street art can have an impact on how we relate to urban public space, and argues that street art is particularly well positioned to affect the way we think and act with regard to the environment. This is demonstrated through the visual and contextual analysis of a number of site-specific street artworks by Spanish artist Isaac Cordal that address and problematize how human beings relate to nature in the urban environment.

Keywords
street art, visual ecocriticism, anthropocentrism, biocentrism, environmental art.

Introduction

The trees along this city street,
    Save for the traffic and the trains,
Would make a sound as thin and sweet
    As trees in country lanes.

[...]
Oh, little leaves that are so dumb
    Against the shrieking city air,
I watch you when the wind has come, —
    I know what sound is there.[1]

Since the beginning of the 21st century, street art has become an increasingly prolific feature of the urban landscape. Concurrently, street art has received growing attention from scholars from a number of disciplines such as art history, sociology and philosophy. Street art is here understood as artworks that are created or placed in public space, or are visible from public space, and are perceived as unsanctioned ("perceived" because it will often be unclear to the casual viewer whether or not an artwork is actually sanctioned). It should be noted that the term "public space" in this chapter is taken to include so-called "publicly accessible spaces", which is to say spaces that appear to be public but that are in fact privately owned.

---

1 - This chapter is based on research that has been generously funded by The Crafoord Foundation and The Gyllenstierna Krapperup's Foundation.

One important point of discussion in academic literature on street art has been the role the context of the street plays in the viewer's interpretation of the artworks and how the artworks may in turn influence the viewer's perception and use of urban public space (Riggle, 2010; Wacławek, 2011). In previous publications, I have argued for what I call street art's potential to turn public space into a site of exploration. The basic idea being that if an artwork is perceived as unsanctioned and ephemeral, as something that should not really be there and might be gone soon, an unexpected encounter with such work can serve as an interruption that has the potential to pull the viewer out of the everyday and increase their awareness of their surroundings. In this way a street artwork can turn the everyday environment into a site of exploration and make people question how they see and use the city (Bengtsen, 2013; 2014).

This chapter expands on the already established notion that street art can impact how people relate to urban public space, and argues that street art is particularly well positioned to affect the way we feel, think and act with regard to the environment. While, for example, news stories, popular science documentaries, and information campaigns based on research conducted within the natural sciences are useful for transmitting facts and findings about the environmental challenges the world is facing, art broadly can involve an audience more subtly on an emotional level. It can address attitudes and lifestyle choices, as well as societal, existential and ethical values that inform our actions and that might therefore have an impact on the environment. This is a point I have previously made when writing from an ecocritical perspective about the studio work of American artist Josh Keyes (Bengtsen, 2015, p. 4). A central argument in the present chapter, however, is that street art holds a special potential when it comes to influencing how we relate to the environment because it is often encountered unexpectedly in the setting of physical urban public space, where surprising shifts in perspective and meaning may inspire further reflection.

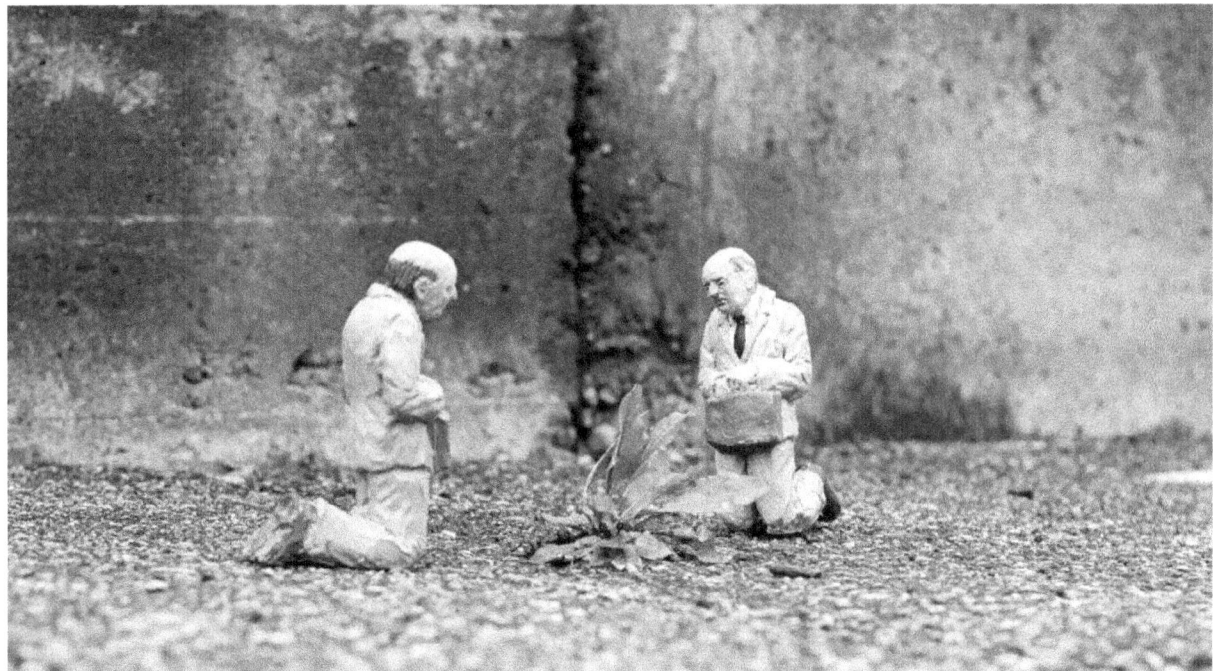

Fig. 1 - Isaac Cordal, no title (2015). Street installation in Stavanger, Norway as part of Nuart Festival. The sculptures in this image are approximately 10 cm tall. Photo: © Isaac Cordal.

Considering how art can affect people's understanding of the relationship between human beings and the environment is vital. As Professor of American Literature Lawrence Buell, who is seen as a pioneer in the field of ecocriticism, argues, "[i]ssues of vision, value, culture, and imagination are keys to today's environmental crises at least as fundamental as scientific research, technological know-how, and legislative regulation" (2005, p. 5). Thus, even though offering the public an intellectual understanding of environmental issues like climate change is undeniably important, eliciting an emotional response in viewers to, for example, the estrangement of human beings from nature may be even more instrumental in facilitating an actual change in behavior.

In this chapter, the relationship between street art and the environment will be explored through the visual and contextual analysis of street artworks by the Spanish artist Isaac Cordal, who is best known for his ongoing project *Cement Eclipses*; since around 2006, Cordal has been placing in public space small sculptures of human beings – often balding, briefcase-carrying, white men in suits – that are either painted in drab colors or are left in the grey tones of the raw material they are made from. While cement was used to create the sculptures at the beginning of the project, the artist has more recently shifted to mainly working with resin.

A common feature in *Cement Eclipses* is the juxtaposition of the small, dreary-looking sculptures with urban plant life (see for example Figure 1). Given the attire of the sculptures, which brings to mind that of archetypical bureaucrats, businessmen or politicians, Cordal's installations can be interpreted as critical comments on the unsustainable, growth-based capitalist society which currently dominates the world economy. The artist's work can be seen as a call for people to re-assess their anthropocentric values and reflect on the affinity of human beings and the rest of the biotic community – that is to say a community founded on biocentrism that includes as its members "soils, waters, plants, and animals, or collectively: the land" (Leopold, [1949] 1987, p. 204). Biocentrism is understood here as the idea that human beings neither stand outside the biotic community, nor above its other members (which all have intrinsic value), and that the collective interests of the biotic community should therefore govern human interest and inform human action (Buell, 2005, p. 134). In stark contrast to the views expressed by Leopold and Buell, according to sociologist Jacklyn Cock, the World Bank has described "soil, water, air, flora and fauna" as "natural capital" (2014, p. 28). Cock argues that this perspective "implies that nature should be measured and valued according to the 'services' it provides (for example, the capacity of wetlands to filter water, the capacity of forests and soil to capture and store carbon and so on)", which "means the expansion of the market into all aspects of the natural world: an attempt by capital – in the name of protection – to effect the last enclosure of the commons – that of Nature itself" (ibid). In other words, the consequence of the World Bank's description, according to Cock, is that nature is valued solely as a resource for human need and profit. Cordal's installations in urban public space can be read as a critique of a legal-rational-oriented bureaucratic system that would produce in people such a utilitarian attitude towards nature, rather than recognize the intrinsic value of non-human members of the biotic community regardless of their perceived usefulness to human beings. This critique can also be related to German sociologist Max Weber's notion that a system based primarily on legal-rational authority leads to a disenchantment of the world and traps the individual in an "iron cage" of bureaucracy ([1905] 2005, p. 123). While Weber's text is more than 110 years old, the modern state is still characterized precisely by its reliance on legal-rational authority, which leaves little room for types of social action that might involve a less utilitarian attitude towards non-human members of the biotic community.

Isaac Cordal: perspectives on the city as a biotic community
The installation depicted in Figure 1 is quite typical of Cordal's more explicitly environmentally oriented artworks created in urban public space. In this and similar installations, the artist seems to be problematizing human estrangement from

nature and the limited space the latter is afforded in the city; Cordal has here placed the sculptures of two balding men clad in grey suits so they are facing what appears to be a dandelion that has pushed through the tarmac of a city street. The men are kneeling, their heads slightly lowered and tilted to the side, and they are both somewhat awkwardly holding up a briefcase in front of their stomachs. The arrangement of the sculptures next to the small green plant, as well as the kneeling position of the bodies, creates an air of reverence on part of the depicted humans in relation to the installation's non-human member of the biotic community. The scenario also invokes a sense of nostalgia and even romanticism, as the seemingly worn-out men gaze with sunken eyes at this vivacious element of plant life that has forced its way into the human-dominated world of the city. The cheerlessness of the scenario is further emphasized by the two decrepit slabs of concrete that, from the vantage point the photo was taken from, constitute the backdrop of the installation.

As is the case with many artists that produce work in the street, Cordal's installations in part create meaning by playing with perspective and existing elements of the urban environment; in virtue of their scale, the human figures draw attention to details such as small pieces of uncultivated plant life, which otherwise often are negligible in size and easily overlooked by people moving in the city. The combination of the miniature sculptures and existing elements of the urban environment creates a visual shift that enables people that come across one of Cordal's installations

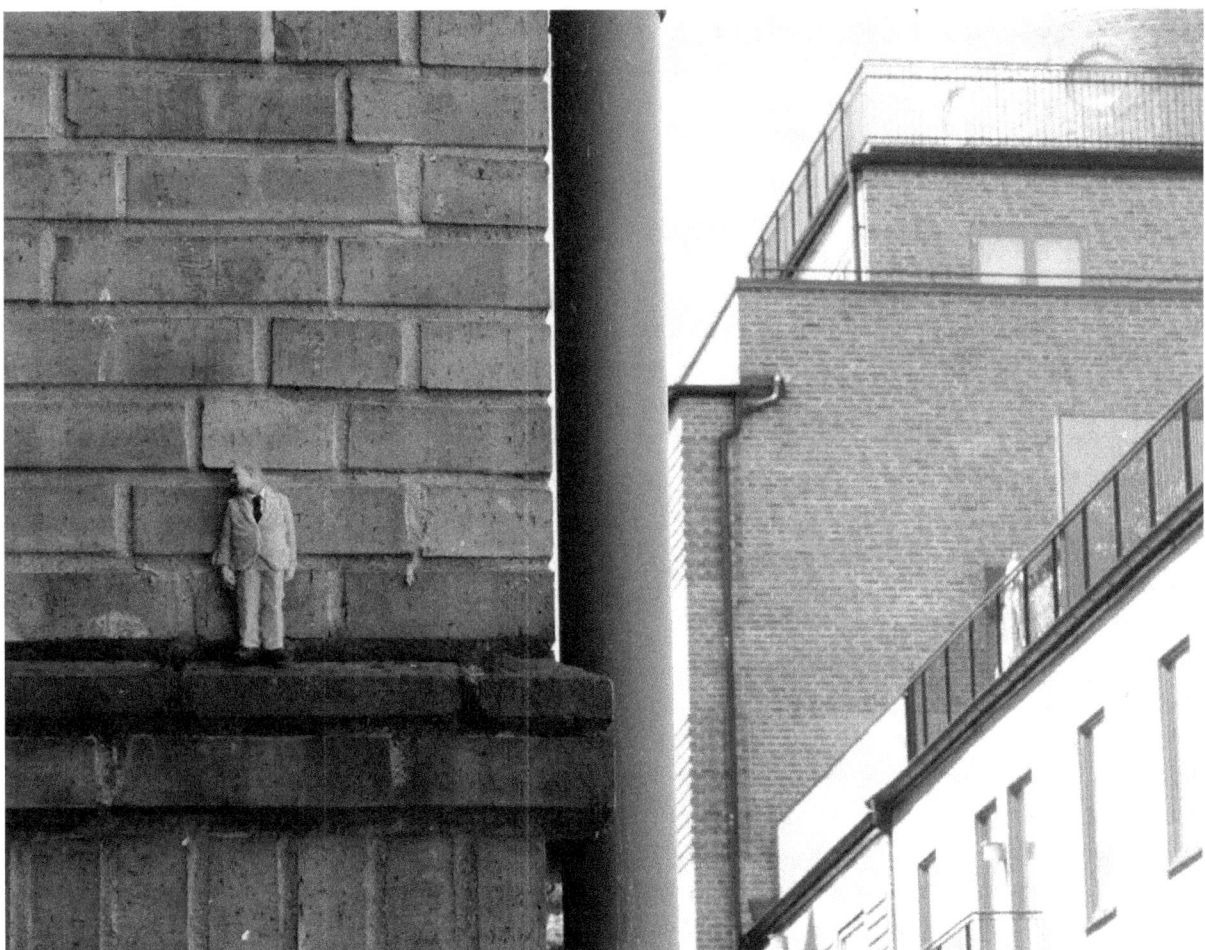

Fig. 2 - Isaac Cordal, no title (2014). Street installation in Malmö, Sweden. Photo: © Peter Bengtsen.

to see themselves and their surroundings from different point of view. As a statement on Cordal's website explains, facilitating such a shift is an important part of the work:

> With the simple act of miniaturization and thoughtful placement, Isaac Cordal magically expands the imagination of pedestrians finding his sculptures on the street. Cement Eclipses is a critical definition of our behavior as a social mass. The art work intends to catch the attention on our devalued relation with the nature [sic] through a critical look to the collateral effects of our evolution. With the master touch of a stage director, the figures are placed in locations that quickly open doors to other worlds. The scenes zoom in [on] the routine tasks of the contemporary human being.[2]

Through the use of perspective shifts and surprising visual disruptions of daily routines, then, Cordal deliberately calls attention to generally overlooked elements of the city in order to create a space for reflection. In the case of the installation depicted in Figure 1, by identifying with, and mentally and emotionally putting themselves in the stead of, the miniature human gestalts, viewers might come to consider their relationship not only with the specific dandelion the artist has incorporated, but also with other non-human members of the biotic community of the city. Further, the combination of the micro-scale of the sculptures with the macro-scale of the city has the potential to create in viewers at once a sense of affinity to, and alienation from, their everyday surroundings and routines. While the drab sculptures can be seen as embodiments of what happens to human beings who are caught in the routines of a reigning paradigm of rationality and efficiency (something that approximates Weber's before-mentioned iron cage), the dreary concrete slabs may represent the contemporary city. The latter is itself a result of the rationalization of society, which has led to the gradual suppression of aspects of all members of the biotic community, human and non-human alike, as the value of actions has come to be measured on a short-sighted, purpose-rational scale.[3]

While some of Cordal's installations in a very explicit manner address the relationship between human beings and nature and promote a biocentric agenda, others are more subtle and may not immediately call for an ecocritical reading if seen in isolation. For example, Figure 2 shows a 17 cm tall standing version of the artist's signature balding man in a suit and tie on a street in Malmö, Sweden. A number of sculptures like the one depicted here were placed around the city as part of the street art festival *Artscape* in 2014. The sculpture is positioned on a row of protruding bricks approximately three meters above the pavement. The size of the sculpture in conjunction with its elevated placement creates the impression of a man standing on a ledge high above the street.

The way the man is depicted – body pressed up against the wall, feet sticking out over the side of the ledge, and head turned to the side as if he is averting his eyes from the drop before him – adds to the sense of the precariousness of the situation. The scenario is reminiscent of someone either being involuntarily trapped on a ledge and trying to avoid falling to their death or apprehensively contemplating suicide. While the installation does not visibly include any non-human members of the biotic community of the city, the human gestalt dressed in dreary-looking business attire can still be interpreted as a representative of our current growth-based capitalist society. His placement on the ledge, then, may be seen as a visual metaphor for the dangers of relying on an unsustainable economic, political and societal system that is too taxing on the environment, and his looking away may be illustrative of our collective unwillingness or inability to face the issues in front of us. The man's possible fall could represent the plunge into an abyss of environmental disaster that may await us all if no viable alternative to the current anthropocentric societal paradigm is found in time. This interpretation is of course further substantiated when the installation is seen in the context of Cordal's larger body of work.

When considering the artworks so far analyzed, it is clear that the context of the city plays a key role in Cordal's installations. Art that seeks to highlight urban public space – and, by extension, the world – as not just host to a community of human beings, but to a wider biotic community, gains poignancy from being embedded in that everyday context, rather than appearing within the confines of the traditional "white cube" of the gallery or museum.

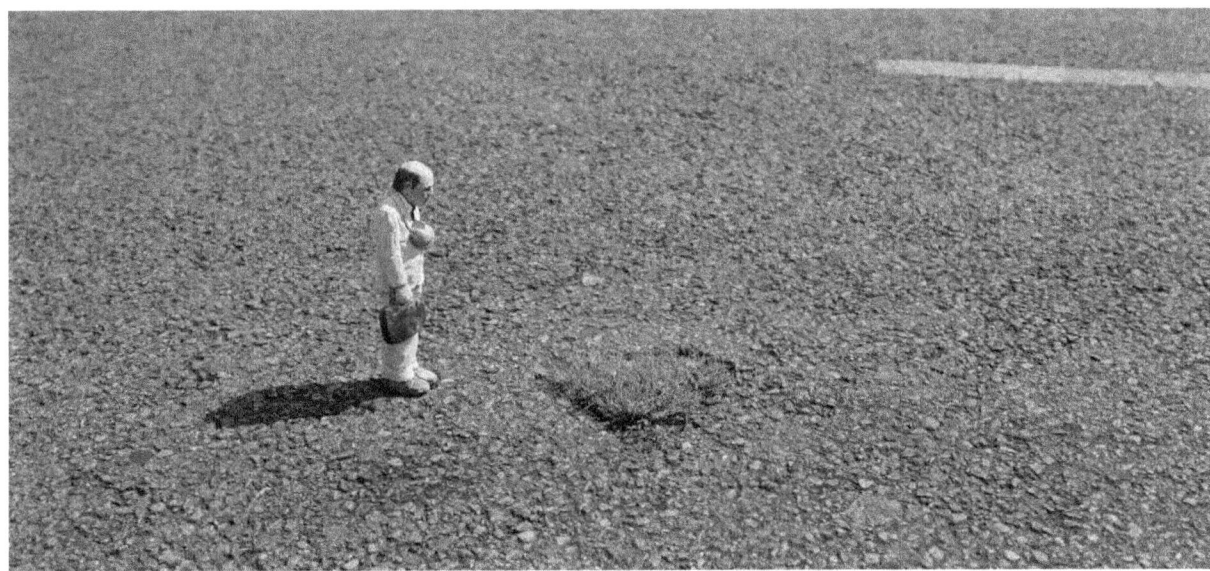

Fig. 3 - Isaac Cordal, no title (2013). Street installation in Nantes, France. Photo: © Isaac Cordal.

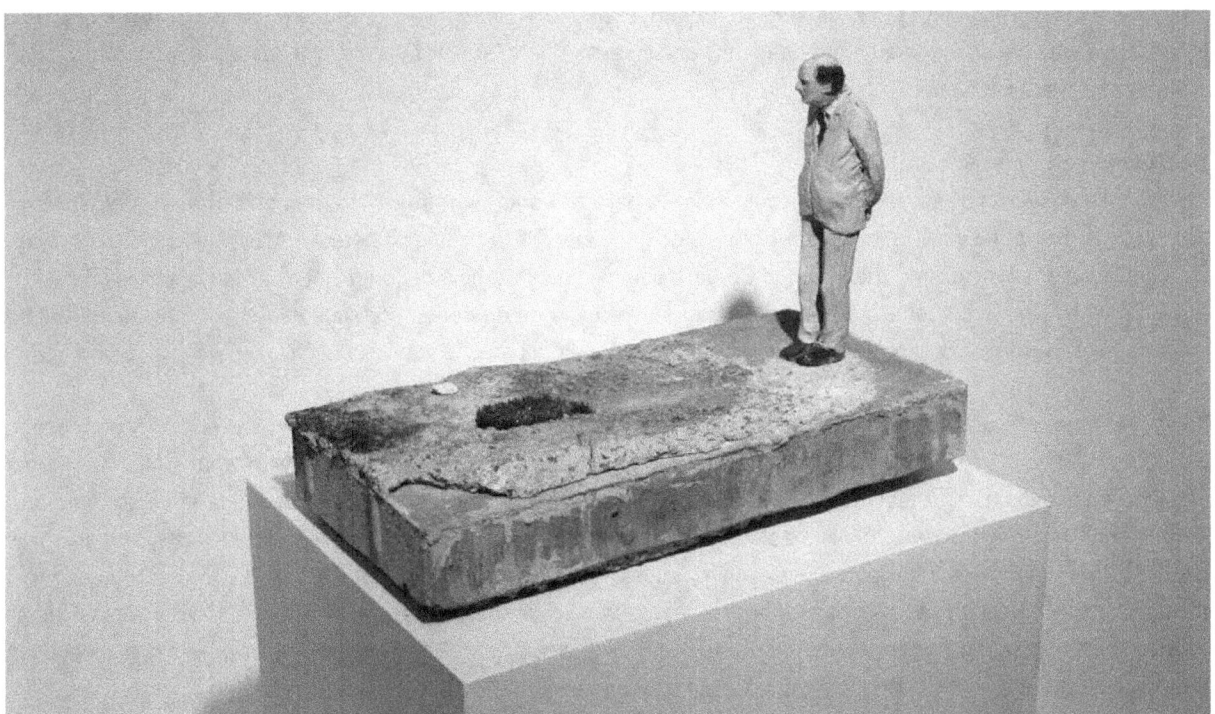

Fig. 4 - Isaac Cordal, *Remembrances from nature* (2015). Resin, plastic and concrete, 19 x 38 x 15,25cm. Photo: © Isaac Cordal.

That the context of urban public space adds meaning to the street artworks becomes very clear when considering the installations depicted in Figures 3 and 4. Whereas the former shows an installation on the street in Nantes, France, the latter is an image of a sculptural work exhibited in a gallery setting. The artworks each feature a different variation of Cordal's men in grey suits, both of which seem to be contemplating a small patch of green grass.

The difference between the two artworks partly comes down to material properties. For example, the use of synthetic grass arranged by the artist in the gallery work creates a less evocative and convincing juxtaposition between the elements that stand in for culture and nature than the inclusion in the street work of real, wild grass that pushes through the tarmac of what looks like a parking lot. Equally significant is that the gallery work is unable to replicate the effect of the expansive space that is the context of the street installation. In the street, it is unclear exactly where the boundary of the artwork is. This makes it easy for the viewer to mentally extend the scenario arranged by the artist to other parts of the everyday environment. Conversely, the base of the gallery work, which seems to be made from a slab of concrete, is clearly delimited. This sets the staged scenario apart from the surrounding environment inhabited by the viewer and contributes to removing the artwork from an everyday context – an effect that is augmented by the placement of the artwork on a white plinth in the white room of a gallery. While it may still be able to convey to the viewer an air of nostalgia regarding the relationship between humans and nature, the isolated gallery work – with its fixed dimensions and inclusion of only human-made elements – betrays the fact that everything is under the strict control of the artist. It does not encourage the viewer to look beyond the artwork itself like the street installation does. As previously pointed out, in the vast context of urban public space the addition of Cordal's sculptures brings attention to otherwise easily overlooked non-human members of the biotic community. The incongruent scales of the elements of the street installation and its surrounding environment play an important role in creating a shift in perspective that can open up a space for critical reflection. For example, the patch of grass can at once be seen as very small (if considered in relation to the expansive context of urban public space) and larger (if seen in relation to the human sculpture). In the gallery setting, on the other hand, the diminutive size of the grass patch is not apparent in the same way because there are no differently scaled elements of everyday life extraneous to the installation that can create a visual disruption.

Documenting the artist's perspective

This chapter has so far discussed how encountering Cordal's artworks in the street may influence the way people relate to the environment and instill in the viewer a more biocentric attitude. It should be noted, however, that photographs of street installations form an important part of Cordal's oeuvre, and that the artist does not always leave his installations in place after they have been documented photographically. In other words, sometimes a street installation will be staged mainly as a means to produce a photograph, rather than as an end in and of itself.

The artwork depicted in Figure 2 is an example of an installation that is intended by the artist to be relatively permanent. This is evident by its elevated placement, which, along with its attachment to the wall with what looks like rubber cement, makes it is hard to reach and remove. In comparison, the installations depicted in Figures 1 and 3 are less permanent. They are placed in a vulnerable position on the ground and are not physically affixed to the site. It is possible, then, that these installations were mainly staged for the purpose of Cordal creating photographs, and that the artist took the sculptures with him after the photos were taken. However, while some of Cordal's installations may be present on the street for only a short time (even by the standards of ephemeral street art), they still have the potential to attract the attention of passersby while they are there.

Seeing the artist's photographs of installations in a gallery or online is very different from experiencing the installations in person in urban public space. First, in accordance with the arguments previously made in this chapter, significant meaning is lost when installations are experienced outside of the everyday context of the street. As I have discussed elsewhere, unexpectedly coming across seemingly unsanctioned artworks in urban public space can be an interruption that instills in the viewer a sense of exploration and encourages engagement with both the artwork and the everyday environment (Bengtsen 2014, p. 150). Second, a photograph offers a single vantage point and a specific framing of an installation, leaving out the majority of the wider context the artwork is embedded in. As with the gallery installation depicted in Figure 4, this can make it harder for the viewer to mentally connect the depicted scenario to other parts of the everyday environment.

The use of the photographic medium may, however, also have potential positive implications for the dissemination of a biocentric way of thinking. A photograph allows the artist to frame the sculptural work and emphasize certain details in a way that helps ensure that the viewer sees precisely what the artist wants them to see. An example of this is the inclusion of the concrete slabs as a backdrop in Figure 1. Exposure to photographs of installations that explicitly deal with the relationship between human and non-human members of the biotic community can also form a background for understanding the installations that are left in place in public space, including those that are more subtle and that would not otherwise immediately call for an ecocritical interpretation. Further, a photo that is spread online may reach a significantly larger audience than the depicted installation itself would have. For example, on Instagram alone, Cordal has more than 28,000 followers who might see, comment on and even repost the images of his street works. In addition, whereas on the street the installations have to speak for themselves, on Instagram (as well as in similar media contexts) images are often accompanied by a text that can steer the viewer's interpretation by making explicit the biocentric agenda of the artworks. While a digital context can in this way add an explicitly ecocritical layer to the depicted artworks, it should be noted that in the constant flow of images on Instagram and other apps, it is unclear what kind of impact the shared material really has. This is of course also difficult to measure in relation to street artworks. However, the argument in this chapter is that the experience of unexpectedly discovering an artwork in urban public space is more likely to create an interruption of the everyday than seeing a post on social media, and therefore also more likely to engage the viewer on a deeper level.

Conclusion

Through a discussion of selected works by the Spanish artist Isaac Cordal, this chapter has argued that street art is in a special position to affect the way people feel, think and act with regard to the environment and non-human members of the biotic community. While artworks in a designated art space like the "white cube" of a museum or gallery certainly can address environmental issues, the particular context of urban public space enables ephemeral street artworks to reach people unexpectedly in their everyday environment. Such encounters can create interruptions in the daily routine of viewers and cause them to pay attention to, and question, their surroundings and values, including contemporary society's predominantly anthropocentric and legal-rational basis for relating to other members of the biotic community.

In the street, Cordal's combination of miniature sculptures and the large spaces of the city creates a visual shift that enables people to see themselves and the culture they are part of from a new point of view. This is an effect that would be difficult to replicate in the confines of a gallery. The context of urban public space adds meaning to Cordal's installations in part because it is not an artificial construct, made solely for the benefit of the artwork or the viewer, but rather is an organic and integral part of the everyday environment where people live. Likewise, while posting images of street installations on social media can help further a biocentric agenda, the impact of seeing depictions of the street artworks in this context is not directly comparable to encountering the installations in urban public space.

As the chosen cases have demonstrated, Cordal's street artworks visualize and problematize environmental issues in different ways. While some installations can be interpreted as speaking to human estrangement from nature by directly juxtaposing sculptures of people with elements of urban plant life, others are more subtle. In the latter cases, however, the frequent inclusion in the artist's installations of dreary-looking, balding, white men in grey suits can be seen as a visual allusion to the impact of an unsustainable, growth-based and legal-rational society on both human life and the wider biotic community. Even when seen in isolation, then, such works may create an interruption in the everyday and cause viewers to pay attention to, and question, their surroundings and values, including their anthropocentric attitude towards other members of the biotic community.

References

Bengtsen, Peter. "Beyond the public art machine: a critical examination of street art as public art". *Konsthistorisk tidskrift/Journal of Art History*, 82:2, 63-80, 2013.

Bengtsen, Peter. *The Street Art World*. Lund: Almendros de Granada Press, 2014.

Bengtsen, Peter. "Until the end of the world? Biocentrism and traces of human presence in the paintings of Josh Keyes". *Journal of Ecocriticism*, 7:1, 2015.

Buell, Lawrence. *The Future of Environmental Criticism. Environmental Crisis and Literary Imagination*. Malden, Oxford & Carlton: Blackwell Publishing, 2005.

Cock, Jacklyn. "The 'Green Economy': A Just and Sustainable Development Path or a 'Wolf in Sheep's Clothing'?". *Global Labour Journal*, 5:1, 2014, 23-44.

Cordal, Isaac. *Cement Eclipses. Small interventions in the big city*. London: Carpet Bombing Culture, 2010.

Leopold, Aldo. *A Sand County Almanac*. [1949] New York: Oxford University Press, 1987.

Edna St. Vincent *Millay. Second April*. New York: Mitchell Kennerley, 1921.

Riggle, Nicholas Alden. "Street Art: The Transfiguration of the Commonplaces". *The Journal of Aesthetics and Art Criticism*, Vol. 68, No. 3, 2010, 243-257.

Wacławek, Anna. *Graffiti and Street Art*. London: Thames & Hudson, 2011.

Weber, Max. *The Protestant Ethic and the Spirit of Capitalism*. [1905] London & New York: Routledge, 2005.

Notes

1 - Excerpt from the poem "City Trees" by Edna St. Vincent Millay, *Second April*. New York: Mitchell Kennerley, 1921, p. 3.

2 - http://cementeclipses.com/about-2/ (retrieved 2016.12.19). The importance of the dynamic between the miniature sculptures and the expansive urban environment is also highlighted in the title of Cordal's monograph *Cement Eclipses. Small interventions in the big city* (2010).

3 - A symptom of this is a tendency to focus on short-term benefits of actions rather than their long-term consequences. This can for example be seen in the way contemporary society to a large extent is run by career politicians who often seem more concerned with their own personal interests (e.g. appeasing voter constituencies to ensure re-election, or securing profitable positions in the corporations and organizations they are meant to regulate) than with making value-based – and potentially unpopular – decisions they believe will benefit the biotic community as a whole in the long-term.

Where (not) to go?
The general intellect between the precarious and resistance

Jovanka Popova

Art historian and curator, press to exit project space
Skopje, Macedonia
Jovanka.popova@gmail.com

Abstract

This text presents a series of cultural and socio-political discourses referring to Jacques Rancière's notion of participation in democratic regimes, which is usually reduced to a question of filling spaces left empty by power. In this sense, the possibilities and limits for the shifting place of art practices are examined. Where can they possibly exceed traditional boundaries and break through institutional terms, transforming everything into a politics of life by producing both: affect and an effect?

Keywords

engaged art practices, protest movement, precariousness, general intellect, immaterial workers.

1. Introduction:

Art that is intentionally produced for institutions, such as museums, occupies a privileged space of politicization, closely related to neoliberal processes. It tends to decrease the effects of neoliberalism, but also takes part in new economic and geopolitical distribution of power. Culture, in general, is employed in order to restore economically destroyed spheres, to promote educational strategies, and to design social spaces. By being used in daily politics as mechanisms of intervention and renovation, contemporary art supports the stabilization of neoliberal strategies by occupying real-life spaces.

The use of freelancers, precarious cultural workers coming from non-profit organizations as representatives of a prospective market for the so-called "creators of culture" also became a trend. Political strategies have stretched their way out through the domain of diverse "cultural options." But culturalization is not only the transmission of political questions into cultural ones. Culturalization tends to become an ideological education for the masses or the subjects of the capitalist order. And the prefix "cultural" is just the neoliberal form of a new social literacy — new expertise or the ones who "know-how-to-do it."

The effort to be critical in the field of cultural production remains untruthful, and it only emerges as an aesthetic of administration, shifting between the market, state, and freelance activism. This kind of critique shows no capacity to abandon its comfortable position, which sets it off from the formal articulation of the needs of "class cultural workers." It does not intervene in real-life activity. Instead, it is the negotiable middle class's interpretation, which only makes a distinction between the conscious bourgeois and the consumer of spectacular kitsch. Critical stance appears as a trademark for the enlightened citizen.

2.

The recent Macedonian government-organized project *Skopje 2014* and the rebellious acts in the arts and protest movements in response to it serve as the case study to examine the possibilities and limits of the shifting place of art practices beyond the institutional. What happened in Macedonia just a few years ago in 2009 was unreasonable and shocking. The government announced large-scale developments for the city center, including a complex of buildings and monuments built in inappropriate public spaces, without consulting professional opinion, without a broader examination of the subject of urbanity or civic involvement. In the government's nationalistic censuring of the past, it replaced the modernist facades of buildings with baroque and neo-classicistic designs – obsolete historical styles that never existed in the history of architecture in Macedonia. An enormous amount of public money was spent on covering modernistic architecture with inauthentic facades. Public space was packed full with numerous sculptures and monuments of disputable heroes from the national pantheon, a newly built triumph arch, and a 22-meter-high bronze statue of Alexander the Great in the main square, which purportedly attests to the antique patrimony of Macedonian people. The project itself reflects the nationalistic, authoritarian regime, populism, and hegemony of the right-wing ruling party. Even though dissatisfaction, especially among intellectuals, had been rising, most people actually approved, or even more incredible, liked the project.

Architecture students initiated the first protest activities. Since then, linked to the protest actions on the level of similar politics, many art projects constituted social activism. Artists actualizing these kinds of projects were dealing with an attempt to intervene in the public sphere in order to actualize or resolve urgent questions in society, in all of its complexity. The results from these kinds of actions were exhibited mostly within the frames of the institutional gallery space.

Starting from the premise of Claire Bishop (2012) that "contemporary capitalism produces passive subjects with very little agency or empowerment," participatory art then "seek[s] to stimulate the public and turn them away from the passive, private consumption of spectacle in favor of creating a shared space for collective social engagement through constructive or symbolic gestures that have social impact and create new alternatives." But, set in gallery space, artworks or projects dealing with activist practices or protest groups are questionable. The projects remain based on re-enactment, and audiences witness the transformation of the effects from the real only as a performance – or art. And, although the languages of struggle, protest, and subversion were extremely dominant in art debates in the last several years, this does not necessarily result in effectiveness in terms of disobedience: these kinds of projects often simulate real social activism with the resonance of implications within the art system itself, but with no real consequences. Gaining knowledge about reality demands a certain distance, achieved through an imposed passivity. So, consequently, the intellectuals who were not confident enough to sabotage and act in a radical way in the system that they criticize, take the voice of the weak and marginalized showing real fascination with their object of study.

Generally speaking, the contradictions of the intellectual stratum can be explained through the contradiction between theory and practice. Intellectuals are a contradictory class, as such. The extreme division in their position is based on the fact that, although they have admission to the establishment of the society through knowledge and the leisure to imagine and rethink the possibilities through art, they do not possess political or economic power. And, although closely introduced to the ruling class of society – through their action and in their lifestyle – they do not conform to them. On the contrary, they often tend to act from the margins, in space close to neither the upper class nor the working class. And here another problem arises in their engagement in the field of art activism: the common understanding that they can also serve within capitalism and, moreover, make a profit from labor stripped of rights. Artists who use their life as material for their work often exploit the marginalized subjects. The examples are artistic and curatorial activist practices that tend to give a voice to those who are silenced in the hegemonic system. So, the question is: Is there a model for an engagement that refers to their act politically more than unaffectedly aesthetically?

The problem, according to Groys (2009), is not that the political sphere of the arts has already become aestheticized. Groys interprets the artistic process of art activism as something that often cedes its territory to a political sphere, that has no need of an artist (as an expert in this field with appropriate education), or the term art as such. When art becomes political, it is forced to make the unpleasant discovery that politics has already become art and that it has already situated itself in the aesthetic field. There is no better example for Groys than the representation of terror itself, which constitutes an image-production machine: the terrorist, Groys (2008: 122-126) argues, consciously and artistically stages events that produce his own easily recognizable aesthetics, with no need of an artist to represent them in mediation. Images of the defeated and humiliated also bypass the need for an artist. Therefore, Groys suggests that the point is not that art should conquer the territory of politics. Instead, it needs to find its way into a territory that is now being conquered by political and economic forces. Consequently, artists dealing with engaged practices, just as curators who became the new critics, unsatisfied with their position, are "forced" to enter public activism or the masses. Mostly, the links between the arts and the protest movements were widely recognized because of the initiating role of the artists from the very beginning, which leads to the old questions about the borders between art and activism expressed in Nato Thompson's phrase "far beyond the arts."

3.

Despite the entertaining appearance of their images on social media, the initial rebellious movements in Skopje in 2016 escalated into a mass protest called the Colorful Revolution. It mobilized thousands of people who vented their anger by throwing paint on the monuments – symbols of the government's oppression and hegemony. "This isn't just a case of protestors writing their anger on walls. In Skopje, the walls themselves are part of the problem," announced the media. And although peaceful in its nature, the movement covered all of the government institutions and Skopje 2014 monuments in multicolor paint.

So, the questions arise: If there is an aesthetics of protest, do we have serial images produced at once as its representation? Does the protest that is being organized around short sequences of images do what Hito Steyerl would call "editing"? Articulation of protest is being held on two levels: the language of the protest or verbalization and visualization; and the same combination of concepts that are shaping the structure of the internal organization of the protest, actually two different types of combining different elements: on the level of symbols and on the level of political powers. What kind of political meaning can come out of this type of articulation?

As argued by historian and art theoretician Nebojša Vilić (2016), after coloring the objects of Skopje 2014, which highlighted their absurdity, the protesters' interventions on facades and on the streets took a new course. First, the image turns into text, the painting to writing. The initial intensive colors poured on the facades, were replaced with more pleasant and enjoyable pastel colors. Thus, the Colorful Revolution of radical, rebellious red and black became pleasant to watch: pink, turquoise, and violet soft as if they were the consensual compromise between colors from the palette. The protests became a kind of consensual compromise between protesters and police; as the protesters' palette of colors softened, the police began to stay indifferent to the act of painting. It is difficult not to notice that the number of protests rapidly increased. The difference toward protests movements from the past and the so called Colorful Revolution, concerning the design and performative elements, taken as a form from arts, is also noticeable, just as the number of people who were involved in it.

Still, being based on the values of liberal democracy, the Colorful Revolution did not dissolve important obstacles. It did not possess the strength for the mass mobilization of different segments of society: one of the conditions for significant political change. Its failure was because of the unequal social groups support, as a represents of the ruling party and its opposition. Hence, the voters of the ruling party (as the counter-protestors in the Colorful

Revolution) are recognized as the most oppressed social stratum in society, the poor and the workers. On the other hand, the protestors, mainly followers of the opposition, who do not identify themselves as workers, marched from the relatively comfortable position of economic security. They emerged as representatives of citizenship. The Colorful Revolution failed to avoid the elitist moment. Mostly through social media, it started to emphasize young and fancy figures with their branded appearances as a counterpoint to the poor and unattractive counter-protesters. As Nebojša Vilić points out, although initially pro-leftist, the Colorful Revolution identified mainly through the concept of citizenship as compromised and consensual social category, was not able to tap into the radical and dissensual oppressed and underprivileged classes. In addition, although there were no elements of authorship identified through the coloring as an artistic act, the statement written on the newly built triumph gate "Macedonia: The art of citizens" confronts the main revolutionary goal, since the art does not include the collective, but the artist/individual as such.

The protest, in political and social terms, was an effort to reconfirm democracy. However, at the same time, it failed to extend its limits as a social act of resistance on behalf of the citizenship represented by precarious workers, or the general intellect. The protest movement failed because it did not reach beyond the borders of the general intellect. The "general intellect," in Maurizio Lazzarato's (2004) terms, is a representation of a social stratum of immaterial workers whose presence is set upon the old modernist presumption: that it is always necessary to draw the line between invention and work, creativity and routine. The protest means "the reactivation of the social body. But the energy coming from protest must be transferred into the real place of production: not just the urban territory, but the bio-financial global network and real life relations." (Özengi and Tan, 2014)

The intellectuals established a zone where breaks occurred in social reality. As freethinkers, they are the most democratic strata but also the leaders (although not in commanding positions) in the most authoritarian spheres, like education and expert governance. They embody society's contradictions between the consolidation and exploitation, between solidarity and the division of labor, or between the intellectual and the material labor. On the opposite, those excluded from the privilege of leisure or liberal education, in constant urge to gain the attributes of intellectual contradictions, exist also. In today's society, this division slowly disappears with the fact that there are more and more possibilities (starting with education again) for everyone to become an intellectual. Meanwhile, the utopia is realized in the opposite sense, when the intellectuals turn into the "immaterial workers."

4.

Hence, the question: Should the "general intellect" be defined through the terms of the most operative form of production under capitalism or is it more important to give consideration of less pragmatic meaning that cannot be reduced to knowledge and qualifications? Will the general intellect ever be in the position to be the avant-garde of protest? Even though precarious, this social stratum still owns its means of production: the general intellect, which is on its own. The general intellect and its embodiment in the immaterial worker, must take up a more avant-gardist position, namely on the side of the oppressed based on its isolation from this same intellectual instrumentalization. In addition, it is finally time for artists, critics, and scholars to stop lecturing and learn how to stand in someone else's shoes. What we need is to critically re-examine the materiality of a world facing ongoing modification, and to join the marginalized in the process of producing an applicable theory that unifies the essential critique with a new form of practice. As Chantal Mouffe (2007) explained: "Today artists cannot pretend anymore to constitute an avant-garde offering a radical critique, but this is not a reason to proclaim that their political role has ended. They still can play an important role in the hegemonic struggle by subverting the dominant hegemony and by contributing to the construction of new subjectivities. In fact, this has always been their role and it is only the modernist illusion of the privileged position of the artist that has made us believe otherwise. Once this illusion is abandoned, jointly with the revolutionary conception of politics accompanying it, we can see that critical artistic practices represent an important dimension of democratic politics." This does not mean, though, as she declares, "that they could alone realize the transformations needed for the establishment of a new hegemony. A radical democratic politics calls for the articulation of different levels of struggles so as to create a chain of equivalence among them."

In order for art to transform into life, it must accept the idea of equality, in Rancière's terms, as he puts it in the *The Ignorant Schoolmaster*: the equality of all subjects, freed from the hierarchies of knowledge, the idea of the equality of intelligence itself. As he declares, emancipation can't be expected from forms of art that presuppose the passivity of the viewer or those that want to make viewers active at all costs with the help of gadgets borrowed from advertising. The practice of art is emancipated and emancipating when it renounces the authority of the imposed message, the target audience, or, when, in other words, it stops wanting to emancipate us (Rancière et al., 2007).

The most radical way in which art can represent a form of social critique is to start to question and transform meaning and the function of the art system itself. We have already become subordinated to a hegemonic idea of what art is and what it does if we agree upon the questions: In what way can art contribute to hegemonic repression; or, what is the way that it can be used in order to give voice to the silenced and oppressed? As Bishop has pointed out, such questions are hegemonic in themselves, as long as they presuppose what art is and what it can do. Ideology is in the question, not in the answer.

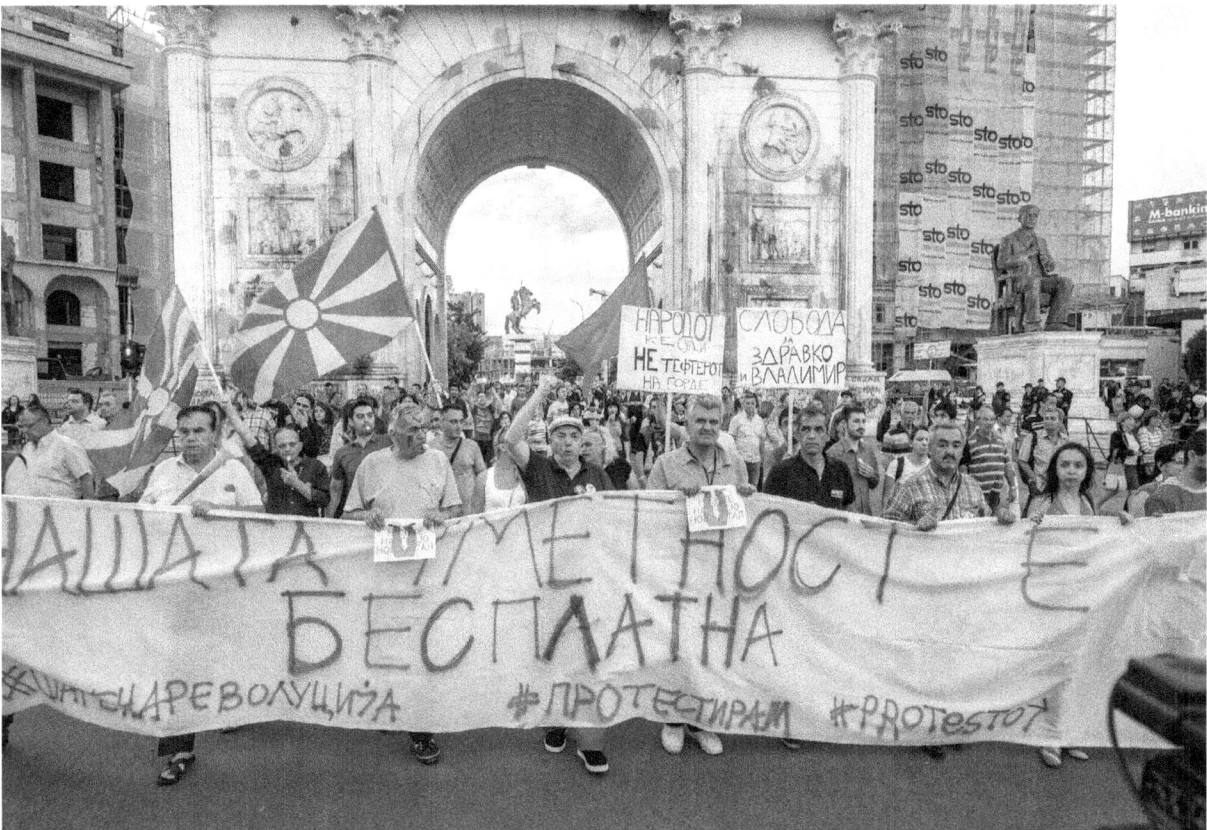

Fig. 1 - Our art is free slogan. "Colorful Revolution" protest movement in 2016 against governmental "Skopje 2014" project. Photo: Vanco Dzambaski.

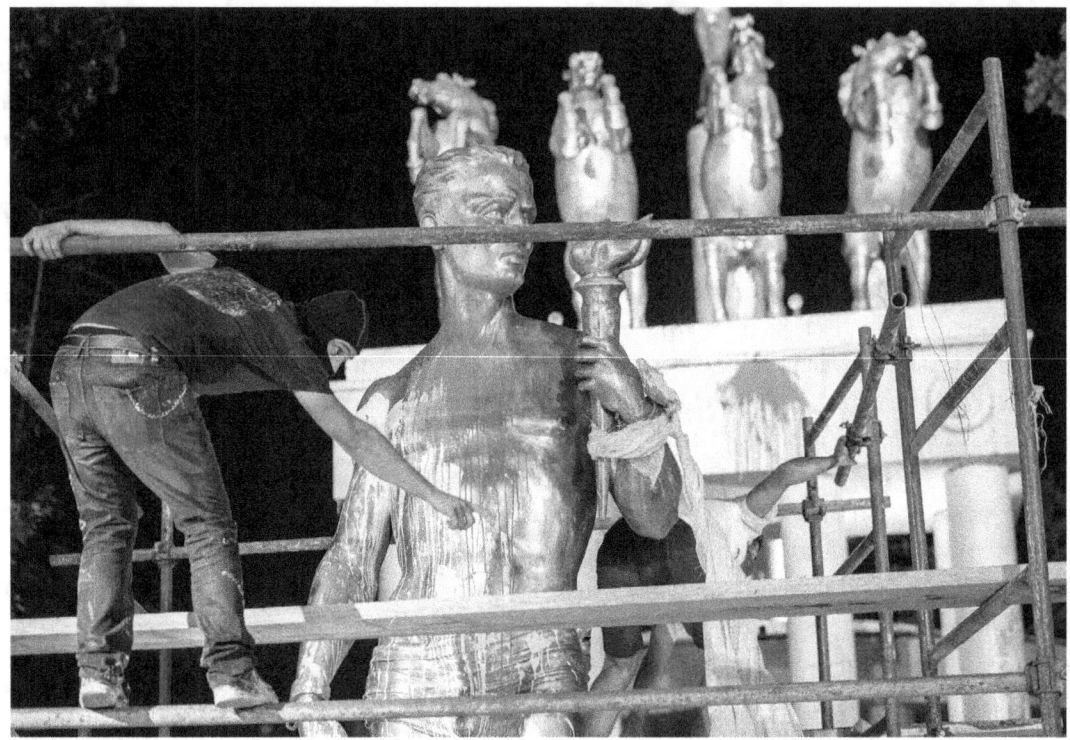

Fig. 2 - Protesters coloring the monument Prometheus which was part of the governmental project "Skopje 2014". Photo: Vanco Dzambaski (2016).

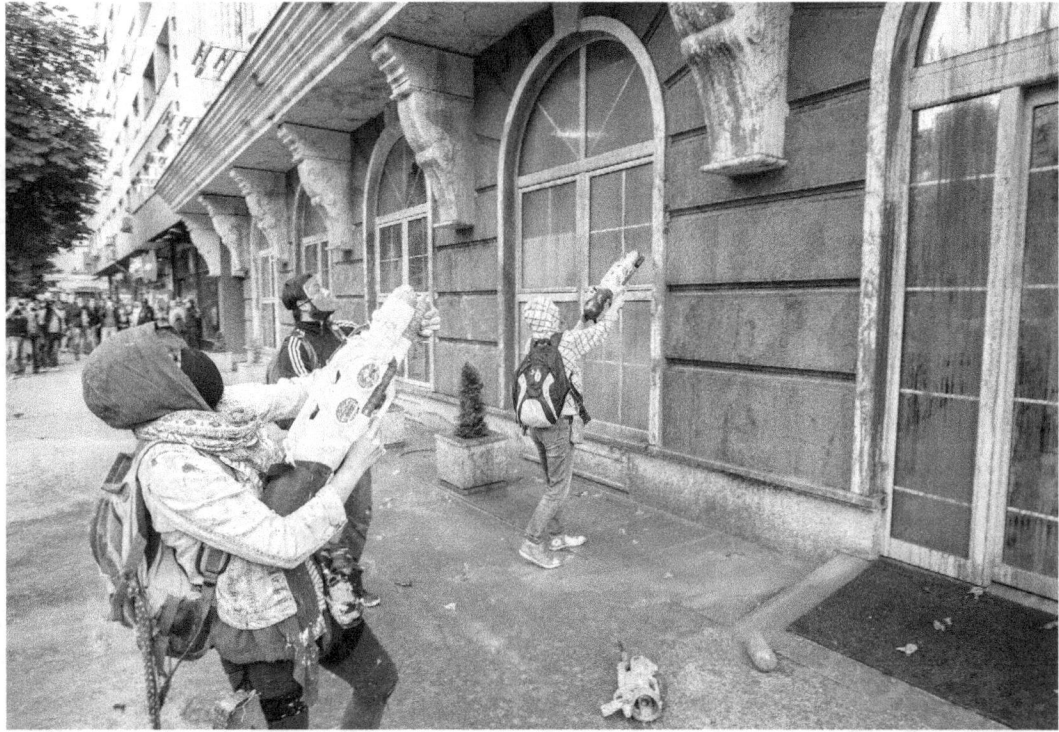

Fig. 3 - "Colorful Revolution" protest movement in Skopje against the government politics. Protesters in front of the Ministry of Justice of Republic of Macedonia (2016). Photo: Vanco Dzambaski.

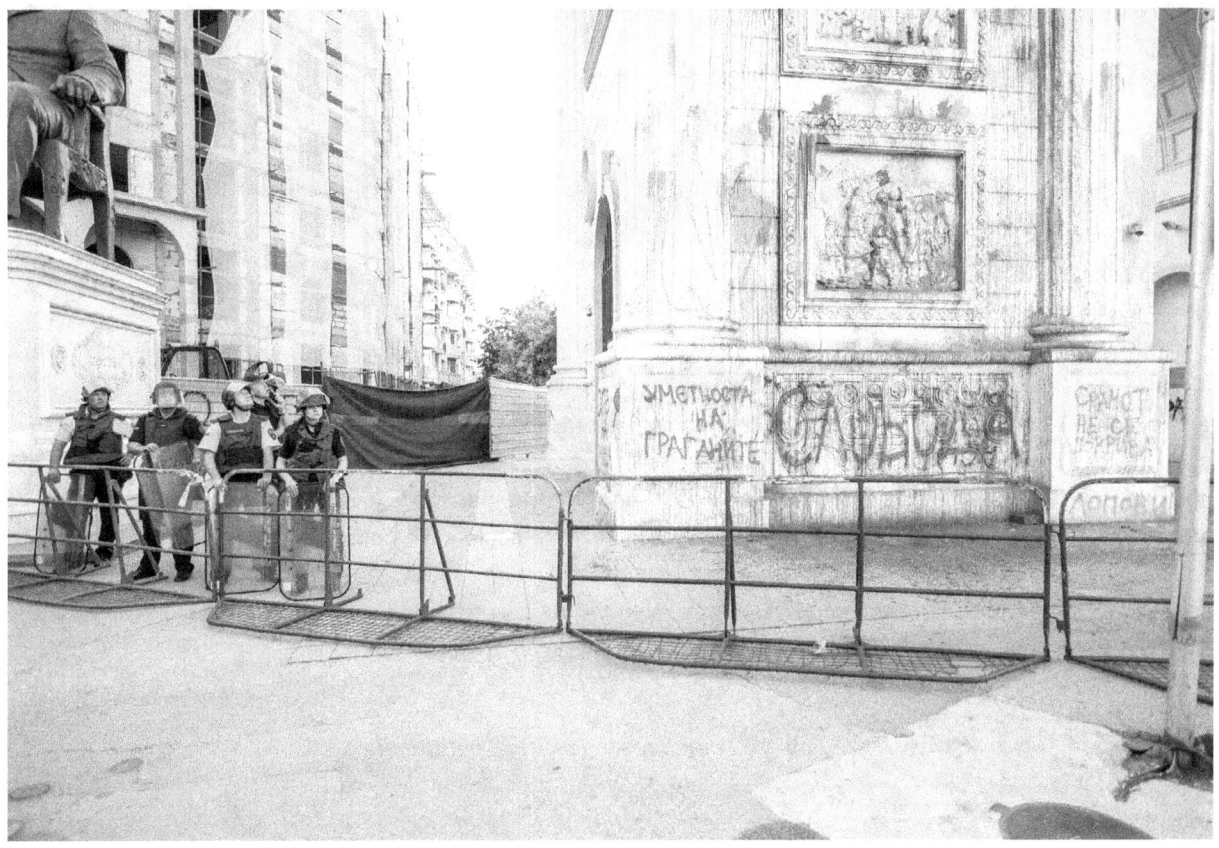

Fig. 4 - Art to the citizens, graphite written at the recently built Triumph Arc in Skopje as part of the governmental project "Skopje 2014" (2016). Photo: Vanco Dzambaski.

References

Bishop, C., 2012. Participation and Spectacle: Where Are We Now?, in: Nato Thompson (ed.), Living as Form: Socially Engaged Art from 1991–2001, Cambridge: MIT Press, 34-36.

Groys, B., 2009. Self-Design and Aesthetic Responsibility, in: e-flux journal, no. 7, http://www.e-flux.com/journal/07/61386/self-design-and-aesthetic-responsibility/.

Groys, B., 2008. Art Power, MIT Press, Cambridge, MA.

Lazzarato, M., 2004. General Intellect: Towards an Inquiry into Immaterial Labor, in: Multitudes, online journal, http://multitudes.samizdat.net/article.php3?id_article=1498.

Mouffe, C., 2007. Artistic Activism and Agonistic Spaces, in: Art & Research. A Journal of Ideas Context and Methods, 1 (2), 3-5.

Nebojša, V., 2016. Facebook project: Status #100 – 66/34, Доста е со "шарената револуција, https://goo.gl/yvLUAP.

Özengi, Ö., Tan, P. (LaborinArt), 2014. Running Along the Disaster: A conversation with Franco 'Bifo'" Berardi, in: e-flux journal, 56, www.e-flux.com/journal/56/60328/running-along-the-disaster-a-conversation-with-franco-bifo-berardi/.

Rancière, J., Carnevale, F., Kelsey, J., 2007. Art of the Possible: Fulvia Carnevale and John Kelsey in conversation with Jacques Ranciere, in: Artforum, online journal, https://www.artforum.com/inprint/issue=200703&id=12843.

The Visual Culture of Football Supporters: The Borderland of Urban Activism and Art

Henrik Widmark

Department of Art History, Uppsala University
Box 256, 751 05 Uppsala, Sweden
Henrik.Widmark@konstvet.uu.se

Abstract

This article scrutinizes the use of visual and performative practices in football supporter culture. It examines how supporters -- by means of graffiti, stickers, tifos (the collective visual manifestations of the supporters in the stands), and performative protests -- claim space in the public space of the urban fabric and on football terraces. Supporters are understood as a public contending and interacting to form society. The specific cultures of supporters and especially the ultras are understood as a subculture and act as such. I discuss the conflict between international commercial football and the autonomous supporter movement. I debate territorial claims, conflicts with society, and means to bring unity in the public sphere of a city by the activities of the supporters.

Keywords

visual culture, urban activism, supporter culture, ultras, sticker art, performance.

Introduction

On 16 March 2014, a demonstration of nearly 10,000 people gathered at Möllevångstorget in Malmö, Sweden.[1] One section of the procession held a large banner that read "Against Nazism." In a photo from the demonstration's start, one can see behind the banner a man holding a two-pin banner in yellow and red with an image depicting a young man fit into the number 03 and "Supras" written below it. In this scene, a protest against neo-Nazi-related violence and xenophobia, one could by the visual language decipher formations that were not usually present at political manifestations. The colors of the main banner, light blue and white, are the colors of the local football team Malmö FF. The colors of yellow and red in the two-pin banner would also have been well known at the local football stadium, understood as the local supporter movement's flirtation with the separatist or provisional movements in Scandia of southern Sweden. The two-pin also marked the presence of one of the major Malmö FF ultras group, Supras, in the demonstration. Through these small visual codes, one could depict a network containing the Malmö FF football team, supporter groups, and the demonstrators. It was also evident how visual signs had moved from the terrace into the streets of Malmö and at the same time actively claimed to be part of the reshaping and control of society and public space.

In the photo, one could also see the visual language of supporter cultures and its subcultural codes: in the dress of the young men standing at the front of the demonstration and the flares that later were lit (Thornton, 2003). This was in a way both an act of solidarity and a show of strength from the ultras movement — the subcultural hard-core groupings within the supporter movement — which was making its presence known. It was not just the colors of the team, it was a subcultural manifestation. Being there in the demonstration, as mentioned however was at the same time a merging of the subculture of supporters and the public protests against violence and racism. It was an active choice to participate in the public sphere. However, through visual codes and performance they stayed true to the idea of the authenticity of the subcultural identities of Ultras, and especially to the authenticity of the Malmö Ultras. The Malmö Ultras and other supporter groups were one of many publics, to use the term of Habermas who attended the protest (Habermas, 1989). Its presence was articulated and preformed through the group's visual marking, just as the different supporter groups did on the terraces and in the streets with graffiti, stickers, banners, tifos, and sometimes performance protests.

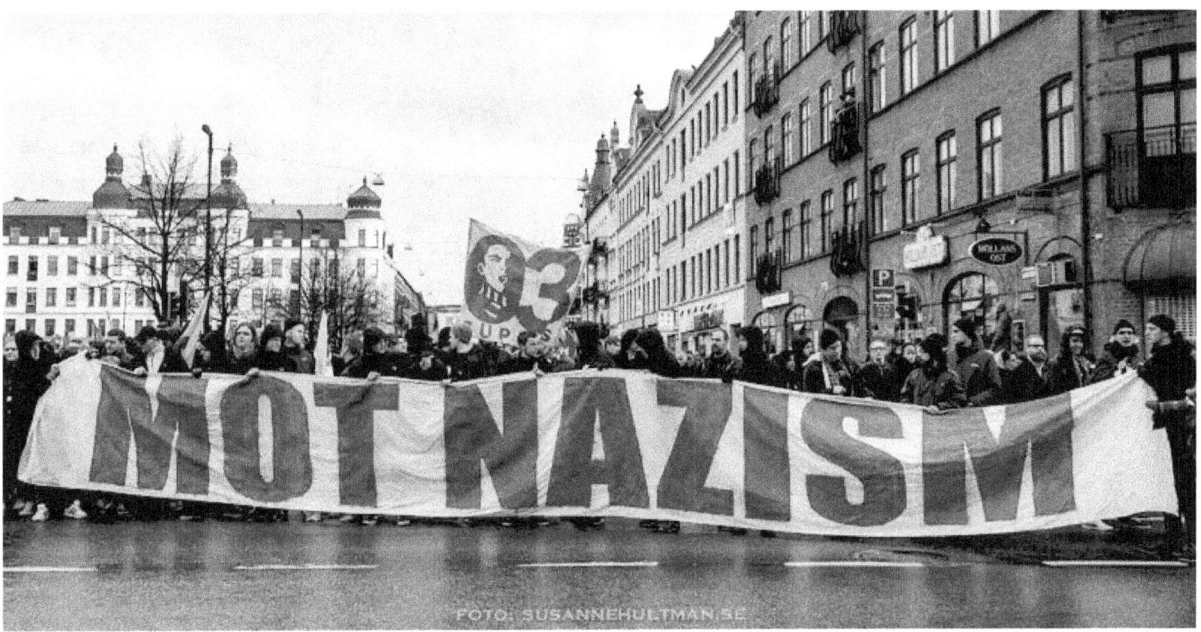

Fig. 1 - Demonstration against Nazism, Malmö, Photo: Susanne Hultman.

Public Spaces and Subcultures

Urban society, and consequently the materiality of public space, is in this article understood as a conglomerate of different, sometimes competing publics that form and shape the urban fabric. Public space is thus formed relationally in the interaction between different contenders or publics (Massey, 1994: 146-156, 2002). This formation of society and public place is both material and visual as well as social. Visual practices and enacted identities pla a major part in the construction of public space. If we focus on urban place, the city, football supporters in most cases as a group connect to the city of their team. To support Malmö FF, one are probably also a keen advocate of the city Malmö.[2]

However, supporters are seldom claiming the right to the city as a political manifestation (Harvey, 2012; Mitchel, 2003). They claim and inscribe themselves in the urban fabric thorough marches to their home ground and at worst through hooliganism in the streets. Mostly, though it is not a bodily presence. Instead, their visual tactics in stickers, tags, and graffiti writing, referring to their supporter group or their football team, mark their presence in the urban fabric. Still it is not in the urban fabric predominantly that the defining of the culture of football supporters take place. It is on the stands of the home ground. It is there that flares, clothes, banners, and chants form their identity. It is a formation that verges on what Dick Hebdige writes in his seminal book *Subculture the Meaning of Style*: "It stands apart – a visible construction, a loaded choice. It directs attention to itself; It gives itself to be read" (Hebdige, 1979). In the football stands, it is expressed in opposition to the opposing teams and through the unity of the supporters. What happened in Malmö in March 2014 was that the identity of the football stands was merged with political activists, political parties, and common inhabitants of Malmö, etc. Interconnectivity formed a new urban place of openness and respect (Massey, 1994: 121). Was it a one-time event or should supporter cultures be understood as forming in a dialogue between the stands and urban place?

Aims

This article discusses the public participation of supporters in the public sphere of football games and the public space of urban areas. It discusses the use and impact of visual and performative practices in the supporter cultures of modern day football. I use the term public sphere as a social nexus where different publics and institutions meet and critically discus and enact society. However, the public sphere is also understood as something reliant on the materiality of public space and place, if it is a football terrace, a street corner or the internet. When being materialized in its concrete meaning of appearing as a material body, society is possible to contest or defended through visual nodes as art or other visual practices. Even though supporter culture could act as art, I must underline that I am not claiming that the expressions of football supporter cultures are the result of artistic creativity or artistic performances. That is, of course, a possibility, but to properly examine that it demands a deeper discussion of similarities and differences, intentions and belongings. To reach my scope, to understand and discuss the supporter cultures' visual and performative expressions, I confine myself to calling them visual practices. The cultures of supporters are an individual or collective act with the double intention of supporting your team and stating identity as well as being an instrument in the construction of a modern urban society.

Modern-day football is part of a commodified market of merchandise and entertainment (King, 2003; Morrow, 2003). Enormous amounts of money go into an industry that has become one of the largest entertainment sectors in Europe. Many football clubs across Europe have become corporate companies with large international shareholders. Players are commodities and supporters are consumers of events. This challenges the basic assumption of many supporter groups: that of representing an authentic football culture where local identity, belonging to a long tradition, and being a genuine alternative in a world where everything is made up of commodities and where a love of a team or even the team in itself can be bought. It is an autonomous subcultural position taken by the supporter groups. In his book the G-word, Jacob Kimvall uses to explain graffiti culture as subcultural a lexical definition as "a smaller cultural group with beliefs, norms, practices and rituals that are different from and sometimes at odds with the larger culture" (Kimvall 2014). The definition is also well suited to understand part of the supporter cultures discussed here. It is slightly vague and open, and as such has the benefit of allowing the differences in the supporter movement still to appear as one movement. As seldom is the case, there are no clear limits between the larger culture of modern football and the subculture of supporter culture.

Rex Scania and the Commodified World of New York FC

To exemplify the difference between the position of the ultras and the commodified, branded market of modern football, let me compare the Malmö ultras group, Rex Scania's visual tactics, and the marketing of a new soccer team in New York.

The team New York FC's owners are an overseas football consortium deeply rooted in globalized international capital. The team lacks a traditional history and its life span stretches one year back before their inauguration into U.S. Major League Soccer. The Ultras group "Rex Scania" has used graffiti as a tactic in the manner of de Certeau to claim the geography of Malmö, to strengthen their identity and to support the team Malmö FF (de Certeau, 1988). This graffiti is to be found on trains and walls, and is frequent on ultras forums and on social media. It has a circulation of its visual production similar to many urban art forms (Bengtsen, 2014). In its expression and cultural belonging, it interconnects to urban subcultures as well as ultras movements around the globe. As such, it relies on the experience of an authentic culture in opposition to mainstream commercial society. When New York City FC announced its first season in New York, it visualized its presence in the city through the signifier of graffiti. The visual language signified urban cultures, youthfulness, and an alternative sport. To a certain extent, Rex Scania's and New York City FC's territorial tactics and usage of graffiti were similar. They both claimed the local city as theirs; they both used a visual language, recognizable as urban, active, and modern to emphasize their identity. Nevertheless, we can be sure of that Rex Scania's members actively engage in graffiti writings and that they are both part of the graffiti and supporter scene — they belong to the urban subcultures. As a direct counterpart, there's New York City FC. To find its subcultural language, it hired an advertising company, and used the large-scale advertising channels to promote it. However, the most fundamental difference is that Rex Scania graffiti is part of an illegal claiming of territory and thus actively engaged in the contesting of public space. New York City FC, on the other hand, has bought advertising space in Times Square and thus commodified football and public space. The subcultural visual tactics of the ultras has rendered them a place on the margins of society and the commercial strategy of NYC FC has further developed the brand and value of a commercial company.

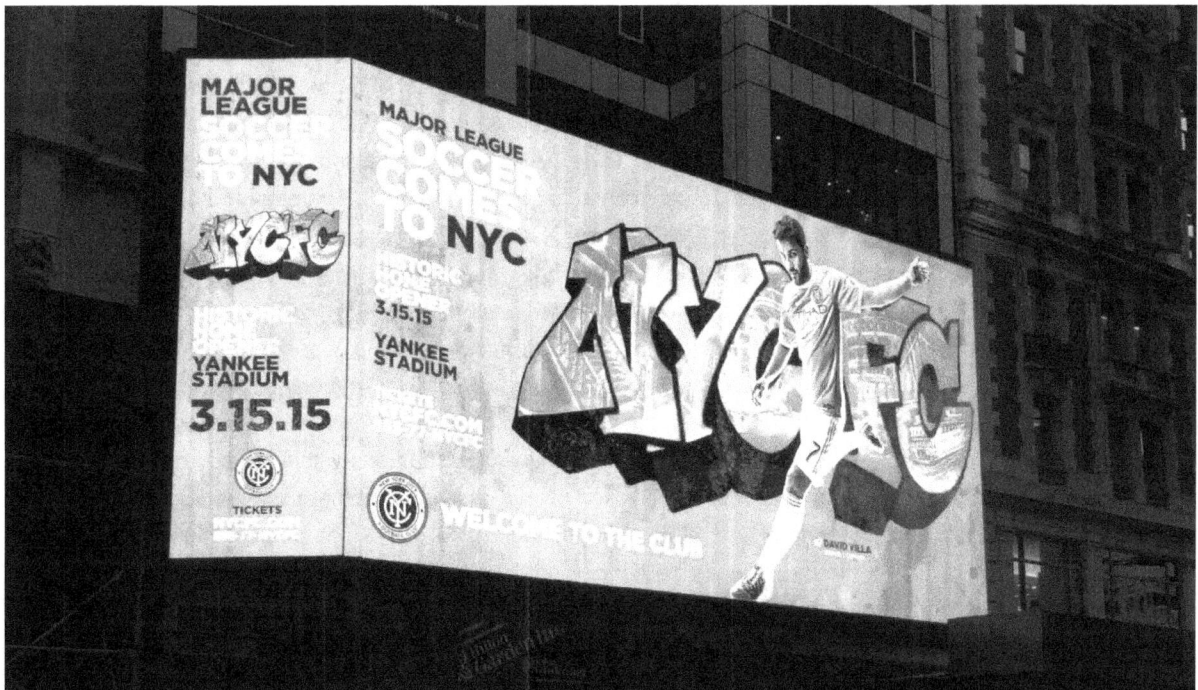

Fig. 2 - Advertisement NYCF, New York, Photo: Henrik Widmark.

Supporter Culture and the Concept of Authenticity

It can thus be concluded that there is a difference between modern-day football clubs and supporter groups being supportive of an alternative to modern football. However, it is not so clear. Football supporters come in many forms and the manifestations of the supporters are also willingly or unwillingly part of the commodified market of modern football. The tifos and the atmosphere created at the games, the reproduction of the team colors in stickers and graffiti are part of an autonomous movement relying on the idea of authenticity. At the same time, willingly or not they are also promoting the team-commodity, football as merchandise and large-scale commercial contracts, brands of football wear, and players as brands. Following the idea of authenticity supporter life is non-profit, idealistic, and based on "true love to your team." It is an ambiguous stand as the teams they support rely on a commercial market. It could be compared to the classical subcultural phenomena of, for instance, the rapid commodification of punk or hip hop styles and identities (Williams, 2011). Authenticity among ultras is stressed by the objects of their culture. Still, it is important to bear in mind that the idea of authenticity is evident among the supporters and prevails through actions of autonomy toward the commercial event-based culture of their teams.[3] Moreover, even the clubs seems ambivalent between the nonprofit ideal and the commercial.

In the case of Malmö, supporter groups, and their team, it is important to remember that Swedish football clubs are regulated non-profit organizations, where one as a member can make one's voice heard at the annual meeting (Kennedy and Kennedy, 2016: 68). This is of colossal importance in the supporter movement. It is possible to hold onto authenticity and belonging in a commodified world. At the same time, to be able to compete on an international level, the clubs also act as commercial companies and are competing on an event market (Kennedy and Kennedy, 2016: 66–70). The football world works differently throughout Europe. Some clubs are organized on the Swedish model and others are multinational companies. At the core of a large part of the supporter movement, what makes the idea of a passionate relation to a football club is "the myth of the club" or the supporter-narration of the club. Their own club could in other words be both part of the larger culture that supporters oppose as well as part of "the myth." The complexity of the identity-construction thus allows both belonging to a commercial field and at the same time opposition towards it. Thus, supporter campaigns can oppose the national football federation, which all clubs belong to, as for instance in the protests against the Swedish football association SVFF after they had imposed harder regulation on flares on the terraces in 2009. At another level are the protests against UEFA, the European football association. In the supporter-protests, UEFA represents an autocratic institution in European football that is also the main promoter of football as a commodity. Still, UEFA is essential to the supporters and the clubs as it is the only transnational association in Europe and the means to compete on an international level. In the Malmö stands in 2015, the protest against UEFA concentrated on corruption and earlier fines for chanting "UEFA mafia" at the referee at an UEFA-organized game. The protest used a caricature of the UEFA logo and the supporters wore the transformed logo on t-shirts in a silent protest. Another example is the tifo from the Polish team Legia Warszawa's terrace. They protested against a UEFA-ruling that the year before had expelled their team from the Champions League for using a non-registered player. These are both locally staged protests against institutions within football but they reach an international scope thorough the earlier mentioned circulation of images in internet forums, and through social media (Numerato, 2016; McLean and Wainwright, 2009). Thus the local geography of the football stadiums is turned into the public space of international football. A possible conclusion from the protests is the positioning in opposition of the supporter movement. Another is that the clubs, the supporters, the market, the national, and international associations all belong to an entangled network that is contemporary football culture.

The Right to Enact Your Culture

National and local regulations, and codes of conduct, set the possibility of action in the stands. Security companies and police enforce these regulations. This order will inevitably lead to confrontations with some of the supporters: breaking regulations with the burning of flares is an important part of supporter culture. There is also disorderly behavior, closely linked to the violent cultures surrounding football known as football hooliganism. Violence is seldom a feature at football games, and is not an essential part of the main supporter cultures. At the same time, it has through media, and the male and macho-dominated expression in supporter groups, been inscribed into the narrative both from the outside and the inside (Spaaij, 2006: 38–46). Accordingly, the illegal acts, as many other subcultural movements' actions, has attracted interest from the police and has often led to open confrontations. The police has become the main enemy to a large part of the supporter movement, both through bad experiences and ill treatment by the police and as a symbol of the oppression from society against their way of life (Spaaij, 2006: 17–49).

During early spring 2016, a pre-season game in Malmö against the Danish team Bröndby created disturbances outside the stadium where small groups from both supporter teams tried to fight. The police eventually stopped the disturbances; in the aftermath, the police, a few months later, searched, and took in custody nine members of the Malmö ultras.[4] At the first game after the action of the police, Ultras from Malmö staged a protest similar to a performance, where a man wearing a police security vest and a pig mask lit a flare during the opening of the game. It eventually led to arrests after the match.[5] The performative protest alluded to the police as pigs and the flare both highlighting that fact, as well as being the far strongest symbol of a resistant culture shaping their own public space. The protest should be understood both as a claiming of territory and a defense of their culture (Kärrholm, 2004). The protest also stressed the importance of the larger ongoing battle against the police, in which the performance on the terrace was one node in a network of visual representations of stickers and banners with the well-known acronyms ACAB and 1312.[6] When calling upon 1312 and ACAB the ultras were joining ranks with, or being part of a heterogeneous network of, hooligans and ultras around Europe, left-wing activists and convicts—to name a few in opposition to the police. In consequence, with the interpretation of the pig-police performance the stickers and banners are all part of the ongoing public critique of the police. At the same time, they mark a material and visual claiming of their territory.

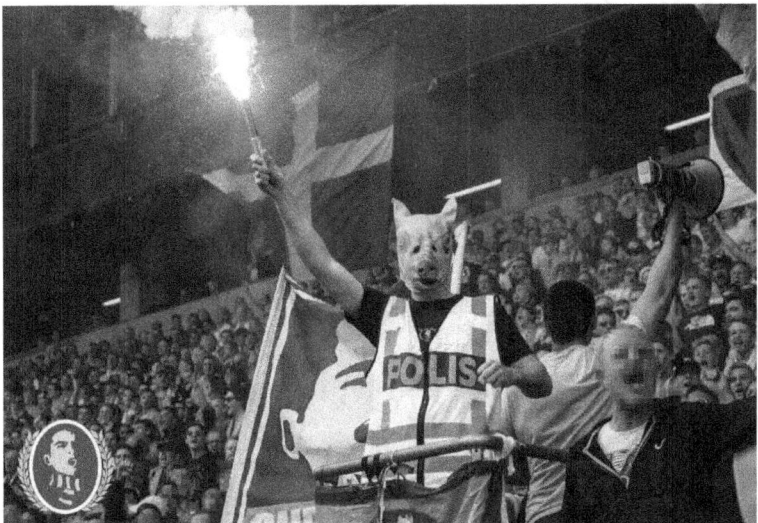

Fig. 3 - Pig mask happening, Malmö
Photo: Supras Malmö.

Bringing the Urban Fabric Together

Not all actions and visualizations are protests. As we have seen in the case of Rex Scania, they are part of a subcultural geography of urban areas or tactics of claiming public space or part of the interconnectivity of urban publics. The interconnectivity and the ongoing visual presence also owns the possibility to unite places and the people inhabiting them. The locality of the city, or the city districts where the clubs are situated are important aspects of what I have called "the myth of the club." Ideally, the football club and its audience represents the whole city and its inhabitants, thus becoming one with the city. In larger cities having two or more major teams, the claiming of the right to the city often lead to conflicts and battles over place, often fought through stickers, graffiti, and tagging. However, not all visual campaigns lead to confrontation.

Going back to Malmö, it is a city dominated by one team, Malmö FF, but it is also a spatially segregated city. On one side you have the thriving areas of the inner city and Västra hamnen, that could be described as ideal parts in what Richard Florida has called the "creative city" inhabited by the "creative class" (Florida, 2002). Their urban counterparts are areas such as Rosengård and Lindängen where unemployment rates are high and where immigrants live. Malmö has a history as one of the most important industrial towns of Sweden, but has during the last decades gone through enormous changes and is today best described as both a young and rich creative city and as an economically and socially weak city, where national media coverage is dominated by violence, unemployment, and a challenging

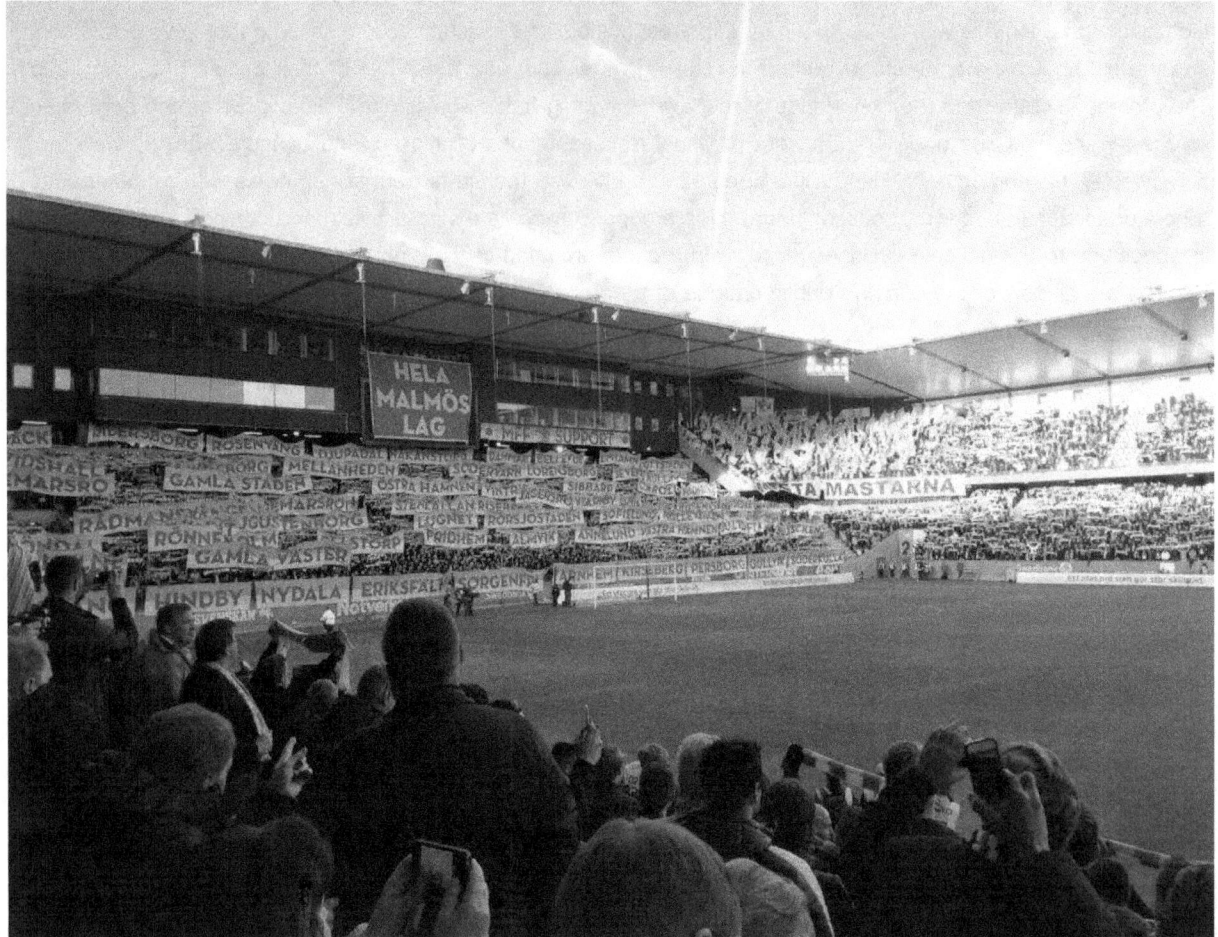

Fig. 4 - Tifo "All of Malmö´s Team, MAlmö Photo: MT96.

situation among immigrants.

The identification and the historical narrative of the football club Malmö FF has traditionally been a part of the Swedish working class. Since the 1990s, supporter groups have challenged the homogenous image and today there is probably few publics in Malmö that can compete with the supporters of the football stadium to fully represent a major part of the city: its districts, social classes, and ethnic groups. In 2015, the Tifo Group MT96 arranged a tifo that concealed the northern terrace completely. The tifo was accomplished as a group performance by the spectators of the northern stands at the new Malmö stadium, one by one, raising signs with the names of different parts of Malmö eventually forming a landscape representing the city with all its different areas as one. They all came together under the banner, all of Malmö's team. It was a tifo hard to misinterpret. The urban fabric with its districts was claimed as part of the Malmö FF territory. At the same time, it pointed out that all of Malmö's inhabitants belong on the terrace. It held local pride but was still welcoming. This time the visual practices and arrangements of the supporters were described as something positive in the media; today local bus companies use images of the tifo on their busses and thus through their routes claim the city space and project the city as being and standing as one with the help of the local team. It does not, of course, change unemployment or hinder social clashes and violence, but it shows the possibility to understand Malmö as one consisting of many.

1.8 The Right to the City – Istanbul

Let us move to Istanbul and the intersection of the streets Sakalar Yokuşu and Mumhane Caddesi in in the district of Fener in late spring 2014 (Widmark, 2016: 173–180). The area consists of mainly multi-storey apartment houses from two to four floors high. Looking down into Mumhane Caddesi, you can see worn-down façades with remains of the traditional wooden paneling. At the intersection, there are two corner shops and at least two restaurants or cafés. It is a lived place of social relations. On the walls of all the houses, there are satellite dishes that could be understood as both signs and material mediators of information that enable communicative meetings all over the world, and they are also thus forming the locus. At this spot Istanbul connects to a global economy, global communication systems, and a global cultural field. In the center of the intersection, on the lampposts, on the cobblestones, on the walls, and even on the street cabinets, yellow and blue colors are present as a sign of the identification of its inhabitants. Just a week before my visit, the football club Fenerbahçe had won the Turkish league and, as a celebration and identification of this historical occurrence, the supporters had remodeled the intersection. The identification of some of its inhabitants with Fenerbahçe had changed the fabric of place. The notion of the action of repainting the intersections appears with a further dimension by using Google maps 'street view'. By using Google maps, it is possible to step back a year in history to 2013, a time when the rival Istanbul team of Galatasaray were reigning champions. The intersection was at the time painted in their colors of yellow and red, and the identification was completely different. Without going deeper into the long-time rivalry between the clubs and their supporters, it is not an exaggeration to depict it as long and often violent. Seeing how supporters depending on who reigns as champions change a place allows us to note existing different identifications within that singular place. The colors of the teams hold the imagining of future victories, and the imagining of a change of colors, and they become part of the constitution of place at that very moment. They do not aspire to be the place of the 'Totenbaum' to use a contested term of Heidegger, where our ancestors' bones are buried, but the place of identification and imagination and the possibility of a different identification the next year (Heidegger, 1971: 156). Regarding the history of the team, we can be sure that the painting of the street corners also are signs of conflicts, of physically contesting publics. As an example of the conflicts, note that some of the Galatasaray paintings of 2013 have scribblings of F.B on them. F.B are the initials of Fenerbahçe, and these scribblings contest the Galatasaray colors in the hope of what is to come.

Coming back to the satellite dishes on the walls, it is also worth remembering that football on a large scale such as that of the Istanbul clubs is a global affair. Spatially, Istanbul football encompasses the whole world. Supporters of Turkish teams have been scattered all over the world through emigration, and new generations grow up with roots that can be traced back to Istanbul. Connectivity through internet and satellite television has made it possible to experience wins and losses in an instant regardless of whether you are in Istanbul or Berlin. Thus, it is also possible to see the satellite dishes as connections to the experience of football with relatives in Berlin or Toronto. Some of them are certainly happy to know that the cobblestones in 2014 are yellow and blue, and some are hoping for change.

The intersection of Sakalar Yokuşu and Mumhane Caddesi is a place of different supporter identifications, but it is also a place under the pressure of gentrification. The intersection is a place that defies a singular identity. The formation of a lived place is full of conflicts. The colored cobblestones of the supporters defy that just for a moment, and perhaps make living there easier. The right to the intersection belonged in 2014 to both Fenerbahçe and Galatasaray—in the imagination of Galatasaray and materiality of Fenerbahçe, and in such it was also a hope for small changes controlled by its inhabitants.

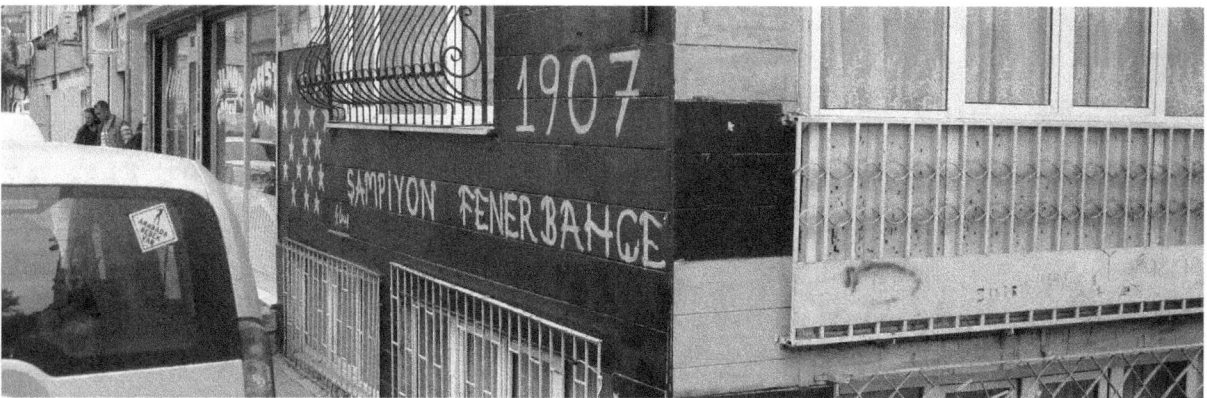

Fig. 5 - Street Graffiti Fener Bahce, Istanbul, Photo: Henrik Widmark.

End: Supporters and Political Activism in the City

Let us conclude back in Malmö, at the rally. It was held because a supporter, Showan Shattak, had been brutally attacked by neo-Nazis a week earlier leaving a feminist midnight rally called "Take back the night". Showan is a well-known left wing activist and a supporter with a background among the ultras in Malmö. On the night after the attack, the first graffiti appeared a few blocks away from where Showan had been attacked, on a roundabout known for its graffiti. In the colors of Malmö FF it held the message in Swedish "Kämpa Showan," translated "Fight Showan" but could also mean "Survive Showan". The graffiti and the stickers that followed soon became viral and spread in ultras and supporter forums around the world. It had gone global and the message was on banners and stickers and on terraces all over the world. In Malmö, the graffiti was as Showan got better changed into Kämpa Malmö alluding the fight against racism, homophobia, and neo-Nazism. The project had thus changed from personal to political. However, Kämpa Malmö also alluded to common chants at the Malmö stands and thus it connected to the support of the local team. Kämpa Malmö became an important slogan that held hope in a city exposed to violence and xenophobia. Thus the chants from the terraces had through graffiti and stickers become political. Doing the reversed travel and going back from the streets into the arena, was though not such an easy move. A banner that had the message: "The MFF–

family stands united against Nazism," was banned from the stands a few days later by the club out of fear of it being too political. In a sense, it was a threat to the non-political values of modern commercial football. Eventually, after an intensive dispute between the supporters and the club board, the banner was allowed. The dispute goes to show that modern football and the politics of the public sphere is not always an easy match even though they are inseparable.

References

Bengtsen, P., 2014. The Street Art World, Almendros de Granada Press, Lund.

de Certeau, M., [1980] 1988. The Practice of Everyday Life. University of California Press, Los Angeles.

Florida, R., 2002. The Rise of the Creative Class and How it's Transforming Work, Leisure, Community and Everyday Life. Basic Books, New York.

Free, M., Hughson, J., 2006. Common culture, commodity fetishism and the cultural contradictions of sport, International Journal of Cultural Studies 9, 1, 83-104.

Gushwan, M., 2016. The Football Brand Dilemma. Soccer and Society 7, 3, 372–387.

Habermas, J.. [1962] 1989. The Structural Transformation of the Public Sphere: An Inquiry into a Category of Bourgeois Society, MIT Press, Cambridge Mass.

Harvey, D., 2012. Rebel Cities: Form the Right to the City to the Urban Revolution, Verso Books, London.

Hebdige, D., 1979. Subculture: The Meaning of Style, Methuen, London.

Heidegger, M., 1971. Poetry, Language thought, Harper, New York.

Kärrholm, M., 2004. Arkitekturens territorialitet: till en diskussion om territoriell makt och gestaltning i stadens offentliga rum (The Territoriality of Architecture: Contributions to a Discussion on Territoriality and Architectural Design within the Public Spaces of the City), Lund University, Lund.

Kennedy, P., Kennedy, M., 2016. Football in Neo-Liberal times. A Marxist Perspective on the European Football industry, Routhledge, London.

Kimvall, J, 2014. The G-Word: Virtuosity and Violation, Negotiating and Transforming Graffiti, Dokument Press, Stockholm.

King, A., 2003. The European Ritual: Football in the New Europe, Taylor and Francis, London.

Massey, D., 1994. Space Place and Gender, Polity Press, London.

Massey, D., 2004. Geographies of Responsibility, Geografiska Annaler, Series B, Human Geography Vol. 86, No. 1.

McLean, R., Wainwright, D. W., 2009. Social networks, football fans, fantasy and reality How corporate and media interests are invading our lifeworld, Journal of Information, Communication & Ethics in Society Vol. 7 No. 1, 54-71.

Mitchel, D., 2003. The Right to the City: Social Justice and the Fight for Public Space, Guilford Press, London.

Morrow, S., 2003. The People's Game? Football, Finance, and Society, Palgrave McMillan, Basingstoke.

Numerato, D., 2016. Behind the digital curtain, Ethnography, football fan activism and social change, Qualitative Research, Vol. 16(5) 575–591.

Spaaij, R., 2006. Understanding Football Hooliganism, Amsterdam University Press, Amsterdam.

Thornton, P., 2003. Casuals: Football, Fighting and Fashion – The Story of a Terrace Cult, Milo Books, London.

Widmark, H., 2016. Walking with Heidegger and Freud in Fener and Balat. Why a progressive sense of place Matter, in: Widmark, H., Widmark, C., Carlsson, S. (Eds.), Istanbul Encounters: Time, Space and Place in an Urban Context, Uppsala university, Uppsala.

Williams, P. J., 2011. Subcultural Theory: Traditions and Concepts, Polity, Cambridge.

Notes

1 - The demonstration was extensively reported in Swedish press. See: http://www.sydsvenskan.se/2014-03-16/tusentals-demonstrerade-mot-nazism; http://www.aftonbladet.se/senastenytt/ttnyheter/inrikes/article18550631.ab.

2 - In global football of today, this is though not always the case (Gushwan, 2016).

3 - This view has been contested. Instead, it is understood as the supporters invest in their team in admission expenditure and so on and thus demand their commodity in return. See: Free Hughson, 2006, 88.

4 - http://24malmo.se/2016/05/11/nio-mff-supportrar-gripna-av-polis-i-samordnad-insats/ Retrieved 2017-02-01.

5 - http://www.aftonbladet.se/sportbladet/fotboll/sverige/allsvenskan/malmoff/article22879057.ab Retrived 2017-02-01.

6 - The acronyms 1312 and ACAB stands for "All cops are bastards."

Urban imaginary & the City

The Man in the Street:
Shadrach Woods and the Practice of "Pedestrian" Urbanism

Johanna Sluiter

The Institute of Fine Arts,
NYU / 1 East 78th Street,
New York, NY 10075 / USA

Abstract

In his efforts to rebuild war-torn Europe and construct vibrant community life, Shadrach Woods advocated for urbanism defined by streets – not only literally, in terms of form, but as metaphor and theoretical concept, as well. Challenging rising building heights and the growing dominance of automobiles, Woods proposed urban schemes organized by pedestrian networks conceived to be experienced at the scale and speed of foot traffic on ground level. Such designs were generated for and by the common man through sociological study of circulation patterns and vernacular architecture, and often drew upon local inhabitants' knowledge. In opposition to modern architects' frequent imposition of top-down masterplans and totalizing images, Woods sought to revalidate streets from the bottom-up by turning attention to everyday life and privileging notions of appropriation and flexibility. These guiding interests underscored his principles of "stem," "web," and "bazaar," while Woods's broader corpus of writings evidences the importance of the street – and the man in it – to his revolutionary urban practice.

Keywords

Shadrach Woods, social architecture, urbanism, street, pedestrian, urban planning, stem, web, bazaar

1.1 Introduction

Across Paris during springtime 1968, clamoring crowds and emblazoned posters proclaimed "Beauty is in the street!" Yet both as observation and philosophical premise, this slogan might have appeared tongue in cheek. Indeed, at that very moment, the city's historic quartiers were being transformed by brazen technocratic projects including the destruction of Les Halles, erection of the Tour Montparnasse, and construction of a stranglehold around the city center in the form of the autoroute Périphérique. Thus, *les rues*, along with the boulevards and arcades that had inspired the likes of Baudelaire and Benjamin were recast from spaces for casual *flânerie* to sites of dramatic confrontation between the historical past and modernizing present, citizens and state bureaucracy, and automobiles and pedestrians.

However, the battle cry was not in jest and its popularity suggested new ways of thinking about the city were gaining mass appeal. Through statement and in action, protesters affirmed the life of the city was in its streets, upending notions of Paris as a precious object or enduring symbol but rather understood as a constantly changing, charged field of spatial praxis. Moreover, the "events" demonstrated that streets formed spaces of negotiation and encounter, whose social and discursive flows better expressed urban reality than a cliché postcard image.

Paralleling Bernard Rudofsky, Kevin Lynch, and Jane Jacobs (the latter of whose *The Death and Life of Great American Cities* stated the urgency of the situation in no uncertain terms), the new generation believed streets provided the premier arena for fostering community and public engagement, and thereby constituted striking alternative to the growing retreat to private homes, private cars, and private lives. At the same time, the streetscape's potential for activism and appropriation was seized upon by sociologists Henri Lefebvre and Paul-Henry Chombart de Lauwe, while artists mobilized streets as location and thematic in their work from Situationist dérives and Lettriste décollages to Fluxus dances and Dadaist graffiti.

Set against this background of political, philosophical, and artistic response, the fact that streets figure so prominently in Shadrach Woods's writings and practice is not remarkable – and is perhaps even less so given his chosen profession. Yet chronological examination of Woods's writings and built work demonstrates that his theories of architecture and urbanism intrinsically tied to streets, street life, and "the man in the street" were prescient and profound. His lifelong exegesis on streets was expansive in scope and varied in focus, uniting organicism, African architecture, and cybernetics. Finally, as an architect and urban planner, streets dually provided catalysts for theoretical concepts and physical spaces for design interventions, while his ideas crystallized widespread thinking about the "everyday" and the "pedestrian." Through both his built and written practice, Woods proposed a decisive break with de facto postwar planning and irrevocably changed the shape of modern urban habitat.

1.2 A Fork in the Road

Like his mentor, Le Corbusier, Woods conceived of architecture and urbanism as inherently intertwined – an ethos likely instilled during his tenure as project architect of the Unité d'Habitation in Marseille (1946-52). Yet soon after the building's completion Woods decamped to North Africa, actively distancing himself from Père Corbu and distinguishing his work from that espoused by other members of the Congrès Internationaux d'Architecture Moderne (CIAM). Whereas the CIAM old guard utilized omniscient viewpoints and aerial photography to structure masterplans from above, Woods studied the context of each project from below: embedding himself in pre-existing communities, conducting surveys with prospective residents, and embracing an ethnographic approach to building and place-making.

Woods further challenged Le Corbusier and CIAM doctrine by disavowing functional zoning and, with it, the sacrosanct orthogonal geometry characterizing modern town planning. In contrast to the omnipresent grid, Woods promoted an urban matrix composed of interwoven and overlapping layers emphasizing connectivity, relationships, and integration, and suggested that the typology best suited to produce such spatial environments were streets. However, he cautioned that "streets" differed from Le Corbusier's "roads," writing: "The street, which was destroyed by the combined assaults of the automobile and the Athens Charter, may be revalidated if it is considered as a place as well as a way from one place to another" (Woods, 1960).

For Woods, it wasn't the aesthetics of streets that mattered but the activities that occupied and were engendered by them. He explained: "What is generally called 'circulation' is not the key to planning" (Ibid). Instead, human-driven patterns – including and in addition to transportation – generated the flows underpinning the urban realm. Of these overlooked conduits he noted, "[They] nearly always seem to be spontaneous, or at least they tend to escape from predetermined paths. They refer to the *real shape* of the network of human activities and not the apparent traffic pattern or road system" (Woods, 1962a, emphasis added). Woods championed these multivalent "streets" as essential features of urbanity, responsible for facilitating communication and community in traditional architecture and capable of promoting sustainable growth in contemporary times. He believed streets uniquely mediated between public and private spheres and could serve as linking appendages between old and new development.

To illustrate his thesis, Woods designed the Nid d'Abeilles and Semiramis Housing with colleagues in the Atelier des Bâtisseurs (ATBAT) [Figure 1]. The residential complex included passages between apartments that functioned as "streets in the sky" enabling movement from one area to another (what Woods called "ways") and serving as sites for congregation, casual discussion, and chance occurrence (what he termed "places"). Located on the outskirts of Casablanca, the architecture distilled the physical form and social activity of urban streets to the domestic scale in attempts to enliven what were quickly becoming prosaic *grands ensembles* elsewhere in the world.

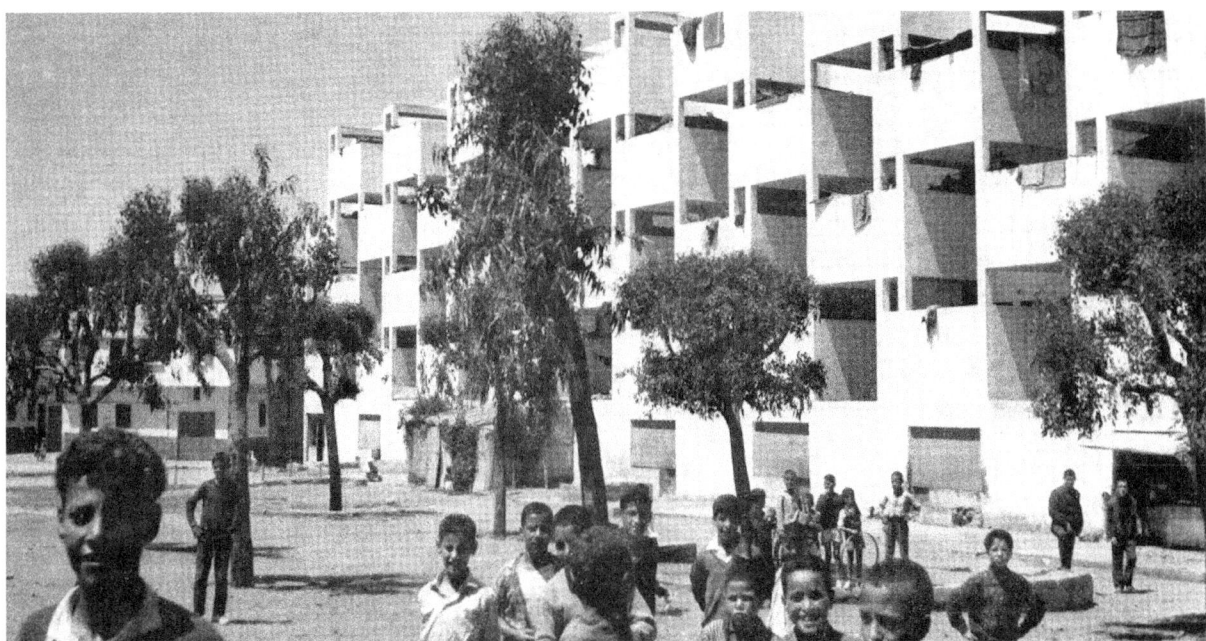

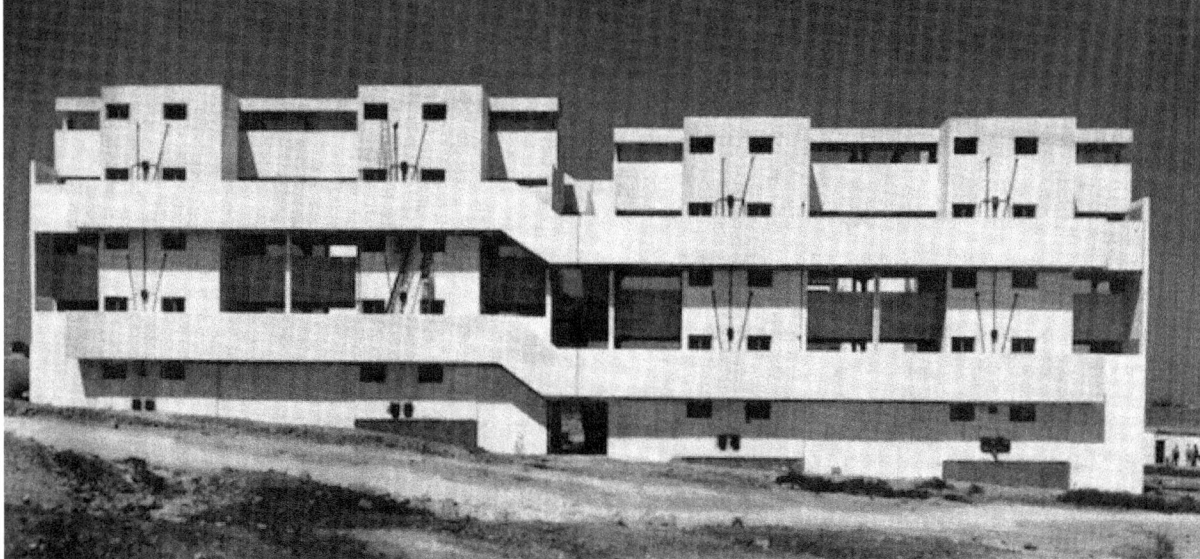

Fig. 1 - View of Nid d'Abeilles (above) and Semiramis Housing (below) in Casablanca (1954).

Subtly paying heed to the diversity of residents' religious practices, the team created a joint sense of individuality and community via the separation and coexistence of public and private spaces throughout the complex. Thus, the design did not result from traditional colonial planning but was a conscious nod to and reformulation of the nearby mountain dwellings and recalled vernacular urbanism in terms of its flexible plan. Unlike fortified, medieval cities in Europe, the residential scheme emulated the size and shape of North African villages with open-ended street networks to encourage evolution and future expansion.

African streets provided example of how to achieve variation within the use of repeated elements. Utilizing this single device, African urbanism yielded a range of permutations, each individuated rather than monotonous or repetitive. Woods reinterpreted these indigenous forms to facilitate dense patterns of habitation while enabling growth and change in the built environment. And although he never explicitly recognized the systemic logic at play, in adopting North African vernacular models to aid his design, Woods also began using fractals: patterns that self-replicate and repeat at multiple scales.[1]

After his early work in Morocco, fractal geometry became central to Woods's thinking. Throughout his career, "streets" broadly considered functioned as his fractal denominator, from corridors in apartment complexes to neighborhood sidewalks, and from regional transportation networks all the way up to immaterial data flows structuring the newly minted cybernetic world. This holistic vision of architecture and urbanism positioning streets as the primary unit of fractal organization had a twofold impact on Woods's practice and philosophy: first, it led him to believe that all architecture is interrelated; and second, as a corollary, that all people are, too. This ideology fueled his commitment to sustainability and equitable living standards, and yielded his core concepts of stem, web, and bazaar, to be discussed.

1.3 Stem

Woods returned to France to found his practice with ATBAT colleague, Georges Candilis, and fellow Le Corbusier apprentice, Alexis Josic, in 1956. Shortly thereafter, the firm won the state-sponsored *Opération Million* competition to expeditiously and economically replace housing stock and build new towns in metropolitan France. In their winning proposal, the studio advocated for a naturally occurring pattern language as existed in North Africa to revitalize the flattened cities of postwar Europe, thereby reversing the assumed direction of colonial knowledge transfer and somewhat ironically causing the firm's first attempts to realize an African influenced *habitat évolutif* to arise under the auspices of the rapidly decolonizing French government.

In the accompanying project text entitled "Proposal for Evolutional Habitation," Woods blatantly condemned Le Corbusier's urbanism, opining, "We have tried to avoid the deadly alignment of the straight line" (Woods, 1959). Yet linear devices were not to be avoided altogether since, "A line is open-ended; it has no dimension, it can change direction at will," and "A linear organization is the truest reflection of an open society" (Woods, 1961). Instead, Woods wanted to subordinate the straight line or pure form to what he considered to be the true determinants of the built environment: inhabitants and their activities.

---

1 - Ethno-mathematician, Ron Eglash, first identified the fractal dimension in African art and architecture. While Eglash's scientific arguments was published after Woods's death, Woods was also aware and observant of the unique systems, geometry, and patterns embedded in African architecture and urbanism. For more, see R. Eglash, *African Fractals: Modern Computing and Indigenous Design* (New Brunswick: Rutgers University Press, 1999).

He believed that cities could be better organized and stimulated by a theoretical principle he termed "Stem" and outlined in an eponymous article. Introducing the concept, Woods lamented how dogmatic personalities had yielded the "present absurdity of treating habitat as a means of self-expression, a plastic universe where houses are building blocks for the child-architect to play with," resulting in "an endless series of virtually identical housing schemes from Stockholm to Algiers," and "a crossword puzzle universe" (Woods, 1960) [Figure 2]. He further attacked modern planning for closed forms that prevented growth and operated in haphazard, additive fashions. Instead, Woods argued that cities and homes should be conceived as comprehensive systems connected by physical streets and information flows, reflecting the era's megastructural aesthetic and popular allusions to cellular propagation.

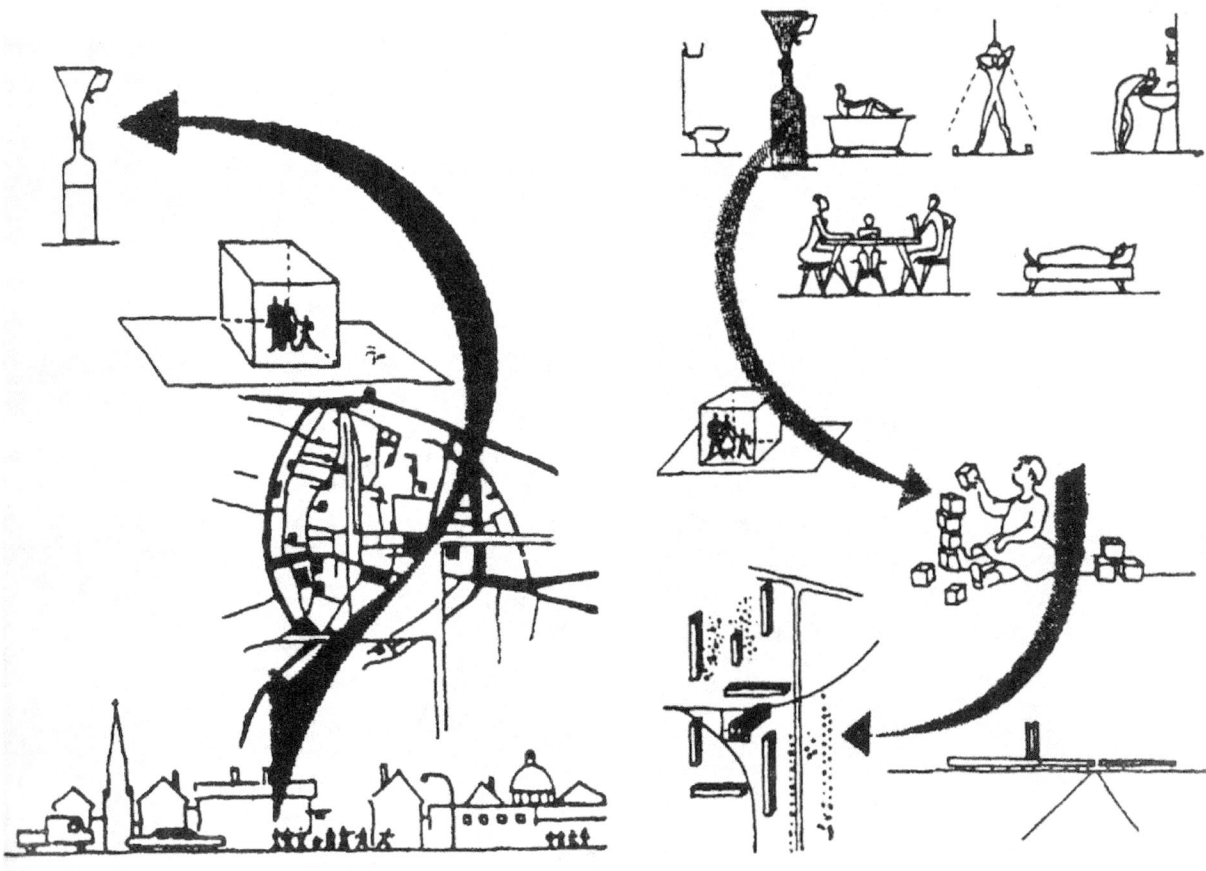

Fig. 2 - "Stem" diagram published in Architectural Design 5 (1960).

At the crux of his argument, Woods stated, "In view of the failure of the traditional architectural tool, *plan masse*, to cope with the accelerated creation of habitat, it is proposed that planning be reconsidered from stem to cluster (rather than from cell to symbol)" (Ibid). He thus concluded, "Stem is considered not only as a link between additive cells but as the generator of habitat. It provides the environment in which the cells may function" (Ibid). While visual description would have helped elucidate the structured growth and conceptual idea Woods was advocating, he only provided evocative cartoons and indeterminate phrases to avoid repeating the very formalism he had previously decried. Therefore, the open-ended nature of stem was intentional and in keeping with his firmly anti-aesthetic position. Although the term could conjure organic associations with a plant branching and rising, it was also meant to spur thoughts of streets and street patterns; as Woods explained, "Its form and spatial content will be different from that of previous streets, but the idea of street (as distinct from that of road) is inherent in the idea of stem" (Ibid).

In project files for a proposed extension to the city of Caen, the stem is immediately visible with its street-like functions clearly articulated and even heralded as "the primordial and permanent function of urbanism" [Figure 3]. Over the course of the design process, stems were replicated from dwelling unit to housing block and ultimately to conurbation; like so many bronchial tubes comprising a set of lungs, the stem repopulated until a new city formed. The diagrams further illustrate how pedestrian patterns led to neighborhood clusters determining the overall scheme for Caen-Herouville. Yet it is important to remember that stem was a hermeneutical concept rather than a specific visual form: while its generative capacities and reformulation of the traditional street were applied across a range of scales and contexts, its shape and appearance were uniquely determined by the uses and users of specific conditions.

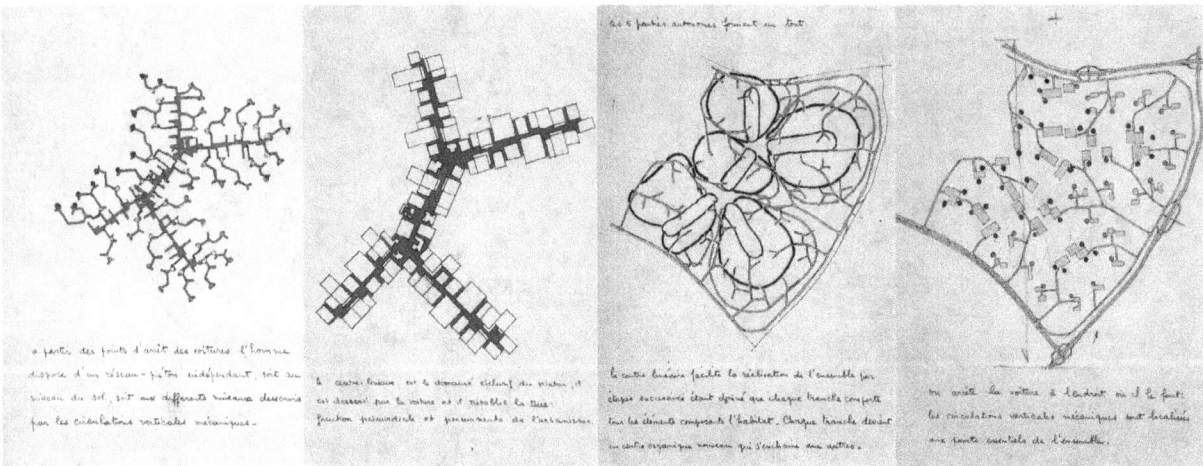

Fig. 3 - Project files for proposed Caen-Herouville development (1961).

Unlike other postwar planners who embraced the carte blanche status of tabula rasa environments, Woods adopted a layered temporal approach, considering a site's past in tandem with its future, and designed with time or what he called "the fourth dimension." For example, since the Caen sub-development was expected to span a building period of fifteen years, Woods developed multiple, independently valid phases (i.e. stems) which would eventually grow to be interconnected. Through the continued addition of new branches and neighborhoods, the city was understood to operate like a living organism; Caen-Herouville would constantly evolve and avoid static form, thereby ensuring its longevity with a flexible skeleton of streets amenable to growth and adaptation by future inhabitants.

The idea that architects should provide customizable, do-it-yourself frameworks rather than finite compositions was essential to Woods's architectural philosophy and he believed that stem represented the first step in achieving this aim. Reflecting upon the Caen-Herouville project he commented, "We needed to discover a minimum structuring device which could be effective for fifteen hundred dwellings but could grow to ten thousand, which could adapt itself to changing conditions, whether these be economic, social or technological, which could then be comprehensible to our clients (that they could use it and find their way in it), and which would allow for adaptation to its physical environment" (Woods, 1964).

Urbanism is a French word, and although my partially Anglo-Saxon heredity rebels at borrowing words from such Latinate sources, I have not yet found a good English or American equivalent. The English have a discipline called town-planning, which is something like urbanism; The Americans have city-planning which is nothing like it. In some places, 'Urban Design' is used to render the approximate meaning of the content of 'urbanism.'

The essence of urbanism, on the most mundane,

practical level, is organization. This is also the essence of architecture. The relationship between architecture and urbanism is that they are parts of the same entity, which might be called environmental design, and that each is a part of the other.

"Urbanism and architecture are parts of a continuous process. Planning (urbanism) is the correlating of human activities; architecture is the housing of these activities . . . Urbanism establishes the milieu in which

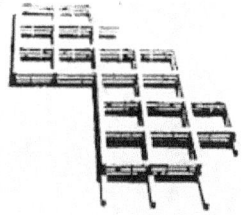

3

Fig. 4 - Excerpt from What U Can Do, Architecture at Rice 27 (Houston, TX: Rice University, 1970), p. 3.

As this statement suggests, Woods prized flexibility above all and analogized the practice of urbanism as akin to a construction site or a permanent work-in-progress to which architects should only provide basic scaffolding. He argued that architecture and urbanism were essentially "organizing processes" and that organization formed the single ethical intervention architects could make to the collective and evolutionary human habitat [Figure 4]. Yet a limited role for architects consequently necessitated greater user participation, from implementation and upkeep, to later revision and modification. Woods explained: "We assumed that the man in the street is the city builder and that the urbanist or town planner, who is an architect, is here to help him, not to supplant him. An urbanist can substitute for a citizen (he is equivalent) but he cannot find within his limited self the wealth of possibilities which are in all citizens. And this is not his job. An architect might design for you a house which would not leak but if he should try to regulate your use of the house you would consider he was exceeding his mission" (Woods, 1964).

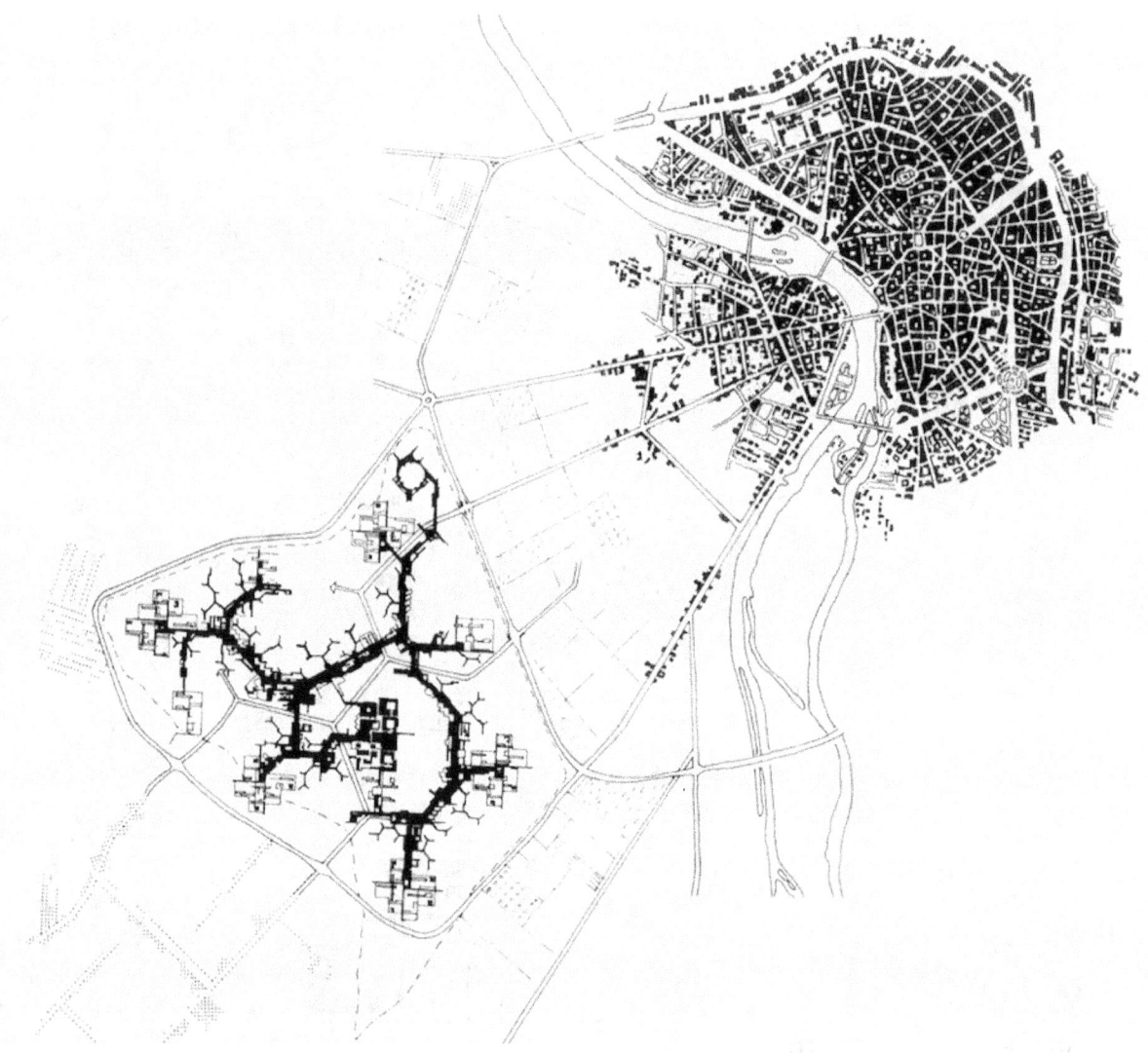

Fig. 5 - Site plan for Toulouse-Le Mirail proposal (1961).

Woods's confidence in his fellow man to become fellow builder was likely due to his early work in Morocco and Marseille, as well as his own unorthodox training in philosophy. As a result, he championed the notion that "the man in the street" and ordinary citizens would become architects as well as occupants of a future global habitat collectively designed from the bottom-up. Furthermore, he believed such an approach to urbanism would require dwellers to collaboratively create both physical and social community along the stem - the site of community-building par excellence. Woods argued that street life instituted a social contract on the most basic level, since "When one walks in the street, one understands very quickly that a certain type of exchange is necessary between people. In order to walk in the street so as not to bump into another person, one must have understood that there are other people; one must already have a social attitude toward others" (Woods, 1967). According to Woods, streets constituted spaces of mutual respect, recognition, and negotiation, while stems served as the primary building blocks of a new urbanism and the first step towards an open society.

1.4 Web

It is difficult not to read Woods's participatory rhetoric in relation to the then expanding field of cybernetics, and in later texts, greater parallels between architecture and technology were made evident. After "Stem" was written to explicate the design process in Caen, Woods published "Web" while working on a satellite neighborhood for Toulouse. There, stems multiplied and spread in numerous directions, not only along a single linear path but outward to form a network without center and northwest to join the city's historical urban fabric [Figure 5].

In the intervening years since Caen, Woods had recognized that a solitary stem could not yield a total environment, rather, a network of stems would be required. He had also become attracted to the democratizing impulse of "webs" both in systems theory and urban planning. These ideas were central to the Toulouse-Le Mirail project and were reinforced in the companion publication in which Woods wrote: "The idea of organization so that no parts are in danger of isolation and none are subject to an a priori over-densification is essential to our thought about what systems can be suitable to the evolving total society" (Woods, 1962b). However, this language of equality did not promote homogenous landscapes; instead, like a decentralized constellation or spiderweb, points of connection and heightened activity would emerge where multiple systems of circulation and organization would intersect.

Toulouse-Le Mirail employed "streets" at multiple levels, with separate systems for automobiles and pedestrians on the ground balanced by public passages on building facades linking apartments, shops, and community centers above; perpendicular to this horizontal activity ran systems of vertical movement facilitated by elevators and stairs [Figure 6]. These multiple circuits were then overlaid, causing independent networks to meet at various "intensity points" yielding a new, polycentric conglomeration. Unlike CIAM-approved functional zoning, where select areas of the city would be occupied at different hours of the day, Woods simultaneously dispersed and linked commercial, residential, and institutional spaces, translating the matrix pattern first outlined in his theoretical writings to the built environment.

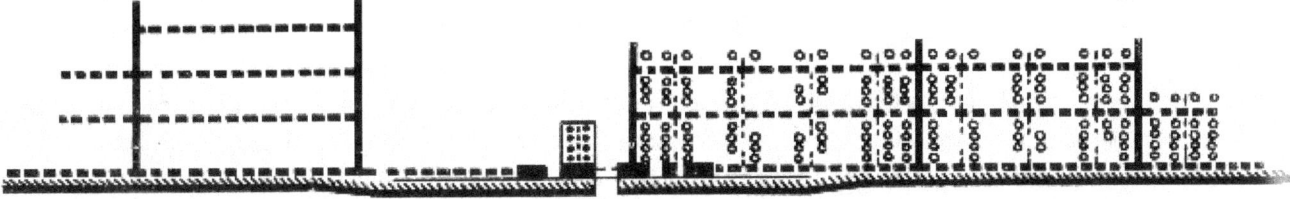

Fig. 6 - Project file illustrating proposed vertical circulation for Toulouse-Le Mirail (1961).

In face of the ever-increasing scale and complexity of his projects, Woods maintained that streets and pedestrians were the essential components of urbanism and announced the primary goal of web was "to re-establish the human scale in planning" (Ibid). Practically, this meant aligning the urban realm with pedestrians rather than automobiles, even at the most elementary level, as when we stated: "The stem remains a pedestrian way – developing at the scale of speed of the man on foot" (Woods, 1964); or when he observed: "In relation to speed, the measure of which is distance, the human scale is the pedestrian who moves at about four kilometers per hour" (Woods, 1962b). With this pedestrian dimension in mind, Woods spaced ancillary features throughout Toulouse-Le Mirail according to the amount of time it would take to walk form one to another; he then calculated such distances in "feet" despite the fact that his colleagues utilized the metric system and larger measurements would have been more practical when operating at the regional scale [Figure 7].

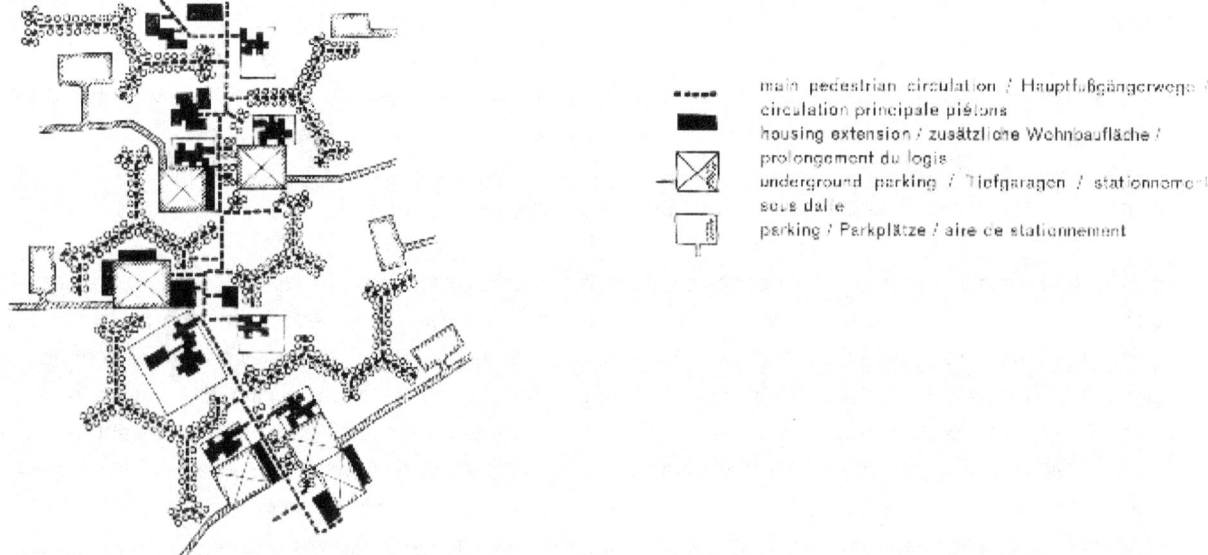

Fig. 7 - Proposed placement of ancillaries along the "Stem" for Toulouse-Le Mirail (1961).

But perhaps the greatest challenge Woods faced was integrating his ideas into existing urban environments, especially those that had embraced automobiles, such as postwar Paris. Although stem and web were theoretically based upon pedestrian networks, reconciling their forms with reality often proved difficult. One of his most ambitious attempts to weave pedestrianized urbanism into a historical city center was the proposed Bonne Nouvelle redevelopment in the heart of Paris. After the municipality relocated the central food markets to suburban Rungis, architects were invited to fill the subsequent void and improve surrounding areas which had long been considered blighted, as evidenced by Le Corbusier's plan to overhaul the neighborhood half a century earlier. Analyzing these proposals side by side is instructive insofar as it illuminates the latent influence of Le Corbusier on Woods's thinking, as well as the many ways Woods sought to break with his mentor [Figure 8]. Performing this visual comparison, Tom Avermaete has noted: "If the 1925 Plan Voisin by Le Corbusier for the same Parisian site seemed to be the blatant illustration of the irreconcilable character of modern urban models and the historic European city, then the Bonne Nouvelle project by Candilis-Josic-Woods seemed to announce a possible reconciliation" (Avermaete, 2005).

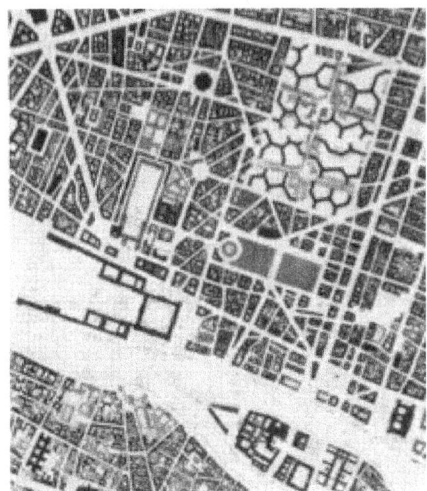 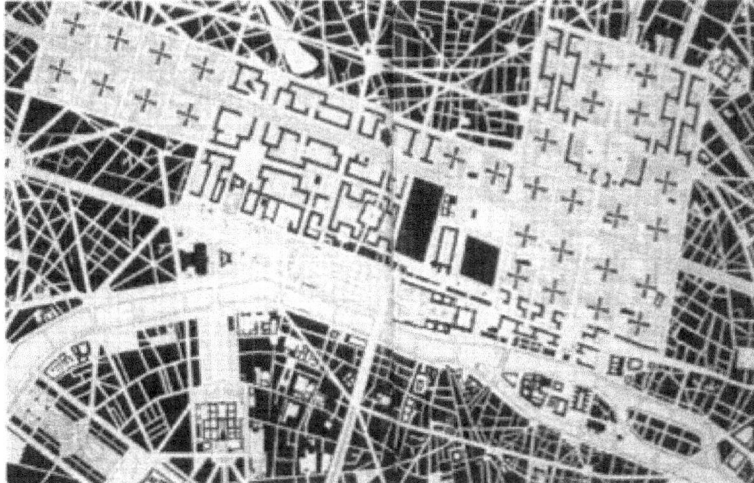

Fig. 8 - Comparison of Woods's proposal for Bonne Nouvelle (1967) (left) and Le Corbusier's Plan Voisin (1925) (right).

As in earlier schemes, Bonne Nouvelle would have created intensity points where the web met with existing neighborhood features such as bus routes, metro stations, and public monuments. The nearby famous *passages* would be echoed in suspended glass arcades linking office and residences across the high-rise development with terraces and outdoor spaces staggered and positioned at varying levels throughout the complex. Woods even proposed an overhead transit system so that upper floors would retain the same level of activity found at ground level below. Yet whereas the stem in Caen grew axially in one direction and the web in Toulouse in two, Bonne Nouvelle signaled an attempt to extend the previously developed systems in three directions and to weave them together in what fellow architect and Team X chronicler Alison Smithson would later dub "mat-building" (Smithson, 1974).

Bonne Nouvelle marked the logical progression of Woods's thinking leading to a more synthetic, unified urban landscape shaped by human practices rather than by compositional means. But, unsurprisingly, this futuristic overhaul never left the drawing board. Further, since Caen-Herouville was not developed and Toulouse-Le Mirail was only realized in amputated form, little of Woods's vision for street-oriented urbanism remains visible today. Due to this lacunae, Woods and his legacy are often reduced to the single built work that forms the closest approximation of his theories herein discussed: in Berlin, Woods wove stem and web together to create what he conceived as a McLuhan-esque "global village" and playfully termed "bazaar."

1.5 Bazaar
The Berlin Freie Universität was designed as a miniature city and was thus intended to provide illustrative experiment of how to deal with broader problems plaguing the urban realm by theorizing issues of city living within the space of the university. Timely circulation was prioritized, as was facilitating interaction between faculty, staff, and students. Additionally, due to its siting in suburban Dahlem, the campus was designed to link town and country by building in accordance with existing urban fabrics and preemptively respond to the rapidly encroaching metropolitan scale [Figure 9]. Finally, as a building intended to house progressive intellectual communities, the university setting provided ideal grounds for Woods to test his notion of social architecture, wherein better building would lead to improved human relations.

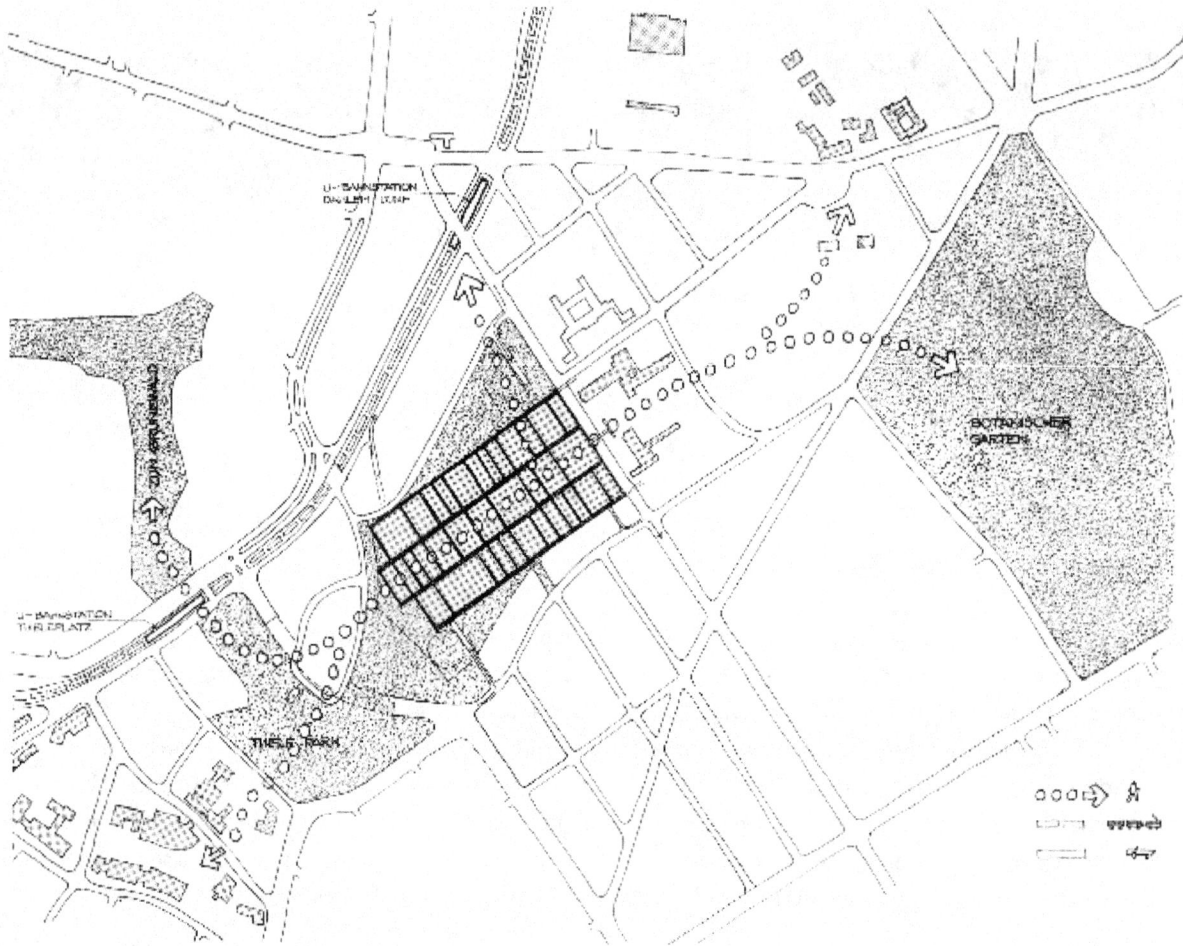

Fig. 9 - Site plan for Berlin Freie Universität (1967).

During the university's construction, Woods contributed to a special edition of the *Harvard Architectural Review* dedicated to the subject of "Architecture and Education." With his text "The Education Bazaar," Woods explained the concepts behind and aspirations for the Berlin project, writing: "Cities represent the future of Western society, and schools represent the future of cities" (Woods, 1969a). He continued: "Teaching and learning are also performing arts, and the city is the theatre of these performances. And just as the other performing arts tend to become stilted and remote when isolated, as in Lincoln Center, so does Education lose its relevancy by being locked up in ivory towers." Lest the metaphor be lost on his audience, Woods then succinctly concluded: "The theatre of our time is in the streets. Education, then, is urbanism. And urbanism is everybody's business" (Ibid).

Woods's altruistic ambitions were reinforced and supported by the university architecture and organization of social practices that would take place therein [Figure 10]. Dramatically flipping the skyscraper model horizontal to avoid vertical isolation and defy hierarchy, Woods inserted a permeable "groundscraper" in its place to encourage movement of bodies and, by extension, ideas, through fluid interpersonal exchanges. He also outfitted the main building with flexible interior and exterior wall panels enabling rooms and points of egress to be reconfigured to accommodate different purposes, activities, and crowds, as well as to provide customizable variety within a modular system. It was hoped that this "open door policy" architecture would facilitate greater collaboration and catalyze the dissolution of disciplinary boundaries within the university providing uninterrupted access to the life of the city beyond, wherein city and university would mutually enrich and learn from one another, and ultimately "intertwine to an inextricable degree" (Ibid).

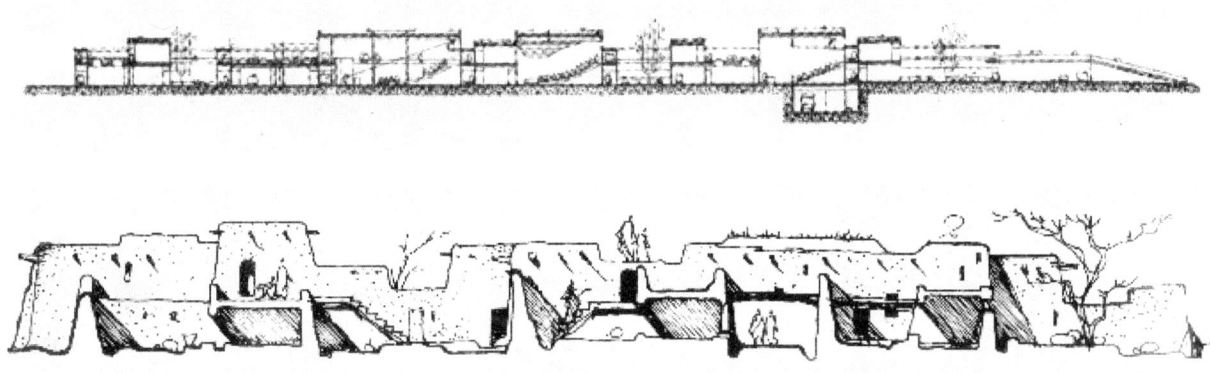

Fig. 10 - Section for Berlin Freie Universität (1967) (above) compared with section of observed dwellings in Chad (1962) (below).

At the core of the Free University project – and the defining architectural feature supporting these manifold desires – is a street network composed of two pedestrian levels overlaid at an angle so that the logic of the grid bends to the will of web [Figure 11]. Outdoor and indoor spaces are peppered between the two systems and are linked by ramps, staircases, tangential views, and hallways, while further activity is encouraged in the interstitial spaces created within alleys and passages providing equivalent to the "ballet of city sidewalks" promoted by Jane Jacobs. In sum, the campus suggested what modern cityscapes and their urban tissues could become, albeit at a fraction of the total scale. The university therefore functioned as a synecdoche or fractal that could be repeated and woven together to produce a comprehensive urban ensemble.

Harkening back to Woods's earlier work in North Africa, the complex invites comparison with a model city comprised of squares, courtyards, and streets, or with an Arabic medina as suggested by the title and ideas contained within the "Education Bazaar" article. Following Woods's untimely death in 1973, Team X collaborator Aldo van Eyck similarly reflected upon his friend's urban practice and the Free University project, stating, "We just used that one word 'casbah' as an image, as a poetic image. We were referring to any kaleidoscopic society where all the functions are more or less mixed, and always said 'casbah' was the final limit. We don't have to literally make a casbah, but we need to be a little more 'casbahistic', by putting things together: and letting things penetrate each other again" (quoted in Forés, 2011).

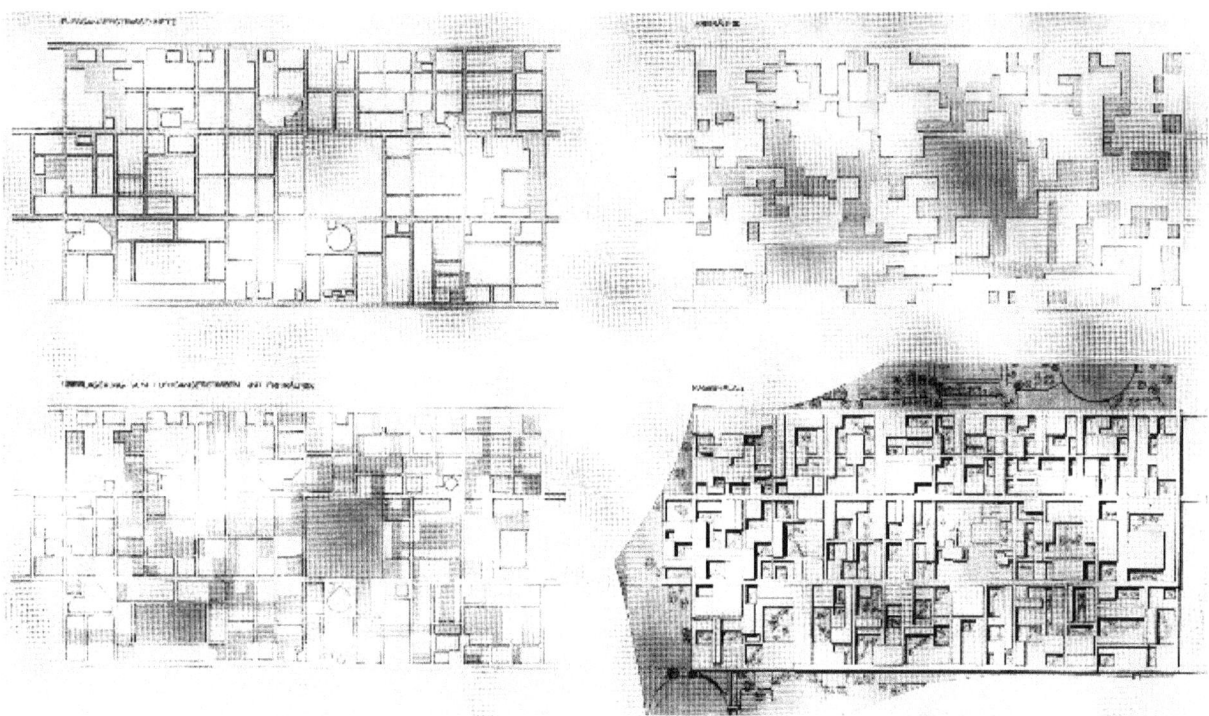

Fig. 11 - Detail of individual meshes and comprehensive overlay for Berlin Freie Universität (1967).

1.6 Conclusion

Perhaps Woods and his ideas of pedestrian urbanism proved too radical for his peers and, later in life, even for himself. (It would be remiss not to mention Woods's final commission for the Lower Manhattan Expressway – one of the most reviled postwar urban initiatives and certainly not a project dedicated to reconstituting the street.) In addition, history has not been kind to Woods's concrete legacy: the central pedestrian *dalle* was never implemented at Toulouse-Le Mirail, while rioting in 2005 forced closure of many of the complex's "streets in the sky"; meanwhile, in Berlin, the installation of code-mandated fire doors radically altered the original nature of the plan and significantly impeded the intended flow of students and ideas within the university.

Yet reverberations of Woods's thinking are being felt and put into practice today, while many of the questions Woods grappled with are as pressing now as they were for his generation. Like other 1960s thinkers, his warnings about sustainability and finite resources have rung true, prompting limited car usage and adaptive reuse projects. Similarly, municipalities around the world have elevated the profile of pedestrian zones and public spaces, as well as pursued well-designed street networks to contain urban sprawl. Pritzker prize winner Alejandro Aravena and his firm ELEMENTAL's low-cost, incremental housing expands upon Woods's model of participation; and the 2016 Venice Biennale British Pavilion addressed the overlooked "fourth dimension" to consider architecture's lifespan throughout construction, use, and its afterlives.

But beyond calling attention to duration, flexibility, and change, Woods's architecture and urbanism for "the man in the street" valued common citizens and the links between all of earth's inhabitants, forcing us to consider the implications of his friend Roger Vailland's observation that: "The world, at the scale of the universe, is an island" (Woods, 1967). Throughout his practice, Woods was committed to pedestrian-oriented urbanism. He sought to build relationships both concrete and metaphysical, and valued the seemingly "pedestrian" by evaluating the vernacular alongside cutting-edge technology.

In a lecture at the Technische Universität Berlin given shortly before his death, Woods called upon architects to avoid reducing urbanism to quantifiable data and to instead observe social practices and provide malleable frameworks for their accommodation and evolution. Questioning his life's work and the future of the profession, he asked: "What can urbanism do, then? Well, first of all it can, and only can, deal with present realities. It cannot be visionary; it is not 'futurible.' But the present reality is sufficiently difficult to occupy us all" (Woods, 1969b). Although Shadrach Woods's philosophy and ethnographic urbanism dedicated to pedestrians and to the "pedestrian" may not have found welcome audience in the late twentieth century, his assessment that "we are all passengers on what Bucky Fuller calls "Spaceship Earth" has proven acutely relevant in today's evermore interconnected world, wherein "The world is a city, and urbanism is everyone's business" (Ibid).

Acknowledgements: The title of this paper reprises Woods's posthumously published text, *The Man in the Street: A Polemic on Urbanism* (Baltimore: Penguin Books, 1975), although the ideas contained therein were equally expressed in the articles, lectures, and built work referenced above. Research was conducted at the Shadrach Woods Archive at Avery Library, Columbia University, New York, NY, USA.

References

Avermaete, T., 2006. Another Modern: The Post-War Architecture and Urbanism of Candilis-Josic-Woods, NAi Publishers, Rotterdam, Netherlands.

Forés, Jamie J. Ferrer., 2011. Mat Urbanism: Growth and Change, Projections: the MIT Journal of Planning 10, 73-84.

Smithson, Alison. "How to Recognise and Read Mat-Building: Mainstream Architecture as it has Developed Towards the Mat-Building," *Architectural Design* (September, 1974).

Woods, S., Candilis, G., Josic, A., 1959. Proposal for Evolutional Habitation, in: CIAM '59 in Otterlo (London, A. Tiranti, 1961), 114-119.

Woods, S., May 1960. Stem, Architectural Design 5, 181.

Woods, S., Candilis, G., Josic, A., 1961. Urbanisme, Carré Bleu 3, 2-5.

Woods, S., 1962. Dwellings, Ways and Places, Lecture, Yale University, New Haven, Connecticut, USA, Spring.

Woods, S., 1962. Web, Carré Bleu 3, n.p.

Woods, S., 1963. The Discovery of Architecture, Lecture, Yale University, New Haven, Connecticut, USA, Fall.

Woods, S., 1964. The Designer's Dilemma, Lecture, Technische Universität Darmstadt, Darmstadt, Germany, Mar. 12.

Woods, S., Vailland, R., 1967. Conversation on Urbanism, Perspecta 11, 54-57.

Woods, S., 1968. Stadtplanung Geht Uns Alle An / Urbanism is Everybody's Business, Projekt 6, Karl Kramer Verlag, Stuttgart.

Urban Art by osa as a Laboratory
New Approaches to Urban Architecture, City Planning, and Community Building

Pamela C. Scorzin

Professor of Art History & Visual Culture Studies,
Dortmund University of Applied Sciences and Arts, Design Faculty, Germany.
pamela.scorzin@fh-dortmund.de

Abstract

Urban art by the Office for Subversive Architecture (osa) functions as an artistic-architectural laboratory. By merging reality and fiction within temporary public interventions and participatory projects osa aims to be exploring new approaches to urban architecture, city planning, and community building that are triggering and evoking alternative and interdisciplinary forms of public engagement, encompassing both creators and recipients, makers, and consumers, inviting everyone to look at, think about, and inhabit the post-industrial city differently, since there has been a huge shift in the discourse of modern cities in general as well as of urban/suburban spaces in particular during the last twenty years. At least, that is true for among those creatives, who occupy themselves professionally with the phenomenon of global metropoles and megacities, i.e. architects and planners, artists, and theoreticians. With this exemplary contemporary urban art collective, it is especially true of a younger generation not so much influenced by the ideological and aesthetic debates of the sixties, seventies, and eighties any longer, but the current actor-network idea.

Keywords/ Tags: osa, new urban art, urban imagination, public intervention, participatory installation, artistic lab, community building, social design, scenography, network idea

1. Introduction: *The Office for Subversive Architecture (osa)*

Over the recent years, the manifold urban interventions and various temporary installations in urban space by *osa - Office for Subversive Architecture*[1] can be seen as a new form of collaborative architectural research, cooperative design experiment, and participatory creation of user-oriented, highly inclusive art which is easily accessible to a wide audience in the public sphere. Public art hereby is utilized as a kind of artistic-architectural laboratory for creating the urban anew with alternative, or rather subversive, forms of ephemeral architecture, temporary interventions, and long-time city planning or identitorial placemaking. Creative responses to specific urban situations and the necessities as well as urgencies of our time beyond "decorative cosmetics" might then open and suggest a new path to greater public engagement and civic co-creation, for example by artistically enhancing the functions and roles of public space in cities or by establishing social interaction and active participation, shared (emotional) experiences, and mutual encounters. The creative reinterpretation and aesthetic transformation of public space by artistic imagination might facilitate the sustainable regeneration of the urban in the end, and even more, discuss the idea of ownership of urban space anew. However, it is not considered a substitute for politics though.

Thus, all started with such a social encounter: The artistic-architectural network group *osa* originated in 1995 as part of a collective student project in Germany at Darmstadt University, in the Department of Architecture, and begun to grow as a self-commissioned, actor-oriented and self-authorized flexible network of several young, not yet fully established practitioners, living and working in London, Hamburg, Berlin, Frankfurt, Munich, Dortmund, Graz und Vienna respectively, but with similar fresh ideas on architecture, urban planning and design. From then on, their consistent aim as a self-organized, yet loosely connected and international creative collective has been to develop an innovative and alternative approach to reinterpret architecture in the city and to foster civic participation within un-commissioned, not directly commercial workings as well as highly transdisciplinary cooperation. From the beginning, their ephemeral, thus mostly temporary, urban art projects and "un-solicited" site-specific interventions/installations have also become a striking form of self-employment as well as self-promotion for getting-up as emerging talents and young members of the so-called "creative industries" — especially by crossing, blurring, and blending the boundaries between art, design, and architecture, varying from minimal or moveable public installations to the construction of actual buildings and huge spaces. Despite their remarkable, spectacular, and often challenging nature, their non-autonomous, legal, and even commissioned urban art projects, however, are mostly not primarily provocative or critical in a cynical or merely activist and deeply political sense. Yet, their urban art projects always focus on the subversive transformation of the actual architectural and historical environment of the city here and now, by critically merging reality with fiction or the artificial as a kind of principle. Herewith, *osa* generates a disruption in the daily-life urban scenery by stopping people in their tracks, making them think, and establishing a surprisingly alternative communication and social dialog in the contemporary cityscape. *osa* therefore develop manifold urban art projects from a strong direct creative response to city site, as a kind of playful attempt to enrich and enhance public space in the contemporary city through different degrees of "scenographic fictionalization" and "real virtualization".

Thus, often "real" urban elements become parts and props of *osa*'s subversive transformations and structural mutations of urban spaces without even losing their original purpose, but then with new performative or scenic components integrated. With much creative fantasy and artistic freedom, *osa* is actually playing with the built modern city as it exists, but revitalizing its dead functions in an impulse of repair and act of optimism, and thus regenerating and reconfiguring urban reality. In so far, their characteristic way of urban hacking, crossing and jamming can also be described as informal "exploits".

2. Some exemplary Urban Art Works by *osa*

The following few exemplary urban art projects by *osa*, discussed in chronological order, shall further illustrate these theoretical preliminaries and give a short insight to their artistic-architectural techniques and specific methods as well as subversive strategies, that are always in direct response to a found and given situation, and in sum, represent a serial method of site-specific interventions and installations, each time according to some already established characteristics of urban art today.

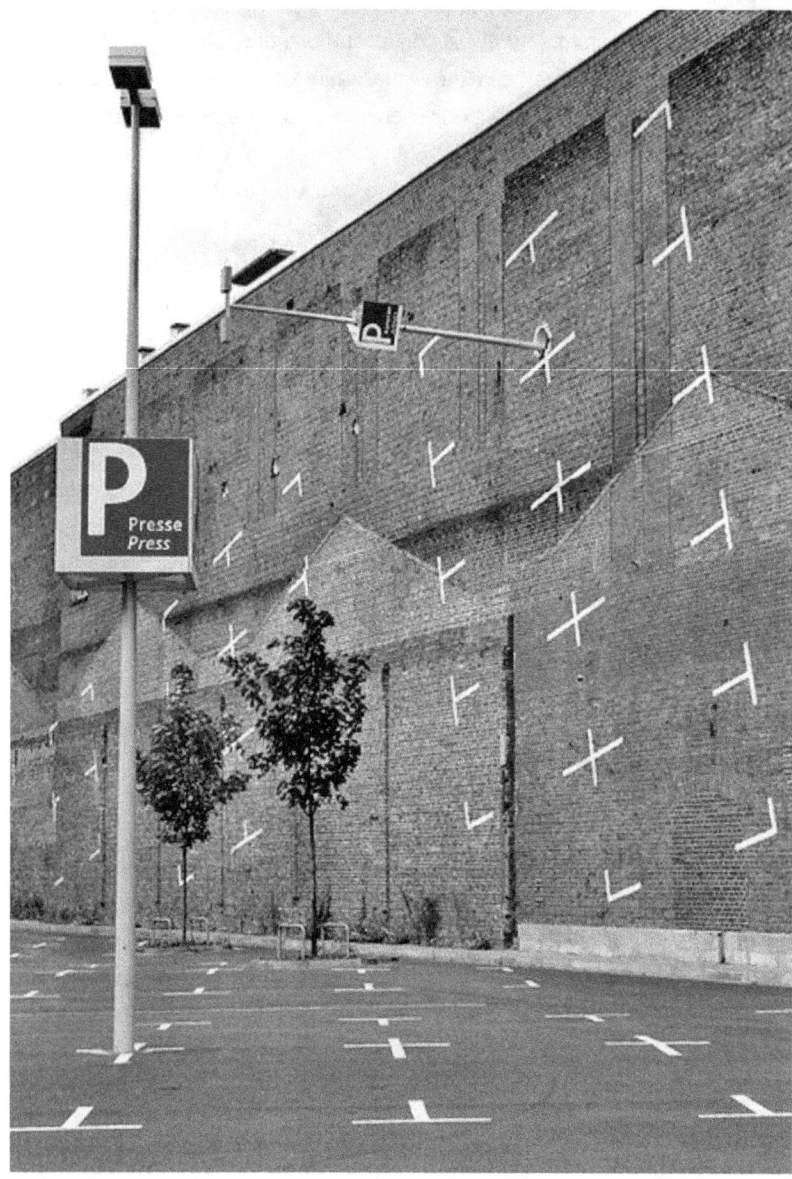

Fig. 1 - osa: Anwohnerpark,
Cologne 2006, Photo: ©osa.

2.1. (Fig. 1) *Anwohnerpark*, Mural, Cologne (2006): Amidst a rather unspecific and desolate quarter in the right bank of the German city Cologne, a transition zone between new-built fairgrounds, old residences, and a mix of former industrial spaces the signs and marks of a dreary parking lot were mirrored in a mural on a flanking huge fire wall. This massive wall probably belongs to the largest art studio complex in Germany, the PlanWerk. In the accompanying artists' statement on their website we read: „Mit der ästhetischen Kraft dieser ebenso alltäglichen wie abstrakten Grafik wird nicht nur ein öffentlichkeitswirksames Icon an prominenter Stelle in einen strukturell schwierigen Stadtraum eingebracht, sondern auch ganz nebenbei das Problem der Anwohnerparkmöglichkeiten bei anhaltendem Druck der Messe auf benachbarte Flächen auf einfachste Weise nachhaltig gelöst."[2] ("With the aesthetic power of this common as well as abstract graphic, a publicly effective icon is not only implemented on a prominent spot in a notorious structurally problematic situation in urban space, but at the same time the problem of the residents' parking possibilities are also being effectively solved in the easiest way working against the sustained pressure from the traffic of a fair area on its adjacent.") Since then miraculously the parking had doubled overnight…

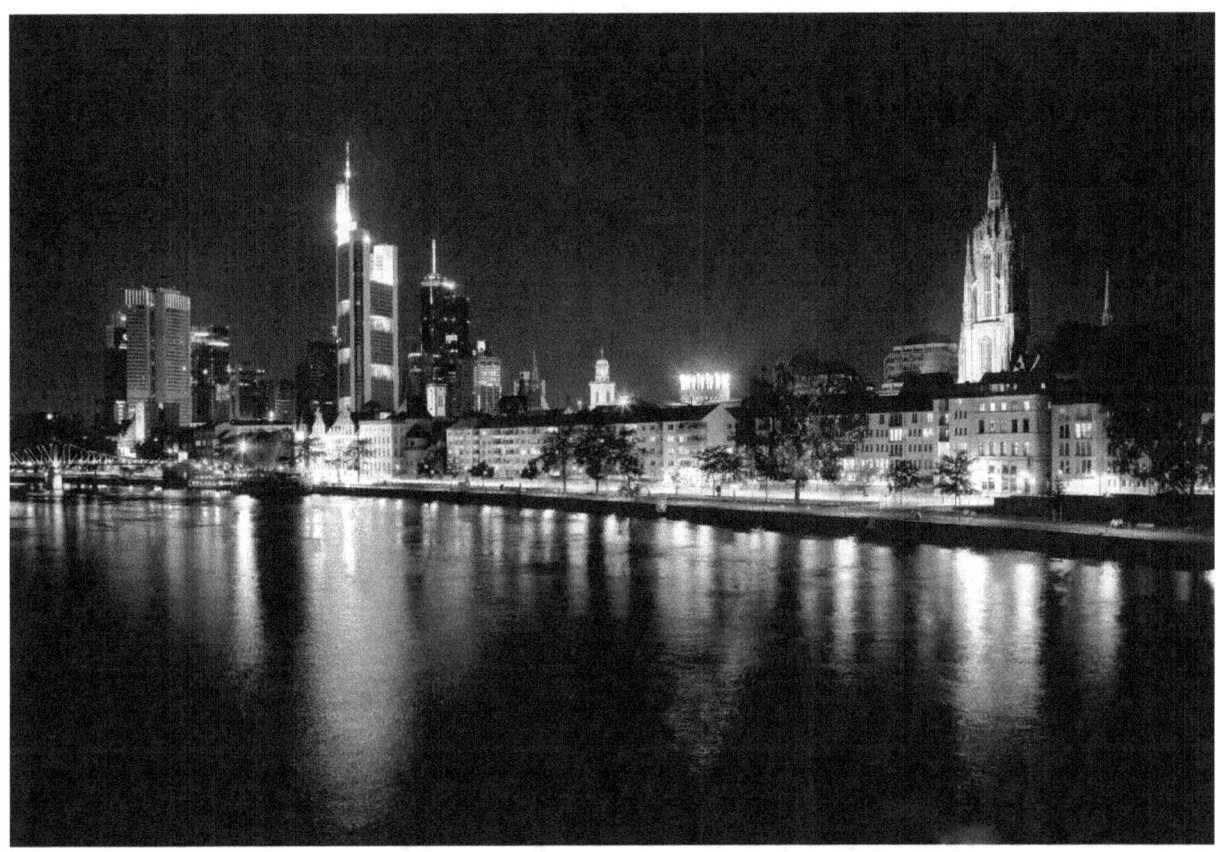

Fig. 2 - osa: Zum Geburtstag gibt's Torte, Frankfurt 2006, ©osa / Photo: Norbert Miguletz.

2.2. (Fig. 2) *Zum Geburtstag gibt's Torte*, Frankfurt am Main, Schirn Kunsthalle, 2. September 2006: This fancy "Happy Birthday Cake", a spectacular, officially commissioned public installation for Frankfurt's Schirn Kunsthalle building, on the occasion of its 20th anniversary, opened on September 2nd, 2006. The gigantic blow-up of a festive party decoration transformed the iconic architecture of the postmodern art building by architecture office BJSS just for one single day and night into its own huge birthday cake. The playfully circular, event design-oriented celebrative scenography was then visible from all over the city in different, multiple perspectives just for a full day cycle of 24 hours.

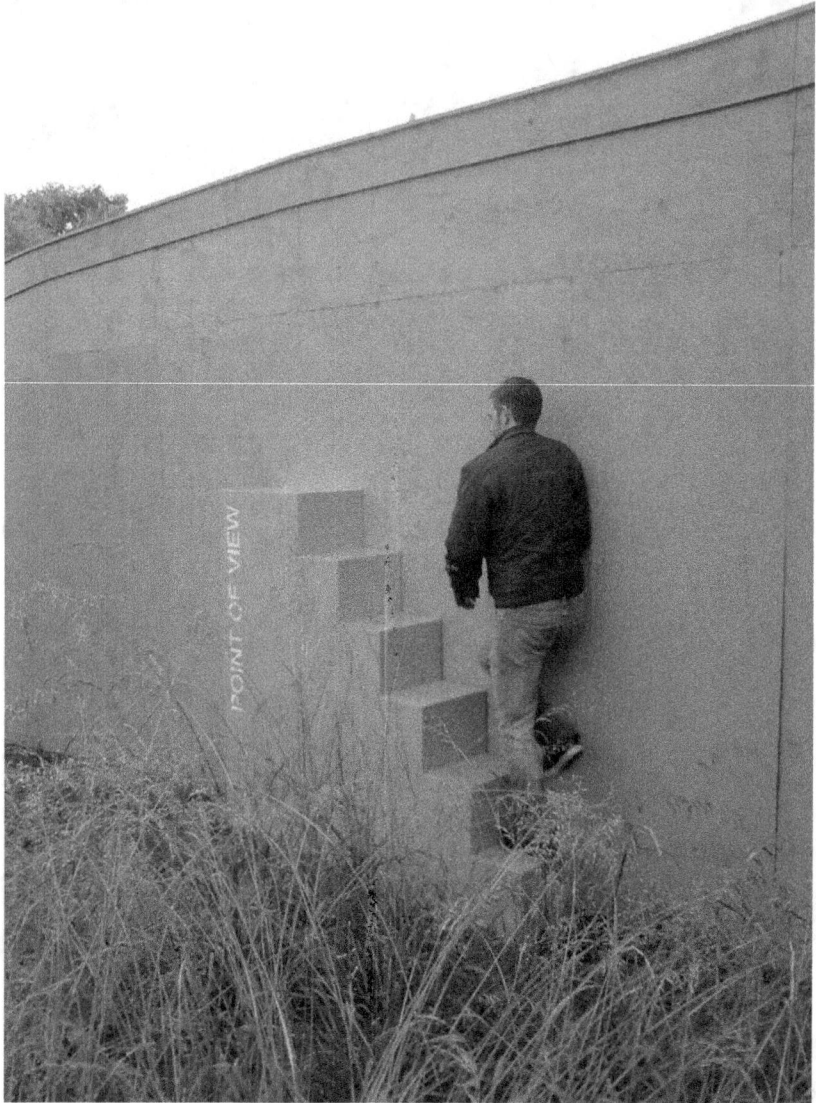

Fig. 3 - osa: POV/ Point of View, London 2009, Photo: ©osa.

2.3. (Fig. 3) *POV/ Point of View*, London (2009): A viewing platform for the 2012 Olympic Games in collaboration with the English *Blueprint* magazine. *Blueprint* and *osa* took direct action and built the first viewing platform for the 2012 Olympics in London. At 6 a.m., on June 12th, *Point of View* was secretly built and erected, without official permission, in form of a stair-like structure painted in regulation Olympic blue. *osa* placed the intervening structure alongside the official fence that surrounded the future Olympic park, not so much in an illegalized act of provocation, but rather as a gesture of friendly curiousness, full openness, and great enthusiasm for the upcoming games — a spirit then seemingly unknown to the many official bodies organizing them and developing the East London site then. So it wasn't just seeking and leaking information about the expensive building program, that is hard to come by. Access to and views of the location were just nearly impossible for the curious visitor and interested public to obtain then. Thus, osa's *Point of View* was installed at the official blue fence on the greenway as an act of parasitage and mimicry, next to the point, where it crossed the Lea River. The integral installation only lasted around 60 hours, during which time it was used by the public, before being silently removed again by the same *Office for Subversive Architecture*.

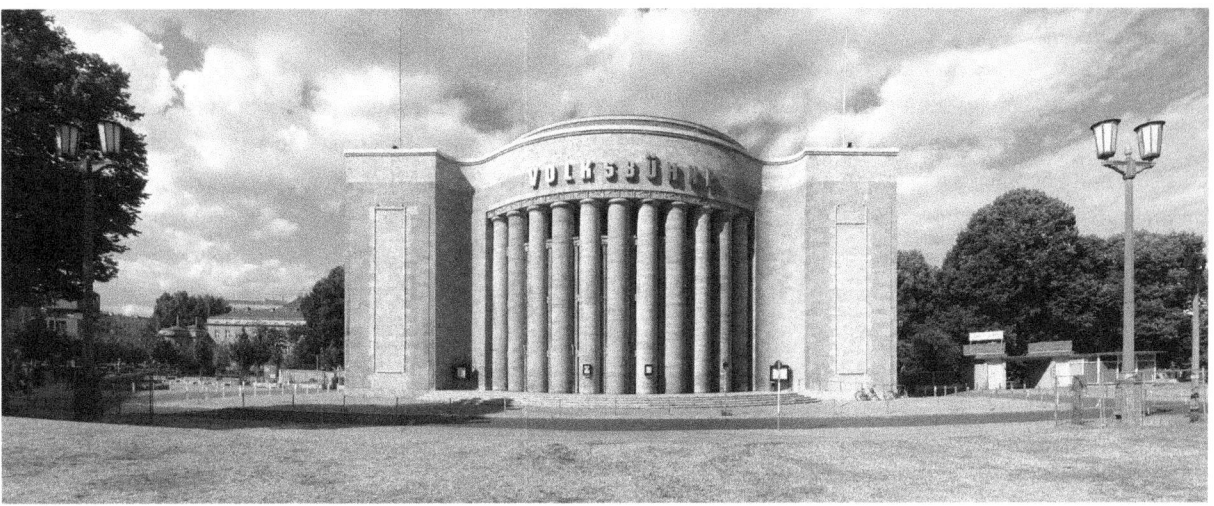

Fig. 4 - osa: Eintritt frei, Berlin 2010, Photo: ©osa.

2.4. (Fig. 4) *Eintritt frei/Entrance free*, Volksbühne Berlin, July 16-August 28, 2010: Some additional fake columns on the front side barricaded the well-known theatre building in Berlin during its annual summer break, while the title of the subversive architectural intervention was paradoxically as well as sarcastically suggesting free admission to everyone… Thus the work seemed like a short, but pointed joke, that further on intimidated the audience, but also provoked general discussions among them, which social groups have access to cultural programs in the city.

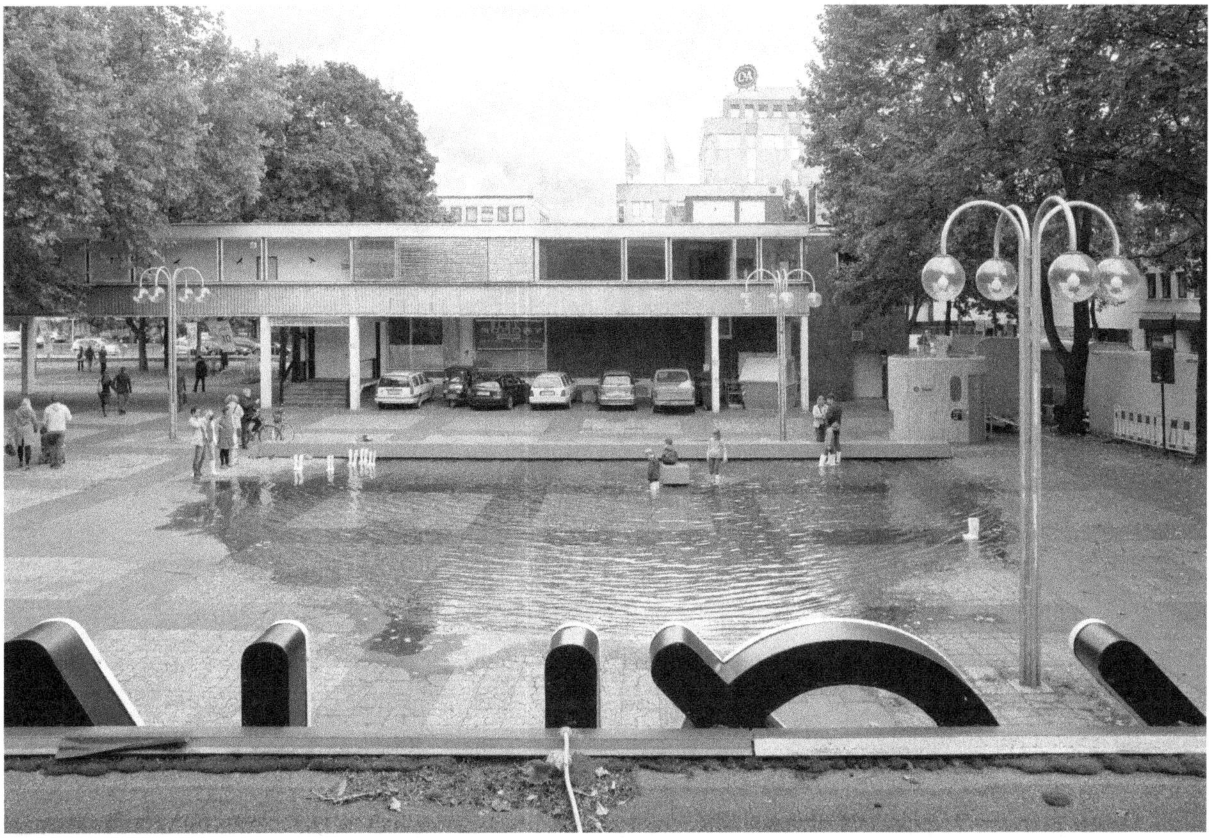

Fig. 5 - osa: Kölnisch Wasser, Köln 2010, Photo: ©Ulrich Schwarz.

2.5. (Fig. 5) *Kölnisch Wasser/Eau de Cologne* has been an interactive urban installation for *plan10*, a well-known forum of contemporary architecture (2010) in Germany: On the occasion of the event, *osa* was proposing an ephemeral water surface in the center of the square in front of the local Schauspiel Theatre. The concept follows the logic of the classical motif of placing a play of water or a decorative fountain in the centre of a square, which in this case will only be a mundane puddle though. As a new interpretation within the current ecological as well as economical climate and its current aesthetics, it not only fits into the somehow neglected appearance of this public square and its dull surrounding elements, it also provides—en passant—a new multi-sensual experience, a moment of a new identity just for the duration of the event. Since the water surface is also offering the spectator new perspectives and reflections of the overall configuration of this forgotten public space. A row of white Wellingtons is inviting the passers-by to interact individually with this urban intervention. The title of the work alludes to a famous Cologne consumer product (Eau de Cologne) whose striking brand color is also cited here.

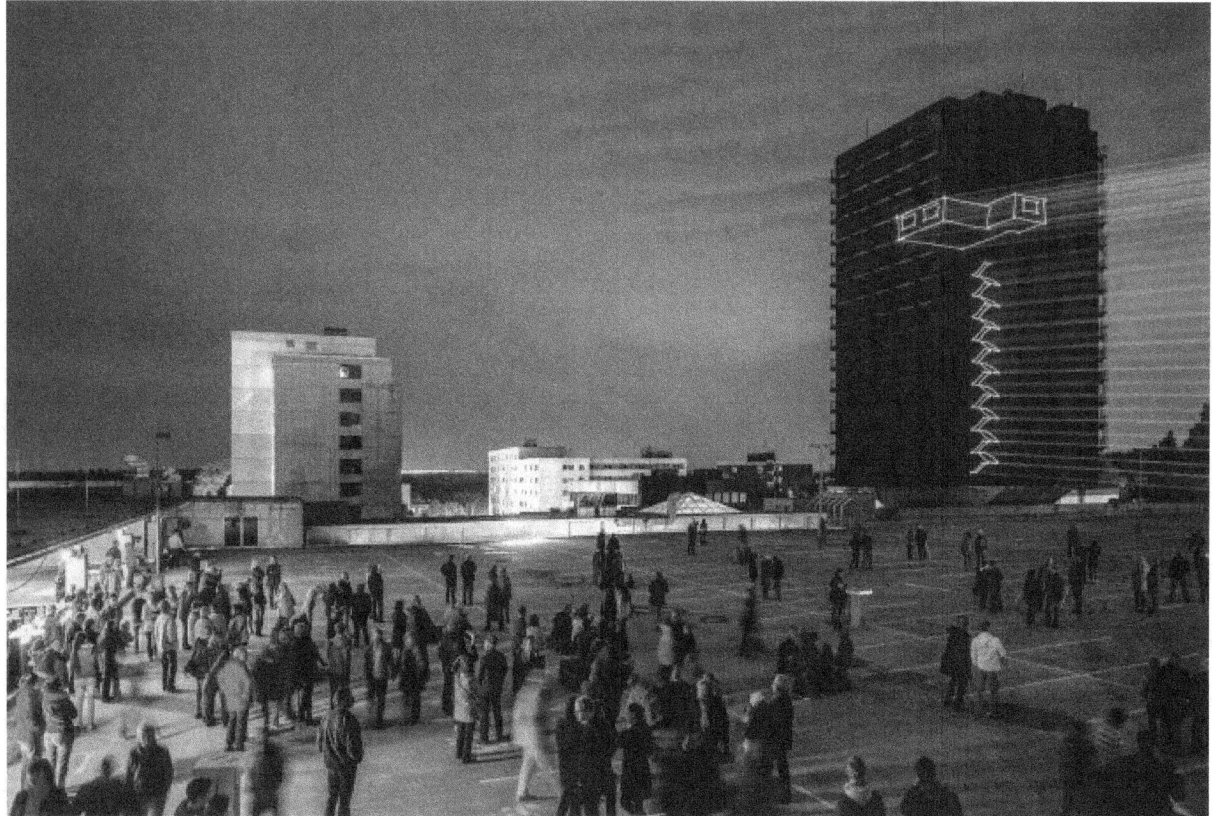

Fig. 6 - osa: Discharge/ Recharge, Urban Lights Ruhr/ Bergkamen 2013, © osa + © Photo: Johannes Marburg | Urbane Künste Ruhr 2013.

2.6. (Fig. 6) *Discharge/Recharge*, Installation/Transformation, Laser, Radio Play, Bergkamen (2013): As part of an Urban Lights Event in the Ruhr area of Germany, *Office for Subversive Architecture* collaborated with artist and philosopher Christoph Rodatz on an architectural performance of light and sound that focuses on a hovering tower block in the center of the Ruhr area city Bergkamen. Simultaneously a landmark and a brutalist eyesore from post-war Germany, this massive urban structure had been unoccupied for about 15 years and was now due to be demolished at the end 2013. As a farewell, the building had been painted matte black signifying its ominous fate, death, and disappearance, but at the same time transforming and reviving the metallic icon into a huge shrouded sculpture above the small post-industrial city "expressing the total absorption of light to symbolize the obliteration of [the tower's] life" and at the same time turning it into a gigantic public screen for the projection of an absorbing laser show at night that tracks the story of this doomed city tower. Interviews undertaken with former inhabitants were transmitted via a local radio channel situated on the top of the dark tower, allowing visitors to tune in on their own devices while enjoying the gigantic spectacle. Since then, the Bergkamen Citytower has disappeared without a trace, as the demolition was completed by the end of 2014.

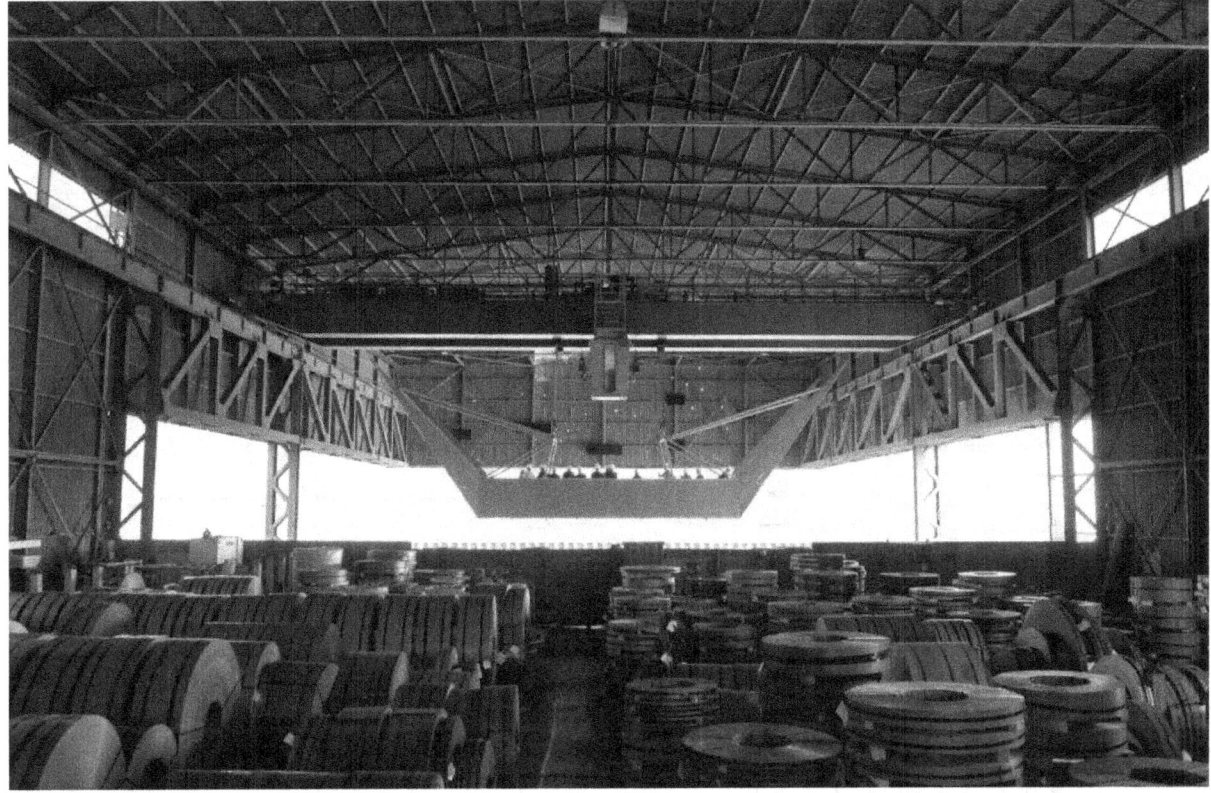

Fig. 7 - osa: well, come, Ruhrtriennale/ Dortmund 2016, © osa + © Photo: Volker Hartmann | Urbane Künste Ruhr.

2.7. (Fig. 7) *well,come*, Dortmund Harbour, 2016: On the occasion of the festival Ruhrtriennale *osa* intervened on the site of the SAZ's steel processing plant in the city harbour of Dortmund. In *well, come*, commissioned for the Urbane Künste Ruhr section, curated by Katja Aßmann, an industrial works building constructed for loading goods is temporarily transformed into a functional walk-on platform, which is as open for encounters as the transshipment point itself.[3]The garishly pink-colored installation vehicle was working as an expression of the manifold movements of goods and people around the globe nowadays: "Tatsächlich widmet sich 'well,come' den Strömen, die um die Welt reisen. In einer Erläuterung zum Projekt heißt es: 'Millionen und Abermillionen Güter sind global in Bewegung. Jedoch wird mehr bewegt als Kapital, Bodenschätze und Waren. Schon immer sind auch die Menschen global unterwegs. Menschen, die migrieren oder einfach reisen, solche, die Geschäfte machen, Menschen, die auf der Flucht sind. Damit ist auch das Paradoxe markiert: Wir befinden uns in Zeiten, in denen alles global unterwegs ist, und gleichzeitig beobachten wir eine Tendenz zur Abschottung.'"[4] ("In fact, 'well, come' is devoted to the streams that travel around the world. An explanation of the project by osa states: 'Millions and many millions of goods are moving globally today. However, more is being moved than capital, mineral resources and goods. People also have always been traveling globally. People who migrate or simply travel, those, who do business, and people, who are refugees. This also marks a paradox of our times: We are in a time ,when everything is on the move globally, and at the same time, we observe a tendency towards foreclosure and new borders everywhere.'")

On the whole, the *Office for Subversive Architecture* should not merely be seen as a professional office or flexible creative network for the global age, but rather as an open laboratory, encompassing both creators and recipients, makers and consumers, inviting everyone to look at, think about and inhabit the city alternatively and anew, since there has been a huge shift in the discourses and perception of cities and of urban/suburban spaces in the last years. At least, that is true for among those, who occupy themselves professionally with the phenomenon of shrinking metropoles and global megacities, i.e. architects and planners, artists, and theoreticians. Within this exemplary contemporary urban art group and their site-specific workings, it is especially true of a younger generation, that is not so much influenced primarily by the ideological and aesthetic debates of the sixties, seventies, and eighties any longer, but by relational aesthetics and the actor-network idea—creating platforms for exchange and new venues by experimenting in real-time micro-nodes, and thus, inviting everyone to look at, think about, and inhabit the modern city anew and differently.

As bottom-up city planners they are actively taking part in current processes of global urbanization with small-scale model transformations and subversive reinterpretations of found urban realities, that build a new form of subtle and striking criticism by activist and subjective artistic self-expression, rather than by sticking to just theorizing and giving big-headed manifestoes. It is all about staging experiments and taking microprobes instead of creating more masterplans.

In the end, in each of these minor single artistic urban explorations and playfully transformative experimentations, which can be compared with small-scale experiments and model arrangements in a laboratory, *osa* are actually altering imaginaries for creating broader real changes in urban spaces, that on a larger scale might be contributing to urban renewal and a new urbanism in the near future. Operating as a dislocated active research collective without one single "real studio space", yet technologically connected, further allows extending the creative process into everyday life, bending the functional structures of a laboratory to the flexible informality of an open and variable creative network, which constantly constitutes itself by an ongoing series of workshop-projects that stimulate social encounters between its audiences in shared moments of social involvement, creative performances, emotional experiences and last, but not least, common spectatorship.

At the same time, when it comes to acting versus planning, here urban planning has more and more turned into a specific form of contemporary urban design, which is also characteristic and significant to the idea of the so-called "creative city" and its constant commercialization and consumerization nowadays. However, new alliances and collaborations between design, art, architecture, and the city—in times of shrinking cultural budgets and rising demands—are forming the "creative city" today. No wonder that sometimes, urban art is already in danger of being instrumentalized for upgrading and up-valuating the city. Creating atmospheres, triggering special experiences, and emotionalizing by visual story-telling are all crucial elements in the play here, while we all observe the continuing decline of public spaces through privatization and commercialization for example, that occupy and even oppress processes of urbanism and urbanity nowadays.

Like with *osa*, this new alternative and subversive form of bottom-up city planning, that pragmatically engages with the modern city as it exists in the here and now, is currently achieved by the art of disruption, which means by developing specific forms and versatile methods of changing perspectives, irritating, hacking, and jamming, by flipping and twisting, re-coding, and reconfigurations, mis- and re-appropriation, fakes and fictions, inclusive as well as participatory scenographic practices, and new innovative models of (inter-)action, that on the whole, relate to the complex demands and central discourses of contemporary urban spaces and redefine them for a global age. Thus, this specific art practice as part of the transdisciplinary urban art genre is not so much a matter of taking over the tasks and routines of professional urban planning, but rather opening up creative alternatives and new experimental perspectives on the larger city-planning as well as the socio-political challenges of migration and globalization today.

Conclusion

What characteristics as specific categories do now define the urban, we may ask further. It seems the old definitions won't fit here any longer—in current processes of urban globalization and in times of transcultural migration. At least, unsolicited architect-artists and unplanned city developers like *osa* do not act as the power controlling urban "revaluation" top-down anymore, but rather as an actively participating, generously collaborating, constructively engaging, socially mediating, and identity-establishing authority highly interested in local expertise. They bridge the gap of seemingly disconnections between the work of architects and urban planners as well as the citizens and the efforts to re-interpret cities made by theoretical disciplines such as the modern social sciences, urban anthropology, political ecology, or political philosophy.

Instead, they also favor the democratization of city planning, and hereby, they are the more challenged with having to operate in two conflicting registers simultaneously: On the one hand, addressing a general public in the city; and on the other, of course, a group of experts, peers or critics with their disruptive experiments and artistic innovations. Since in the end, the temporary interventions and participatory installations are judged like any other public art—whether they be original, aesthetically surprising, unprecedented, striking, skilled, innovative, or authentic, and somehow contributing to any relevant current discourse or political issue of our time.

osa's sometimes entertaining and playful interventions correlate to professional processes of city planning, developing, and implementing new structures and functions for cityscapes insofar as their subversive and highly intellectual approach, combined with an artistic will to create refined, complex, and subversive aesthetics as well as alternative identities for the city, generate surprisingly new functions and roles to public spaces as well as to the public sphere in general, thus becoming alternative communicative nodes and social venues in a given territory by virtual fictionalization as well as by factual virtualizations.

Here finally, their creative appropriations as well as misappropriations of the existing modern city in the here and now contribute on an exemplary micro-scale to some major problems of today's notions of contemporary urbanity.

Be experimental, and just try it!

Endnotes

1 - See all urban art projects by *osa* documented on their official website under http://osa-online.net/. Many thanks to Oliver, Anja, Karsten, Bernd, Britta, Anke, Ulrich und Sebastian from *osa,* who have answered so many questions about their work over so many years now.

2 - See artist statement on http://www.osa-online.net/de/flavours/strange/plan06/anwopark/about.htm [Accessed July 2017].

3 - See the full description and video documentaries of the latest project *well,come* on the official Website of Urbane Künste Ruhr on http://www.urbanekuensteruhr.de/de/projekt/2016-wellcome and https://www.ruhrtriennale.de/de/produktionen/wellcome [Accessed July 2017]. See further Renate Puvogel: "Städte des Ruhrgebiets. Die Rolle der Kunst. Gutes und gut Gemeintes. Ruhrtriennale - Festival der Künste in der Metropole Ruhr, 12.08.-24.09.2016", in: KUNSTFORUM INTERNATIONAL 242, 2016, 280-282. And cf. Simone Melenk on http://nordstadtblogger.de/die-fuenf-tonnen-schwere-kunstinstallation-wellcome-von-urbane-kuenste-ruhr-im-saz-dortmund-im-hafen-ist-eroeffnet/; and Frank Kaltenbach: "Soziale Architektur. Grenzgänger zwischen Architektur und Kunst" on https://www.goethe.de/de/kul/arc/20869612.html [Accessed July 2017].

4 - See https://www.fh-dortmund.de/de/news/2016/08/kunstinstallation-schwebebahn-lockt-in-den-hafen.php [Accessed July 2017].

References

Pop, S. et al. (eds.), 2016. What Urban Media Art Can Do: Why When Where & How, avedition, Stuttgart.

Falkeis, A. (ed.), 2016. Urban Change, Social Design - Art as Urban Innovation, Birkhäuser, Basel.

DeShazo, J. L. et al. (eds.), 2015. Developing Civic Engagement in Urban Public Art Programs, Rowman & Littlefield, Lanham.

Laiser, J. et al. (eds.), 2015. Urban Place-making between Qualitive Research and Politics, Berghahn Journals, New York/ Oxford.

Young, A., 2014. Street Art, Public City: Law, Crime and the Urban Imagination, Routledge, London.

From Urban Interventions to Urban Practice:
An Alternative Way of Urban Neighborhood Development

Renée Tribble

hcu hamburg, Überseeallee

16, 20457 Hamburg, Germany,

renee.tribble@hcu-hamburg.de

Abstract

This text seeks to contribute to the topic of urban art from the perspective of urban development. It explores the qualities of urban interventions as a method employed by urban practitioners to emancipate people to fully appropriate space in the sense of Henri Lefebvre's right to the city. This practice has become more and more common among smaller groups of architects and planners, but is still predominantly used within the art practice as reflected in Assemble's recent winning of the Turner Price. Even though the work of these urban practitioners can clearly be described as an alternative practice of neighborhood development (cf. Holub, 2010), it often still opposes official governmental urban development planning. The paper will therefore show qualities of urban practice differentiating it from urban neighborhood planning while adding certain values to communities, which could not be achieved in other ways.

Keywords/ Tags: urban intervention, urban practice, alternative neighborhood development, urban practitioner, neighborhood planning, urban art, urban art practice

1. The notion of urban intervention in urban planning

In art, architecture, and urban planning, urban interventions have become synonymous with temporary actions in urban space. Referring to Borries et al. (2012) in their glossary of interventions the term "urban interventions" is considered as a collective term for a "generous amount of different practices" and for "new subversive uses of space" in architecture, urban planning, strategic marketing, art, and also activist and socio-cultural strategies. In architecture and urban planning, urban interventions are considered as instruments in urban development attributed with the cultural reconstruction of public spaces, making the processual transformation of the city tangible and requalifying the location as well as creating a new image of the space (Akbar and Scholz, 2008). Since the research on "urban catalyst" (2001–2003) and "shrinking cities" (2002–2008) characterized the phenomena of creative appropriation processes and the potential of spontaneous urbanity of temporary architectural, artistic, and cultural interventions in vacant buildings or declining urban areas, interventions are regarded as adequate instruments to open new perspectives for structurally weak, low-investment areas (Oswalt, 2004; Senate Department for Urban Development and Housing Berlin 2007; Hayden and Temel, 2006; BMVBS, BBR 2008; Akbar and Scholz, 2008). However, their strategic development potential is almost exclusively linked to areas that are not covered by the usual development tools of city planning and real estate management (Oswalt et al., 2013). With the urban interventions award introduced by the Senate Department for Urban Development and Housing of Berlin in 2010, urban interventions were provided with a promising innovative force encouraging new models for cooperation between different actors involved in the participatory process of designing urban development (Senate Department for Urban Development and Housing Berlin , 2010). Here, the definition of urban interventions in urban planning was extended to include cooperation and participatory design, in light of the fact that architects and planners have adapted urban interventions as tools for urban development but also as strategies for working within social space.

In urban planning, urban interventions are still predominantly used in the development of brown fields or declining neighborhoods—especially in the context of *Zwischennutzungen* (meanwhile uses) in areas lacking sufficient economic demand to develop projects with the usual real estate market investors. Used as part of the planning process, these interventions represent a welcome way of experimenting in a mostly "static" planning environment (Karow-Kluge, 2010). There are a number of major advantages associated with such approaches in urban planning. Firstly, urban interventions can often be implemented much more quickly than projects following the usual planning processes thus acting as starting points or indicators for change or new activity. The second advantage relates to the conventional structure of planning administrations, which is focused on outcomes. At the beginning stands a political goal, which an administration is then tasked to deliver. Almost all the steps to be taken in this process are predefined. An urban intervention follows a contrary principle: it's only temporary, it's a test, it's a "laboratory"—it breaks with existing planning patterns. It provides an important tool for areas where planning is too restrictive to enable progress. And there is another, more practical aspect: as interventions are temporary. They can act outside existing policies and regulations or at least explore how much these can be stretched under the given circumstances. Sometimes interventions can even help to define and test new regulations. Using practices that relate to "art" can sometimes also makes it easier to gain planning permission. Another important advantage of urban interventions is their participatory character. The German term *Mitnahme*, which is usually used as an important objective of planning processes, relates to this aspect. It literally means taking someone's hand to leading that person through the process to a point where an agreement or at least understanding of the proposed goal is reached.

Further aspects of urban interventions in urban development are city marketing and social neighborhood development. In city marketing, urban interventions are used to develop the brand of a city, as they successfully produce images and narratives. In social work and neighborhood management, urban interventions are used to get in contact with people or gain easier access to certain projects or programs.

2. A broader understanding of urban interventions as art in the public interest
The notion of urban interventions as a practice of urban art is lost, however, where it is simply used as an instrument or tool. Urban interventions in the field of architecture and urban planning have hence sometimes been criticized as "pocket revolutions," producing micro solutions for everyday problems of marginalized communities (BAVO, 2007). Interventions should rather be understood "as a self-reflexive and a culture of change promoting practice of urban art that understands the given as generated and thus transformable" (Krasny and Nierhaus, 2008). As urban interventions are a practice of urban art and thus as art in the public sphere one can expand the term urban art into public art (Hildebrandt, 2012). The term public art summarizes art practices interfering with urban development processes by involving the art viewers into the third paradigm of public art practices: *art in the public interest* or *new genre public art* (NGPA) as Miwon Kwon (1997 schematically distinguishes it.[1] Her definition is based on Suzanne Lacy's widely known publication *Mapping the Terrain* (1995):

---

1 - The two others paradigms are (1) art in public places and (2) art as public spaces.

It actually is a genre of public art work, not in the traditional sense, referring to a monument places in a central area of the city, but because it deals with the public in an interactive way. [...] This construction of a history of new genre public art is not built on a typology of materials, spaces, or artistic media, but rather on concepts of audience, relationships, communication, and political intention.

Kwon (1997) defines "art in the public interest (or `new genre public art'), [as] often temporary city-based programs focusing on social issues rather than the built environment that involve collaborations with marginalized social groups (rather than design professionals), such as the homeless, battered women, urban youths, AIDS patients, prisoners, and which strives toward the development of politically-conscious community events or programs."

The following terms in the two citations warrant a closer look: city-based programs, social issues, collaborations (with marginalized social groups), development of politically-conscious community events or programs, deals with the public in an interactive way and concepts of audience, relationships, communication, and political intention. Such descriptions indicate that urban interventions are potentially *the* main practice of urban art widely discussed among all disciplines working in an urban context and within the field of public realm.

When looking at the transformation of actual space, the previously cited definition of Krasny and Lierhaus (2008) offers another interesting perspective: If we take the urban as generated and transformable—then transforming the actual space may be the key intention. If that is the main point, the question that arises is: how do artists actually achieve it?

3. urban interventions – a methodology of urban practice

In the following, the qualities of urban interventions are highlighted as a methodology employed by urban practitioners to create self-determined and appropriated space within the public realm. This art of urban action can be considered a common urban practice, which is no longer applied exclusively by artists, but by multiple disciplines intervening in urban space. It is indeed those qualities of urban interventions that originate in urban art, which make them a methodology enabling urban practitioners to produce urban space in the sense of Lefebvre's right to the city.

The idea of urban practice discussed in this paper has evolved from urban art and has shaped a type of alternative community-led development, which is operating in parallel to municipal urban planning. This kind of practice creates a neighborhood driven development, which is both locally specific and truly participatory, as it provides strategies that respect and fulfill local needs while allowing space for the community to fully appropriate the spaces. However, this practice is often still associated solely with the fields of art and culture. This is also reflected in the funding sources for such projects: they are often financed by cultural institutions in the context of biennials, art festivals etc.

"Urban practice" can be defined using four categories originating from art, which are all rooted in art history, but could qualify neighborhood planning alike. There are four characteristics associated with urban interventions as a method in alternative neighborhood development: co-production, local specificity, alternative reality, and positive moment.

3.1 Co-Production

Silke Feldhoff (2009) describes the deliberate inclusion of recipients of art or the local population as co-thinkers— and thereby co-producers—of an artistic project as follows: "As a result, 'participatory' means the unintended, for the time being only potentially enabling active participation, and 'social relations' describes the objective of a work. 'Participative', however, means an active participation that has actually taken place, thus describes the result of an action of a project" (Feldhoff 2009, own translation). While the term "participatory"' describes the possibility for involvement in a project, "participative"' refers to active participation, functioning as a main driver in the process, without that a project could otherwise not have been realized.

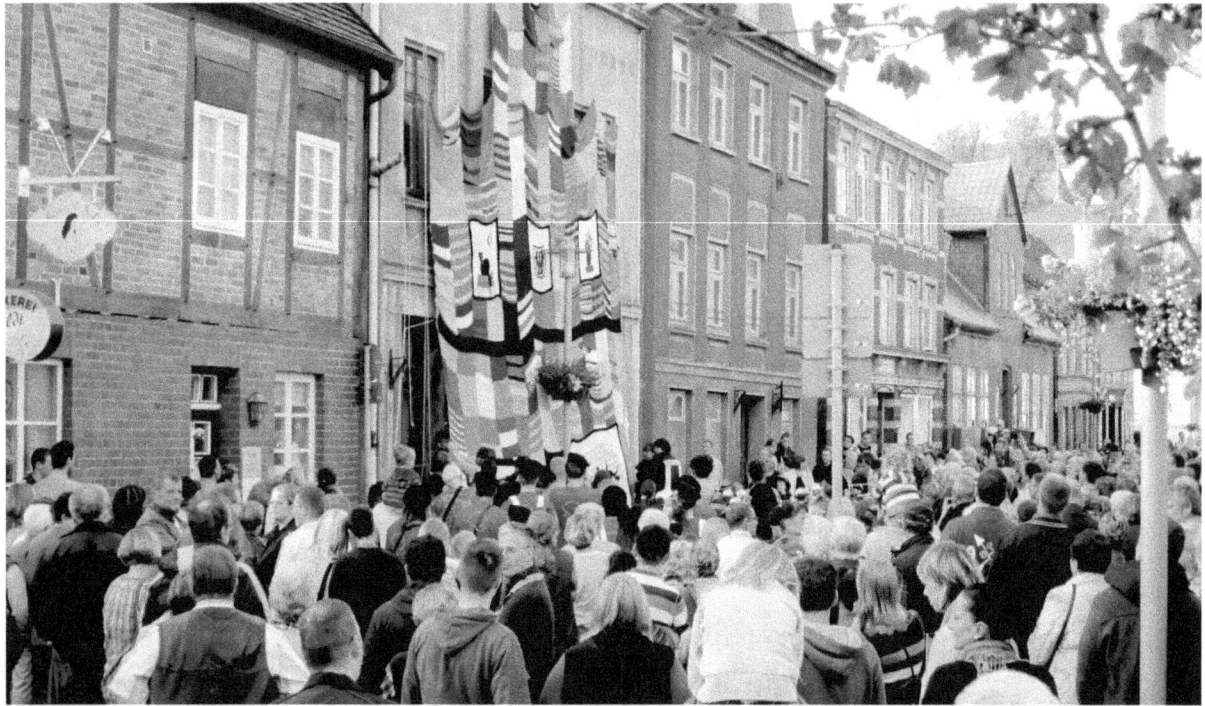

Fig. 1 - Große potemkinsche Straße: a project by Ton Matton et al" ©. Photo: Michael Kockot.

Feldhoff also shows much more detailed than I can describe it now, how the concept of the art viewer as a co-producer has developed throughout art history. Due to the changed visual habits and art conceptions triggered by Duchamp's *Bicycle Wheel* in 1913, the discussion with the art viewer has become a subject of artworks. With his ready-mades, Duchamp challenged museum visitors, who had to learn to perceive an everyday object as art, due to its placement in the context of a museum. The next challenge for the art recipient came with Concept Art, in which the relationship between the artist and the viewer is discussed even further. The conceptual artist Timm Ulrichs speaks of the co-producer (Ohff, 1971, own translation) because art is created in the mind. The social debate on participation in the 1960s and 1970s also led to artists examining participatory practices. The artistic aspect of happenings and environments are other forms of the inclusion of the art viewer in the art production. However, through the social upheavals of the 1970s, urban regeneration processes also became the focus of artistic urban practices. Trisha Brown's *Roof Piece* Performance (1973) and Gordon Matta Clark's *Cuttings* (1974/75) are commonly referred to. In the years that followed, the debate about the city and social conditions played an important role. In 1995, Suzanne Lacy introduces the term "New Genre Public Art" for so-called art in the public interest (in addition to art in the public space and art as a public space). And Paula Marie Hildebrandt (2012, own translation) describes it as "socially engaged, participatory, relational, dialogical, situational and collaborative art practice," which is associated with the politicization of art.

The long-term discussion with the artist's own role as well as with the role of the art viewer leads to intervening on the same level or as actors or representatives equal interests. The urban practitioner's own interest is of no more importance than the interest of other (informal) space users. In stark contrast to "co-producer" the term Mitnahme is often used in urban planning participatory processes. The first means to cooperate with someone: you contribute in a shared work with someone in a self-determined way; whereas the latter means to get an opportunity to act: one can take action, and it is nice if one does, but it's someone else who provides the possibility to do so.

3.2 Local Specificity

In his lecture on *Urbane Praxis*, Frank Eckardt (2013) unfolds three structures that determine urban practice. An intervention becomes authentic by connecting to the local in three aspects: firstly, the political structures, which form the circumstances one is working in, secondly, the material structures, the local material and conditions—the autochthonous—one uses and reacts to, and thirdly, the perception, which interprets the structures within the project and puts them into a narrative.

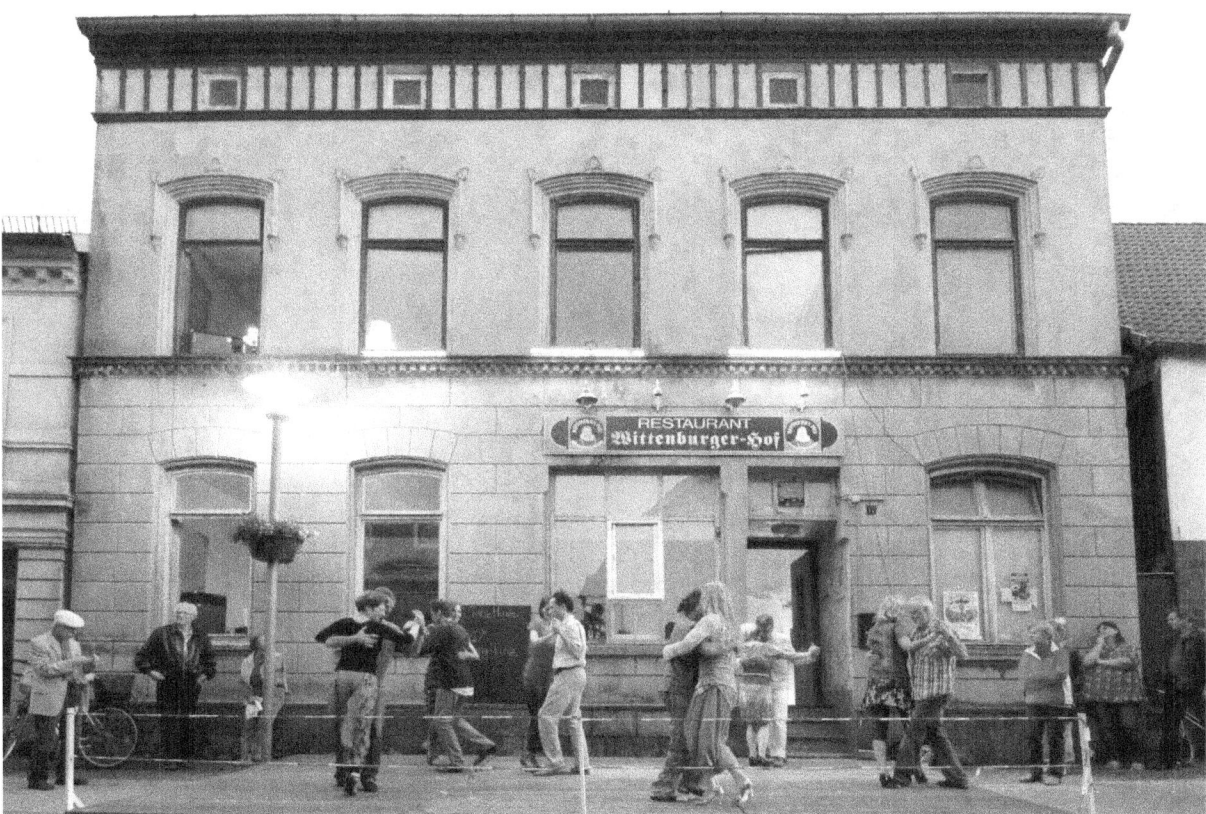

Fig. 2 - Große potemkinsche Straße: a project by Ton Matton et al" ©. Photo: Michael Kockot.

As a structural condition of urban practice, Eckardt (2013) introduces the "structure of the material," which he describes as autochthonous. The term autochthonous originates from ethnology and refers to the "found at the present location" or "at the found place originated." The examination of the found or found on the site is a central property of urban practice. In urban interventions, the improvisation found on the spot determines the improvisation. Spontaneity and improvisation are not arbitrary, but arise in response to the specificity of the premises, to existing local materials, and the prevailing conditions on the ground. The intervention thus acquires its authenticity through the uncovering and displaying of local conditions. This perception allows new interpretations of the created structures telling the process. The urban intervention is embedded in the narrative. This is all the more supported by the fact that the local knowledge of the inhabitants of a site is included within it. Through the narratives, the different perspectives on a place change—and in return, the latter change the narratives. Eckardt (2013) describes this as "the production of meaning and reinterpretation in the aesthetic, the emotional as well as the functional at the same time" (own translation). This reinterpretation occurs chronologically and linearly as a kind of chronology of urban practice from idea—experiment—experience—knowledge. Through the repetition of that chronology—the circuit of improvisation—a new knowledge is created at every step of the project: the localized and personalized knowledge of the urban practitioner. The result is a subjective, localized, and spatial knowledge that is enriched by the continuous circulation of improvisation in the intervention and has its origin in the inherent knowledge of the local (the knowledge of the inhabitants) as well as the creative, spatial knowledge of the urban practitioner. This is what makes urban practice authentic and offers the opportunity to really embed local specificities in the proposed solution.

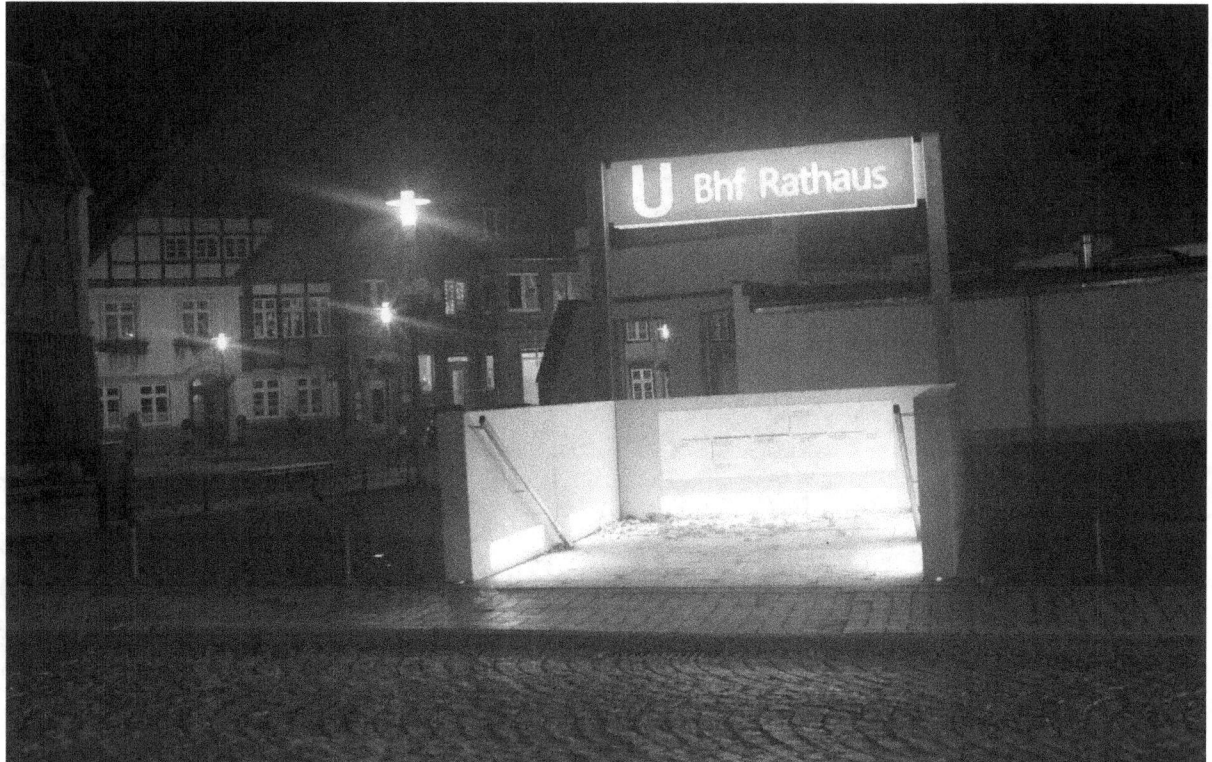

Fig. 3 - Große potemkinsche Straße: a project by Ton Matton et al" ©. Photo: Michael Kockot.

3.3 Alternative Reality

Art has a special role in society that differentiates it from other human practices. This is mostly due to the self-purpose of art. Art has no other purpose than itself. Although this quality is essential for art as it allows free creation, art is also a "highly productive reflexive practice" (Bertram, 2013, own translation). Niklas Luhmann explains "self-referentiality" in art as follows: art creates its own value system by creating specific conditions that apply to it. Through the consistent implementation and pursuit of these conditions, artists create works of art, which are subject only to these, their own laws. This creates a reality parallel to everyday reality. The reality of everyday life can be reflected by not only recognizing the reality of an artwork but also by recognizing another reality. As a result, one can suddenly see his or her own reality abstractly and as only one of different possibilities. Art thus produces alternative possibilities of reality and visualizes prevailing social conditions. Through the artistic process, those conditions become visible and—once visible—can be interrogated (cf. Baraldi et al., 2008).

Urban interventions also show an alternative reality by offering new spaces for a limited period of time. They allow other uses and offer new functions and thereby a different coding of a space. From now on, this space tells a different story, in which other things are possible. Urban interventions enable this alternative reality not only through reflection, as it is the case with works of art in, for example museums, but also through immediate experience and appropriation. As a result, the interventions are not only a form or an object, but they become a possibility. Thus, urban interventions are developed in a participatory manner and through the collaborative and active creation of places of spatial production. They therefore represent a method to produce space and serve as an instrument for a participative approach.

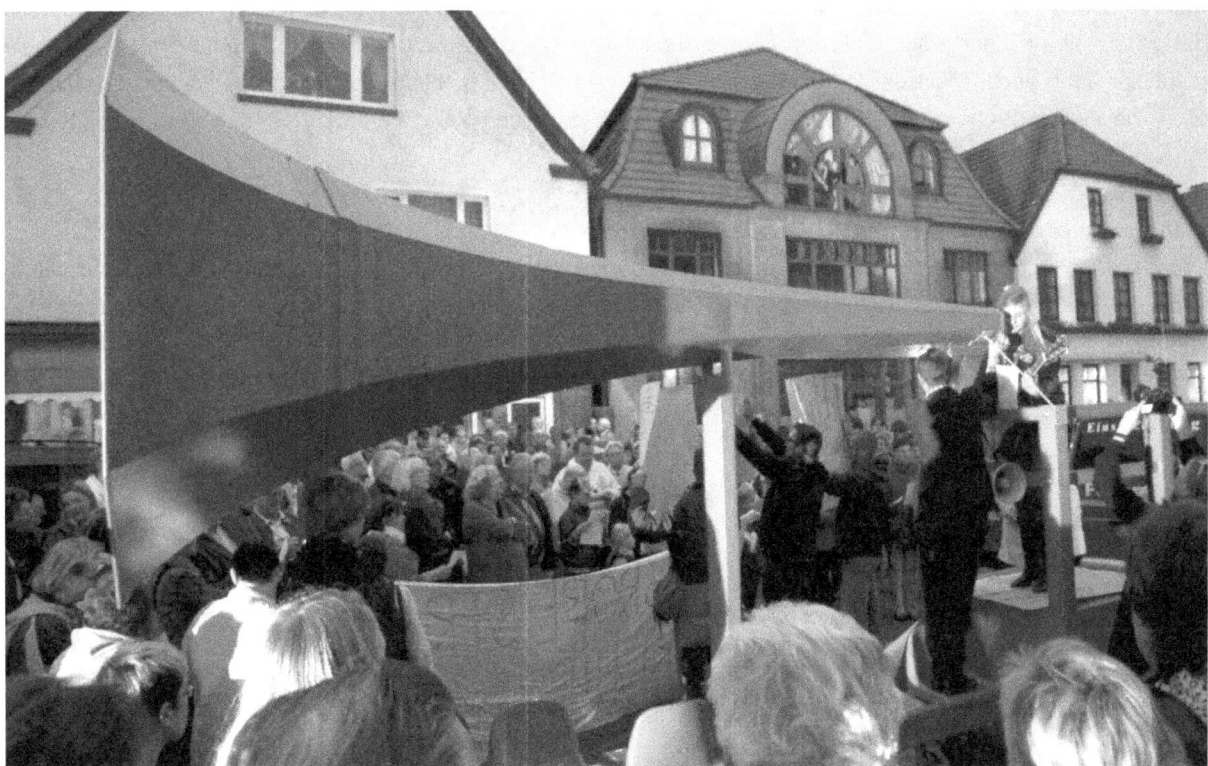

Fig. 4 - Große potemkinsche Straße: a project by Ton Matton et al" ©. Photo: Michael Kockot.

3.4 Positive Moment

Positive moments describe a crucial turning point within processes. The "moment" has come, when a particular interest meets a wider context, a wider understanding. This moment is often connected with the gathering of people, for example at a neighborhood party, a neighborhood assembly or any kind of platform, which launches a broad and fruitful discussion of interests. The "positive moment" is also important for legitimacy issues and democracy discussions of urban practice, because it testifies, that a topic is of broader understanding and support in the neighborhood and no singular interest any more. David Harvey (1996) refers to the concept of "militant particularism" by Raymond Williams to explain a positive moment within a political process, when societal values are developed from a particular set of interests:

> This idea suggests that almost all radical movements have their origin in some place, with a particular set of issues which people are pursuing and following. The key issue is whether that militant particularism simply remains localized or whether, at some point or other, it spills over into some more universal construction. [...] In other words, in this view foundational values and beliefs were discovered in particular struggles and then translated onto a broader terrain of conflict. It seems to me that the notion of community, viewed in this way, can be a positive moment within a political process. However, it is only a positive moment if it ceases to be an end in itself, ceases to be a thing which is going to solve all of our problems, and starts to be a moment in this process of broader construction of a more universal set of values which are going to be about how the city is going to be as a whole.

Urban practice thus employs urban interventions to identify spaces of opportunities, to address questions about the design of reality in a comprehensible and low-threshold manner, and to transform a given place from the conceivable to the nameable and the feasible. In this process, addressing a singular problem can lead to a common understanding of the development goals of the district. And affected individuals can be encouraged to get involved from the start through the platform building process.

4. Urban practice in the realm of neighborhood development

Urban practice uses urban interventions as a methodology, and therefore offers qualities that are crucial for successfully implementing a truly local, supported, and successful neighborhood planning process. I would like to conclude with the statement that urban practice shouldn't be absorbed by urban planning administrations but should be acknowledged as a neighborhood development strategy with an outcome that has the same relevance and importance as an urban development concept or master plan commissioned by the municipality.

In urban practice the integration of local people, their knowledge and approach is just as important as the artist's own. Due to that the project is developed in a way that it allows the people involved to actually decide on how the space is going to be determinded and used. They decide about the function and what the project is going to be like. Sometimes they even build and construct it. They transform the existing—and with the first dinner or party they also use the space. So already during the implementation of the project the space is used by the end users in the way they decided to use it. To summarize again: they first determine the space, then transform it themselves and are finally the ones who use the space.

These three steps describe a process of space production in the sense of Henri Lefebvre's right to the city (Anderson, 2011). This process is what actually connects all the urban interventions I understand as important for urban neighborhood development. They all share the understanding of how to produce, change or create an urban space. In this sense, urban interventions are not a kind of art practice that happens accidently somehow, somewhere, and sometimes, but instead are a method[] for urban practitioners to reach the particular kind of space production in the sense of Lefebvre that I mentioned before. Therefore, this urban art becomes *urban practice*, a practice that investigates and highlights issues and produces relevant effects for neighborhood planning in an alternative way and sometimes in parallel to municipal neighborhood planning.

References

Akbar, O., Scholz, R., 2008. Interventionen als urbane Strategien, in: IBA-Büro (Ed.), Die anderen Städte: IBA-Stadtumbau 2010 = The other cities, vol. 7: Interventionen = Interventions, Stiftung Bauhaus, Dessau.

Anderson, N. M., 2011. Social Infrastructure as a Means to Achieve the Right to the City, in: Architecture Conference Proceedings and Presentations, Paper 18. Architecture at Digital Repository @ Iowa State University. Retrieved from http://lib.dr.iastate.edu/cgi/viewcontent.cgi?article=1017&context=arch_conf, [14.07.2015].

Baraldi, C., Corsi, G., Esposito, E., 2008. GLU : Glossar zu Niklas Luhmanns Theorie sozialer Systeme, Suhrkamp, Frankfurt am Main.

BAVO, 2007. Always choose the worst option: artistic resistance and the strategy of over-identification. Cultural Activism Today: The Art of over-Identification, (3). Retrieved from http://www.potentialofficeproject.org/wiki/images/7/79/Overidentification.pdf [19.08.2017], in: Wilson, M., 2012. Zwischen Pest und Cholera: kritische Infragestellung „neuer urbaner Praktiken", in: Planning Unplanned. Exploring the New Role of the Urban Practitioner, Begleitheft zum gleichnamigen Symposium, TU Wien, 19.-20.11.2012, Wien.

Bertram, G., 2013. Kunst als menschliche Praxis: eine Ästhetik. Suhrkamp, Berlin.

Borries, F. von et al., 2012. Glossar der Interventionen: Annäherung an einen überverwendeten, aber unterbestimmten Begriff, Merve Verlag GmbH, Berlin.

BMVBS, BBR, 2008. Bundesministerium für Verkehr, Bau und Stadtentwicklung. Zwischennutzungen und Nischen im Städtebau als Beitrag für eine nachhaltige Stadtentwicklung, Bundesamt für Bauwesen und Raumordnung, Bonn.

Eckardt, F., 2013. Urbane Praxis Vokabeln für eine kreative Wissenschaft – für eine reflektierte Gestaltung. Retrieved from http://www.uni-weimar.de/projekte/2G13/2g13/debatte-symposium-panel-eckardt/, [02.07.2015]

Feldhoff, S., 2009. Zwischen Spiel und Politik: Partizipation als Strategie und Praxis in der bildenden Kunst, vol. 1. Universität der Künste Berlin, Berlin.

Harvey, D., 1996. Contested Cities: Social Process and Spatial Form, in: LeGates, R. T., Stout, F. (Eds.), The City Reader, 5th ed., Routledge, London, New York, 230–237.

Haydn, F., Temel, R., 2006. Temporäre Räume: Konzepte zur Stadtnutzung, Birkhäuser, Basel.

Hildebrandt, P.-M., 2012. Urbane Kunst, in: Eckardt, F. (Ed.), Handbuch Stadtsoziologie, VS Verlag für Sozialwissenschaften, Wiesbaden, 721–744.

Holub, B., 2010. Für wen, warum und wie weiter? In: Dérive, 39. Retrieved from http://www.derive.at/index.php?p_case=2&id_cont=905&issue_No=39, [02.08.2016]

Karow-Kluge, D., 2010. Experimentelle Planung im öffentlichen Raum, Reimer, Berlin.

Krasny, E., Nierhaus, I. (Eds.), 2008. Urbanografien: Stadtforschung in Kunst, Architektur und Theorie, Reimer, Berlin.

Kwon, M., 1997. Public Art and Urban Identities, retrieved from: http://eipcp.net/transversal/0102/kwon/en, [20.02.2017], originally published as: For Hamburg: Public Art and Urban Identities, in: Müller, C. P., Könneke, A. (Eds.), Kunst auf Schritt und Tritt, Kellner Verlag, Hamburg, 94–109.

Lacy, S. 1995. Mapping the Terrain: New Genre Public Art, Bay Press, Seattle.

Ohff, H., 1971. Galerie der neuen Künste: Pop, Happening, Hard-Edge, Neo-Surrealismus, Kritischer Realismus, Minimal, Ars Povera, Kinetik, Post-Painterly-Abstraction, Land-Art, Electronic-Art, Op, Project-Art, Process-Art, Fluxus; Revolution ohne Programm, Bertelsmann, Gütersloh.

Oswalt, P., 2004. Schrumpfende Städte, Band 1 – Internationale Untersuchungen, Hatje Cantz, Ostfildern-Ruit.

Oswalt, P., Overmeyer, K., Misselwitz, P., 2013. Urban Catalyst: Mit Zwischennutzung Stadt entwickeln, DOM publishers, Berlin.

Rode, P., Wanschura, B., Kubesch, C., 2010. Kunst macht Stadt: vier Fallstudien zur Interaktion von Kunst und Stadtquartier, second edition, VS Verlag für Sozialwissenschaften, Wiesbaden.

Senatsverwaltung für Stadtentwicklung (Ed.), 2007. Urban pioneers: Berlin: Stadtentwicklung durch Zwischennutzung = Temporary use and urban development in Berlin, Jovis, Berlin.

Senatsverwaltung für Stadtentwicklung Berlin, 2010. Urban Intervention Award Berlin 2010, Oktoberdruck, Berlin.

Partners

Connect. Create. Care
URBAN NATION MUSEUM FOR URBAN CONTEMPORARY ART

The URBAN NATION MUSEUM FOR URBAN CONTEMPORARY ART is a globally unique center of urban contemporary art in Berlin.

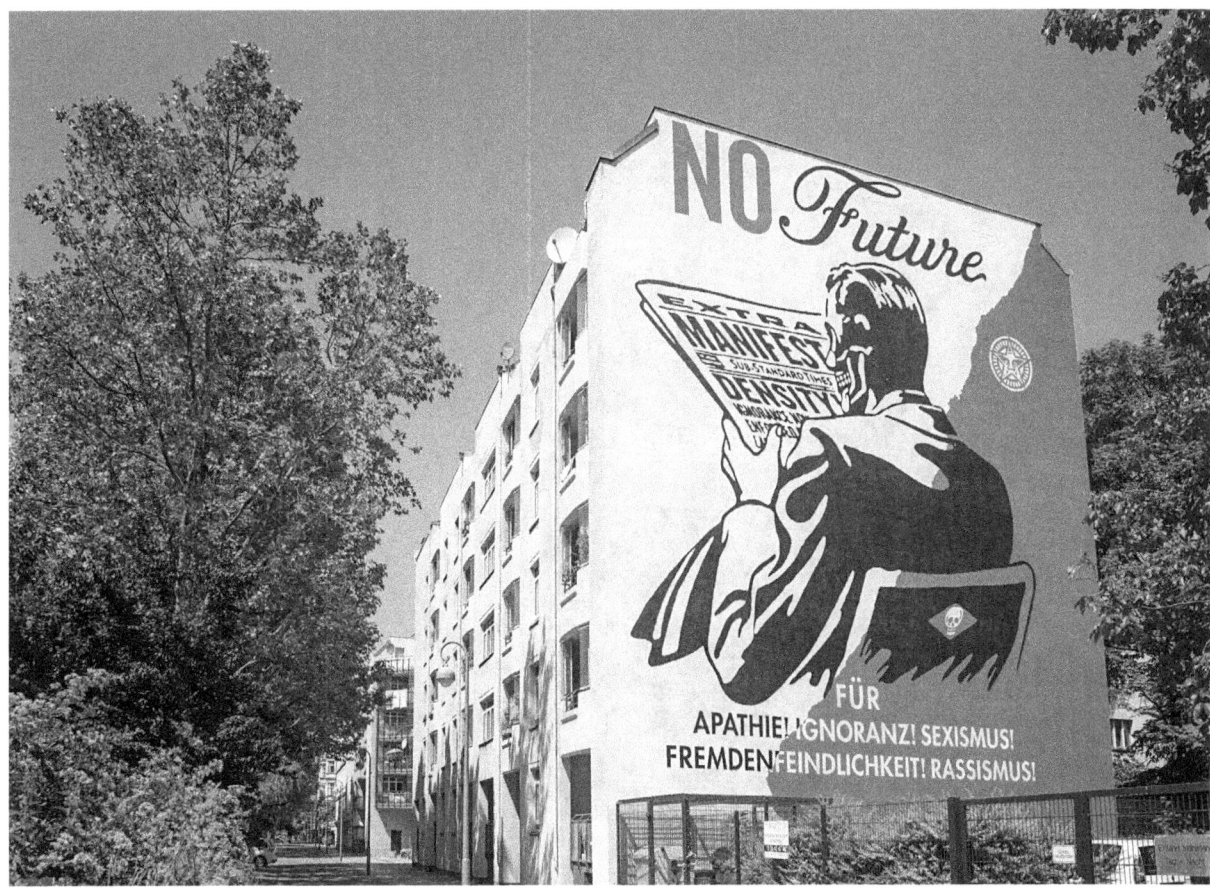

Fig. 1 - Shepard Fairey: No Future, One Wall, Frobenstrasse. Photo: Nika Kramer/URBAN NATION.

Over the last four years, the façade of Bülowstrasse 7 has featured regularly changing works by international and local urban artists such as Shepard Fairey, D*Face, Maya Hayuk, and The London Police. The artworks created throughout Berlin under the auspices of URBAN NATION and executive director Yasha Young since 2013 form the centerpiece of the collection. In addition, the URBAN NATION MUSEUM FOR URBAN CONTEMPORARY ART is home to the unique book collection of the renowned photojournalist Martha Cooper, whose pictures document the birth and development of graffiti and urban art in recent decades.

Instead of just conserving, the museum also encapsulates the original idea behind temporary urban art. Changing murals will be exhibited on mobile elements on the façade of the museum and will subsequently become part of the URBAN NATION archives. The museum's interior also makes for unusual experiences: URBAN NATION is literally moving the street indoors. A gallery catwalk stretching across the two stories of the museum interior makes it possible to look at the exhibits both from afar and close up.

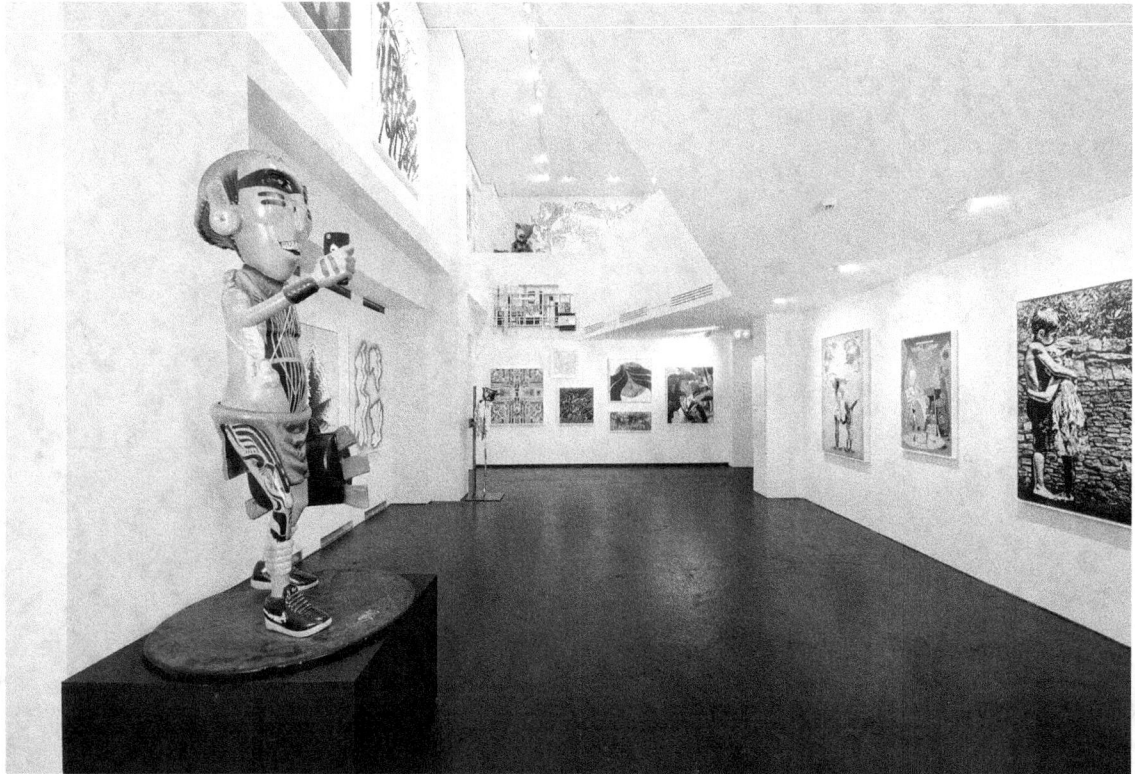

Fig. 2 - URBAN NATION - Inside. Photo: Sabine Dobre.

The museum's leitmotif is "Connect. Create. Care." It is much more than just an exhibition space: in addition to showing ever-changing works by international and local street artists, URBAN NATION also offers a novel platform for encounters, exchange, research and education related to urban street art. Artists' residencies on the upper floors of the building allow up-and-coming artists in particular to live and work in Berlin for three to six months. Their creativity have free rein at URBAN NATION.

Situated in the heart of Berlin, which is home to a high-caliber and highly active art scene, the museum filled a vacuum in international art by providing a permanent access point for one of the most important art forms of the 21st century. URBAN NATION was initiated by the non-profit foundation Berliner Leben. The internationally renowned curator Yasha Young is its executive director.

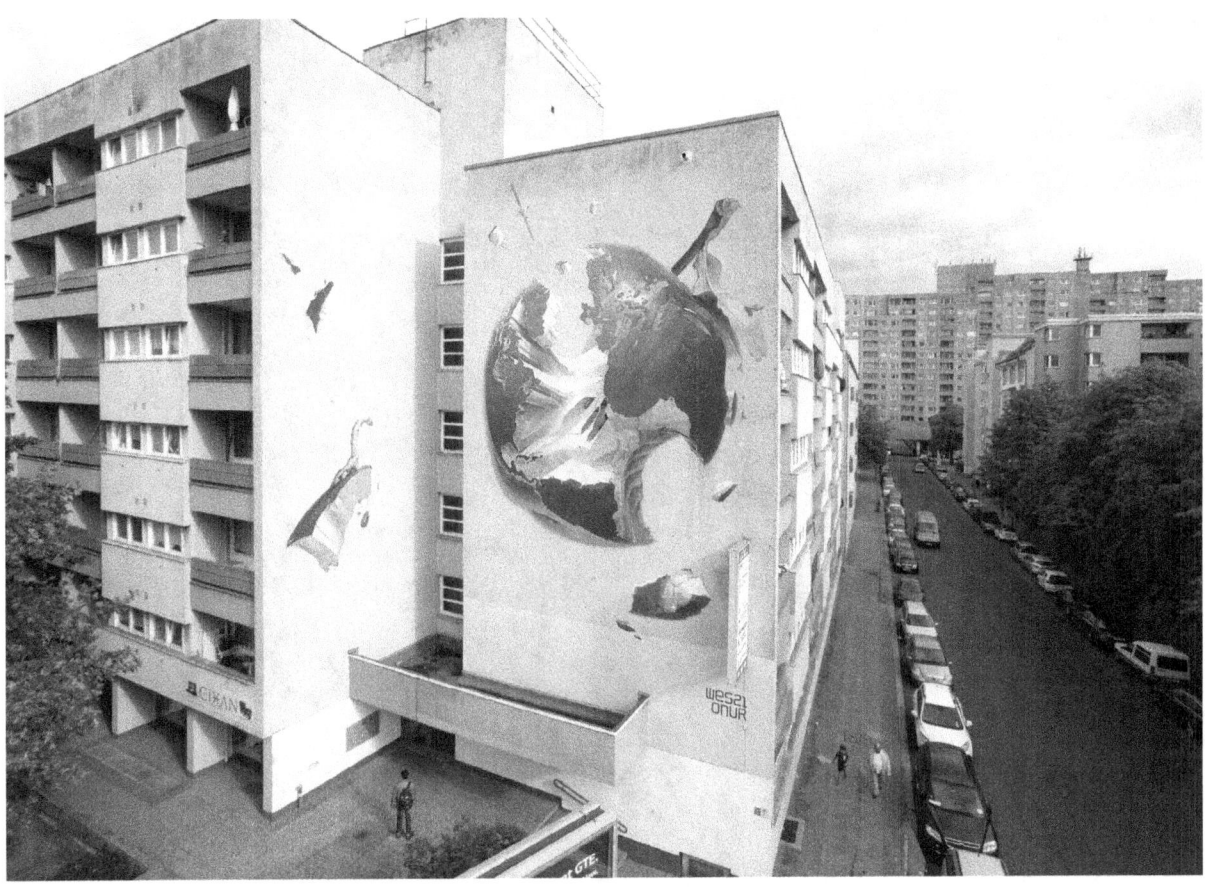

Fig. 3 - Wes21 / Onur: Sweetest Sin, One Wall, Berlin, Kreuzberg 2015. Photo: Prince Boogie.

URBAN NATION MUSEUM FOR URBAN CONTEMPORARY ART
Bülowstrasse 7
10783 Berlin
Telephone: +49(0)30 32295989
Opening hours:
Tue – Sun 10am – 6pm
Admission: free
Barrier-free access

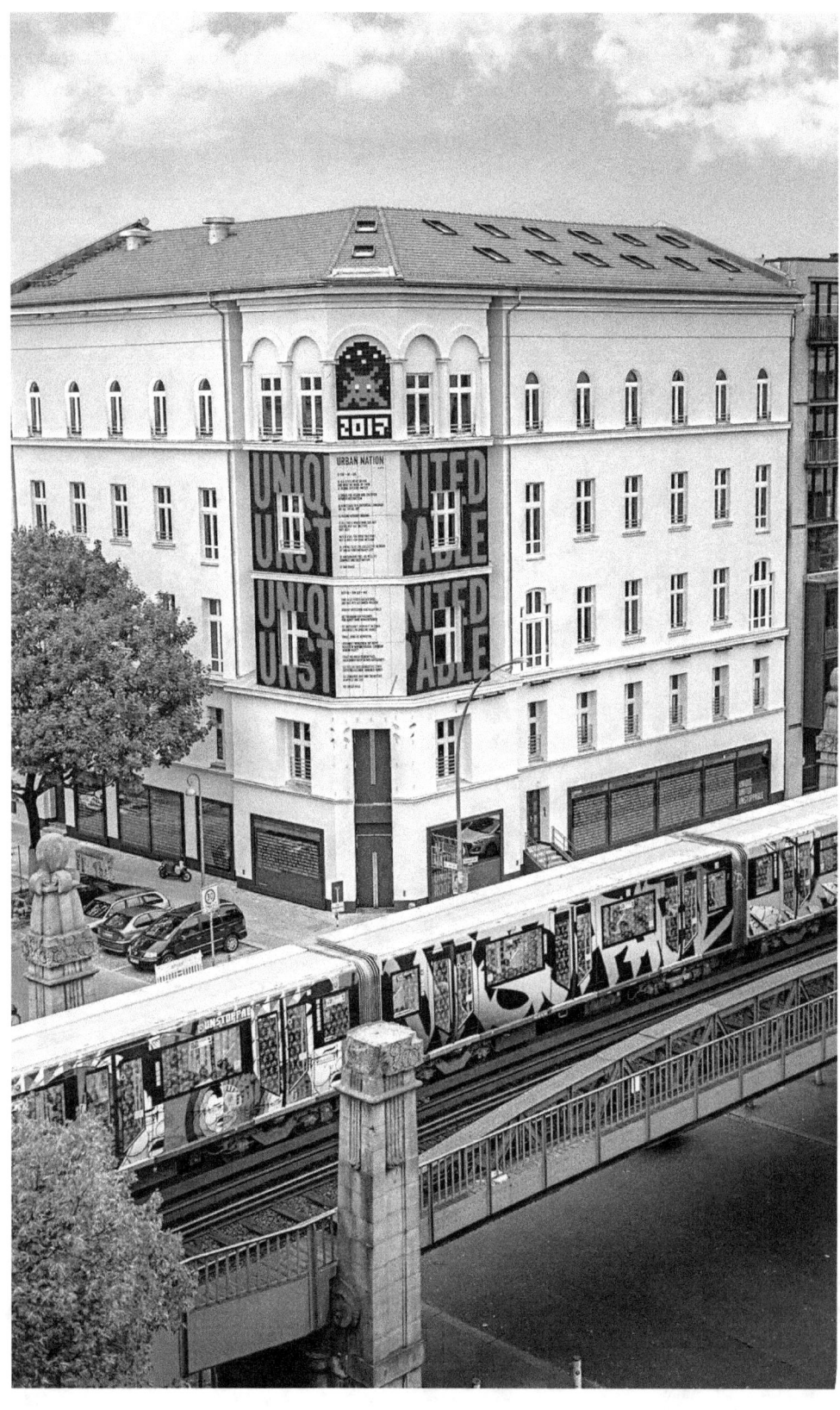

Fig. 4 - URBAN NATION - façade
Photo: Nika Kramer.

"Works without future perspective (…) are fast interventions without impact" - or the idea of a travelling urban art library to document the development of contemporary muralism

Jens Besser
urban script continues, Dresden, Germany
jens@anartchy.com

Abstract
In 2014 the mural project meeting Time for Murals took place in Dresden. The question of the origins of the new muralism was a result of numerous discussions about the future of mural festivals. That's why the wish for a historical reappraisal of the new muralism in the form of a travelling urban art library emerged: a library that is not fixed to a place, but can travel to across all oft he world's continents.

Keywords: contemporary muralism, documentation, research of mural history

In 2014 the mural project meeting Time for Murals took place in Dresden. The question of the origins of the new muralism was a result of numerous discussions about the future of mural festivals. Nearly all festivals (and their organizers) are based on illegal activities, such as graffiti or uncommissioned painting on walls. But their origins have been inadequately documented and poorly analyzed. According to public opinion, the new muralism is only based on legal activities. That's why the desire was expressed for a historical reappraisal of the new muralism in the form of a travelling urban art library: a library that is not fixed to a place, but can travel to all continents.

The key element of the travelling library would be a digital archive. It would serve to to collect analogue information mediums such as graffiti magazines, photos, videos, newspaper articles, and sketches. All analogue mediums are digitized on-site.
The origin of the new muralism lies in the era before the massive spread of digital media when most artists documented their works on film. To protect their anonymity, the library needs a hatch or a "confessional box" where photos or films can be left, digitized and instantly given back anonymously.

A research team would accompany the library. The team would order the library to make it usable. Additionally, the team could archive the street art of the cities to which it travels. Researchers could travel along the paths of artists, be present at events (such as festivals or art projects) or just archive contemporary street art.

Furthermore, the library could function as a meeting point, place for discussions and exchange or starting point of guided tours.

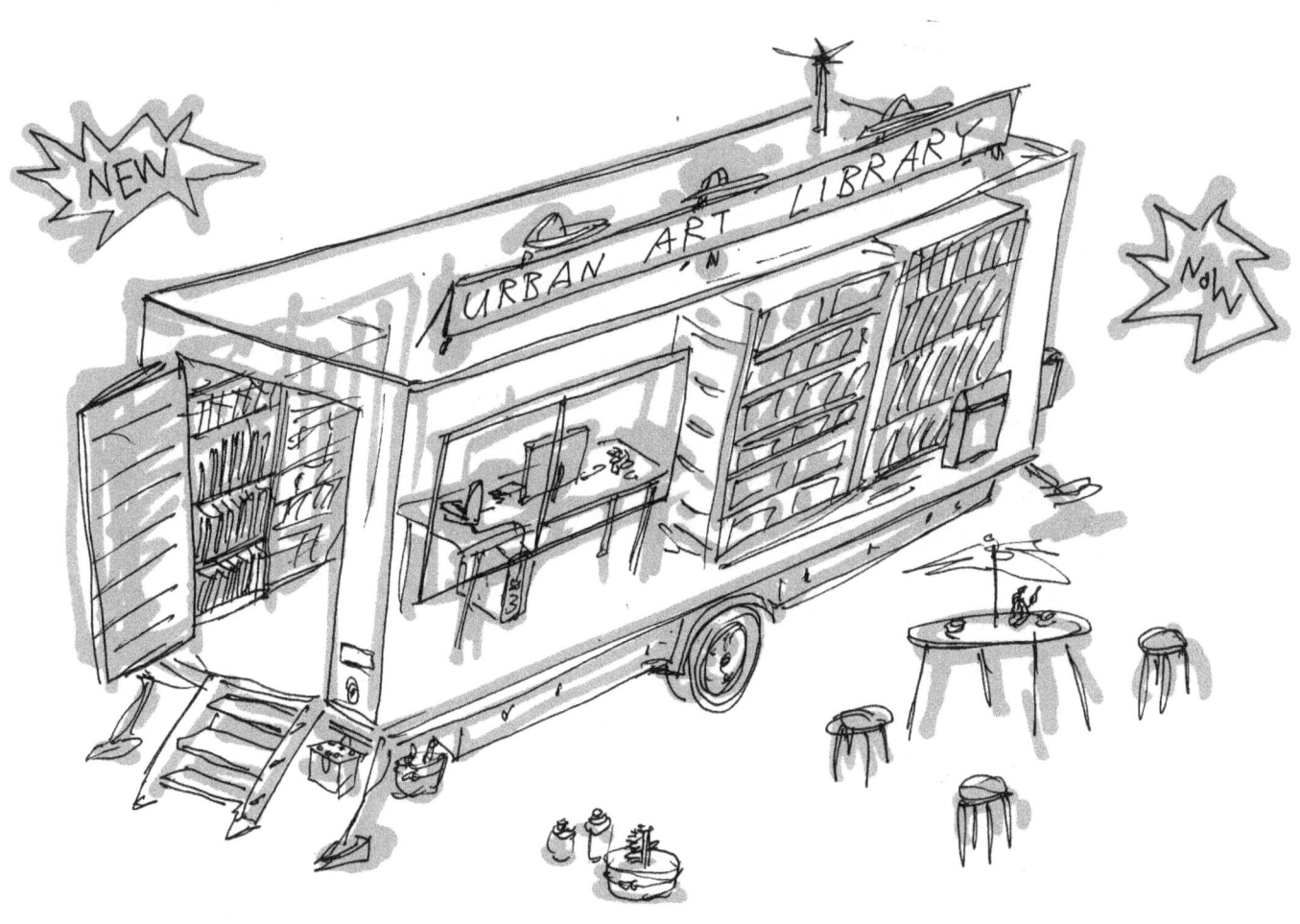

Urban Creativity
International research topic

info@urbancreativity.org

Whether considering them an aggression on the city and its users, whether building them as not only a sociological and anthropological response but also, a creative one to the architectural environment, over the past decades, graffiti and street art have re-centered debates about urban public contemporary art and creativity.

However, and even though a consensus has not been reached (and probably never will), the focus on these creative practices and their actors has increased considerably. The debate around these practices, had being both preceded and followed by exhibitions in museums, galleries and other institutions. Also inside the academia, and the editorial quadrant, several authors have focused their attention and research in graffiti and street art ranging from the most renown names and angles to the most remote and non-traditional geographies.

Due to the maturity of the local ecosystem and to global dynamics, Lisbon has been put on the map of such manifestations and evolutionary movements. Taking advantage of a de-centered perspective to the occidentalized ways of doing, centered in the timeless qualities and well balanced in the cardinal points of world dynamics.

In the aftermath of the 2014 Lisbon International Conference, it became clear due to the large number of contributions from distinctive disciplinary fields that the research methodologies are in fact unique. The advanced studies of Street Art & Urban Creativity (SAUC), interdisciplinary and transnational approaches are "topographies" that we are continuously welcoming in order to further advance this already expanded field for research.

In the present critical context of the need for aligning our cities with a sustainable future, all contributions will make a difference. Every day in our cities there are many tensions and misguided use of resources both from citizens and authorities, which could be avoidable with a better access to the already existing knowledge.

We organize activities, conferences and publications aimed at researching and applying knowledge about urban art and creativity, graffiti and street art. Taking further the concretion and production of murals, public art, installations or performances, studying them and organizing their realization with a view to reflection and innovation in the context of the better development of cities.

SAUC Journal, is the first and, to date, only publication that uses the designation Street Art in its name. In partnership with a vast network, referenced and indexed at the most relevant platforms, supported by a scientific committee with more than 20 members from 12 countries, with more than 200 articles published, and with an average production of 70 new articles per year, it is the regular scientific publication that is best positioned to make recognized the work of researchers who have city, graffiti, street art, or urban creativity as research object.

Evolving into a research platform of gathering between need and capacity, we are both a knowledge producer or a knowledge seeker, check us on:

Urbancreativity.org

www.ingramcontent.com/pod-product-compliance
Lightning Source LLC
Chambersburg PA
CBHW082106220526

45472CB00009B/2073